Richard Wagner's Essays on Conducting

Eastman Studies in Music

Ralph P. Locke, Senior Editor
Eastman School of Music

Additional Titles of Interest

Analyzing Wagner's Operas: Alfred Lorenz and German Nationalist Ideology
Stephen McClatchie

Bach to Brahms: Essays on Musical Design and Structure
Edited by David Beach and Yosef Goldenberg

Brahms and the Shaping of Time
Edited by Scott Murphy

Brahms's "A German Requiem":
Reconsidering Its Biblical, Historical, and Musical Contexts
R. Allen Lott

Lies and Epiphanies: Composers and Their Inspiration from Wagner to Berg
Chris Walton

Othmar Schoeck: Life and Works
Chris Walton

Wagner and Venice
John W. Barker

Wagner and Venice Fictionalized: Variations on a Theme
John W. Barker

Wagner's Visions: Poetry, Politics, and the Psyche in the Operas through "Die Walküre"
Katherine R. Syer

Wagner and Wagnerism in Nineteenth-Century Sweden, Finland, and the
Baltic Provinces: Reception, Enthusiasm, Cult
Hannu Salmi

A complete list of titles in the Eastman Studies in Music series
may be found on our website, www.urpress.com.

Richard Wagner's Essays on Conducting

A New Translation with Critical Commentary

Chris Walton

UNIVERSITY OF ROCHESTER PRESS

The open access version of this publication was funded by the Swiss National Science Foundation

First published 2021

University of Rochester Press
668 Mt. Hope Avenue, Rochester, NY 14620, USA
www.urpress.com
and Boydell & Brewer Limited
PO Box 9, Woodbridge, Suffolk IP12 3DF, UK
www.boydellandbrewer.com

ISBN-13: 978-1-64825-012-5

ISSN: 1071-9989 ; v. 175

Library of Congress Control Number: 2020952166

This publication is printed on acid-free paper.

Printed and bound in Great Britain by
TJ Books Ltd, Padstow, Cornwall

For Eva Rieger, in gratitude and admiration:
scholar, friend, *Jubilarin*

Contents

Illustrations

Figures

Acknowledgements

This book is a result of the research project "Annotated Scores" based at the Bern University of the Arts HKB, funded by the Swiss National Science Foundation (SNSF), and run in partnership with the Royal Academy of Music in London. I am grateful to the SNSF for both their funding and their uncomplicated organization, and to my colleagues at the HKB for their untiring support, primarily Thomas Gartmann (Head of Research), Martin Skamletz (Head, Institute Interpretation) and (in alphabetical order) Daniel Allenbach, Christine Bolzli, Sabine Jud and Kai Köpp. I have profited much from conversations with Christoph Moor, my doctoral student at the project, and with Anselm Gerhard of the University of Bern, Moor's co-supervisor alongside me. Nicholas Saul and Robert Vilain kindly offered advice on matters of *Germanistik* relevant to Wagner's reception of contemporary ideas in the sciences and humanities. Barry Millington generously offered to comment on sections of my manuscript, and his astute advice and criticism proved of immense help in the later stages of my work. Peter Jost kindly provided information on Wagner in French translation. If it were not for my longstanding friendship with Raymond Holden AM, professor at the Royal Academy of Music in London, neither the Bernese research project nor this book would have come about; we first discussed annotated conducting scores over twenty years ago when I was head of the Music Division at the Zentralbibliothek Zürich, and I have since learnt far more from Ray than I could ever acknowledge properly. I also owe thanks to his colleagues at the Royal Academy, Tim Jones and Jonathan Freeman-Attwood—both, I'm delighted to say, contemporaries of mine at Christ Church, Oxford back in the mid-80s—for actively supporting the collaboration between Bern and London. I have also benefitted from Tim's vast knowledge of Mozart's music and Mozart scholarship.

The speakers and participants at the two conferences that were part of our research project—at Bern in November 2018 and in London in April 2019—all contributed to the present volume in different ways, either directly or indirectly, and I am grateful to them for sharing their knowledge and expertise: Roger Allen, Regina Busch, Christopher Fifield, David Gleeson,

Raymond Holden, Henry Kennedy, Malcolm Miller, Christoph Moor, David Patmore, Peter Quantrill, Lena-Lisa Wüstendorfer, and Frits Zwart. Aside from the Bern project, I owe much to my conversations with Thomas Rösner, Artistic Director of the Beethoven Philharmonie in Baden bei Wien. Discussing Wagner (and much else) with Eva Rieger always opens my mind in ways I hadn't before imagined; this book is dedicated to her as a small token of thanks. I am also grateful to the numerous institutions that provided source materials for our project and images for this book: the Nationalarchiv der Richard-Wagner-Stiftung Bayreuth (in particular Sven Friedrich, Kristina Unger and Tanja Dobrick), the British Museum (Elizabeth Bray), the Staatsbibliothek Preußischer Kulturbesitz (especially Martina Rebmann and Roland Schmidt-Hensel), the Zentralbibliothek Zürich (Heinrich Aerni, Stefan Dell'Olivo, Urs Fischer, Daniel Gloor, Heidi Kaufmann, and Angelika Salge), the Arnold Schönberg Center in Vienna (Therese Muxeneder), the Österreichische Nationalbibliothek (Thomas Leibnitz, Eike Zimmer, Hans Peter Zimmer and Birgit Suranyi), the Thomas-Mann-Archiv of ETH Zurich (Rolf Bolt), RIPM (Richard Kitson) and the Vera Oeri Library of the Musikhochschule Basel, especially Markus Erni for his inestimable assistance in getting me access to the online RIPM database. The photograph reproduced here of Wagner's baton was kindly provided by John Keller via its former owner, Hannah Jo Smith, to both of whom I owe my thanks. I am also lucky to reside in a city with a first-rate library, whose staff have over the past years been unfailingly helpful and courteous; I should like to thank Allard Eekman and Ian Holt of the Zentralbibliothek Solothurn and especially its former director, Verena Bider, for their invaluable assistance in my research endeavors. Here I must also thank the composer Urs Joseph Flury, as over the course of many conversations his vast knowledge of the repertoire has been of immense help to me. Markus Kiesel kindly introduced me to the recordings of Nikolai Golovanov, which are a source of delight. The music examples in this book were typeset by Sebastian Meyer in Basel. I also wish to thank Klaus Wallnöfer and his family for generously allowing me to consult the archives of his grandfather.

I must also express my gratitude to the musicians with whom I worked during the years when I was still active in the practical field, especially the singers (in Cambridge and Oxford, then in Zurich, when I worked as a freelance choral accompanist, then later as an occasional répétiteur with members of both the Opera Studio and the main ensemble of the Opera). Like most students of my day at the abovementioned universities, I occasionally took to the podium myself, and circumstances meant I returned to it thereafter on an ad hoc basis, even as late as my first year as head of the music department at the University of Pretoria in 2001. But I learnt more from being privileged to play under first-rate conductors such as Charles Dutoit, Riccardo Chailly, and others when I was in the National Youth Orchestra of Great Britain, then later in CUMS in Cambridge. I especially remember Kirill Kondrashin, whose astonishing aura changed my blasé teenage notions about the "charismatic conductor" being supposedly a figment of the Romantic imagination. Perhaps my most vivid memory, however, is of Vernon Handley conducting us in Elgar's First Symphony at Cambridge. He missed the actual concert through illness, but his final rehearsal was a masterpiece of musicality, erudition, good humor, and people-management, all of it possible because he simply knew the score inside-out. We also endured the best and the worst of composer-conductors, though they shall remain nameless here. These practical experiences, while now long past, have all helped to inform the present book, and I am grateful for them.

Chris Walton, Törbel and Solothurn, Michaelmas 2020

Abbreviations

Editions

CWT   Cosima Wagner, *Die Tagebücher*. Edited by Martin Gregor-Dellin and Dietrich Mack. 2 vols. Munich and Zurich: Piper, 1976–77.

ML   Richard Wagner. *Mein Leben*. Edited by Martin Gregor-Dellin. Munich: List Verlag, 1977.

SB   *Richard Wagner: Sämtliche Briefe*. 25– vols. Vols. 1–9 edited by Hans-Joachim Bauer, Klaus Burmeister, Johannes Forner, Gertrud Strobel, and Werner Wolf. Leipzig: Deutscher Verlag für Musik, 1967–2000. Vols. 10–25 edited by Martin Dürrer, Margret Jestremski, Isabel Kraft, Andreas Mielke, and Angela Steinsiek. Wiesbaden: Breitkopf & Härtel, 2000–.

SSD   Richard Wagner. *Sämtliche Schriften und Dichtungen*. 6th edition (*Volksausgabe*). 16 vols. Leipzig: Breitkopf & Härtel, [1911]. References to Wagner's writings in this book are generally made to this edition, as this has become standard procedure in the Wagner literature. However, I also refer to specific earlier editions of his writings where this is relevant.

Instruments and Voices

fl   flute

ob   oboe

cl   clarinet

bn   bassoon

hn   horn

tpt   trumpet

trbn   trombone

tmp	timpani
vn	violin
va	viola
vc	violoncello
db	double bass
pf	piano
S	soprano
A	alto
T	tenor
B	bass

Author's Note

All translations into English are by the present writer, except where stated otherwise. Richard Wagner originally entitled his conducting essay *Über das Dirigiren*, the last word of which, after the German spelling reform several years later, was consistently spelt *Dirigieren*. Here the later form is used throughout, as it has become common practice to do so, except when the title is used in quotations.

Introduction

Mr. J. S. DWIGHT, Editor of the *Boston Journal of Music* (Massachusetts), is entertaining his readers with a somewhat loose translation of that miserable piece of egotistical coxcombry and absolute nonsense, the pamphlet called *Ueber das Dirigiren*, by Herr Richard Wagner. What, in the name of Music, does any sensible American care about such stuff?

—*The Musical World* (London), July 2, 1870[1]

Our friend ... wonders that we waste our time ... Pray do not be alarmed; we never dreamed of undertaking to translate the whole work, or even the larger part of it; that would indeed be a thankless and a dreary task.

—Dwight's reply to *The Musical World* in his own journal, July 30, 1870[2]

The initial response to Richard Wagner's principal essay on conducting, *Über das Dirigieren*, published in Germany in 1869–70, was hardly enthusiastic, neither in the German-speaking world nor elsewhere. But within just a few years, Wagner's ideas on conducting, here so summarily dismissed, came to dominate the discourse in a manner that is arguably unparalleled in the history of musical performance. And while the tortuousness of Wagner's prose makes one sympathize with the above-expressed opinions of the essay in question, no less than three more men (one German-American and two English) would embark on translating it within a quarter-century of its initial publication (though only two of them would complete the task). The story of how Wagner came to write about the art of conducting, and of the reception *Über das Dirigieren* and its sister essays were accorded at home and abroad, is told in detail in the second half of this book.

---

1   Anon.: "Occasional notes," *The Musical World* 48/27 (July 2, 1870), 446–8, here 447.
2   [Dwight] (1870): 286.

Wagner committed his principal ideas on conducting to paper over the space of just some eight years in the late 1860s and early 1870s—thus on either side of the centenary year of Ludwig van Beethoven, the composer who loomed largest over Wagner's project to codify the art of interpretation. The present volume offers the first-ever complete, unexpurgated translations into English of all of Richard Wagner's writings on conducting since William Ashton Ellis published his multi-volume translation of Wagner's prose at the close of the 19th century. Wagner's texts are presented in chronological order according to their date of completion, so that the reader can trace the development of his ideas. As is explained in the accompanying essay, none of these texts can be properly understood on its own, but only in the wider context of Wagner's prose. In hopes of elucidating that context and of making these texts more readily comprehensible to modern readers, my translations here (unlike those of my Victorian precursors) are annotated extensively, and also quote where necessary from other writings by their author (see, for example, the instance on p. 33 in *Über das Dirigieren* where Wagner refers his readers to an earlier essay, assuming that they will take the trouble to look it up; I instead provide the relevant passage from that other essay in a footnote).

The primary aim of this annotated edition of Wagner's writings is not to document their textual genesis, but to illustrate their impact and reception history. To this end, I have based my translations on the versions that Wagner published in his own edition of his collected writings in the 1870s (which was in any case the venue for the first publication of Wagner's report on conducting Beethoven's Ninth Symphony in Dresden and his reminiscences of Spontini, both of which he had extracted from his autobiography *Mein Leben*). Wagner does touch elsewhere on issues pertaining to conducting (for a discussion of these texts, see the section 'Writing on Conducting—Mania, Helmsmen, and Theory' in part II), but the essays in the present volume encompass his most important statements on the art. Only in the case of his essay on Spontini have I refrained from offering the whole text, since much of this essay deals with anecdotal, biographical matters of no direct bearing on our topic.

In line with my endeavor to document the impact of these writings, my footnotes also refer on numerous occasions to texts on conducting by later authors who drew upon Wagner's ideas (often unacknowledged, sometimes to the point of plagiarism). I also occasionally refer to specific recordings when a later conductor has seemingly followed Wagner's instructions for a particular work, even when those instructions were themselves based on a misunderstanding (such as Wagner's erroneous *diminuendo* towards the close of Weber's *Freischütz* Overture, which was kept by some conductors, but repudiated by others, as explained in footnote 84 in chapter 3 below). For reasons of space, these references to recordings are not comprehensive; I offer them only when they seem particularly pertinent to the topic at hand.

A Note on the Present Translation

The essays in this volume have all been translated more than once since they were first published in German in the late 1860s and early 1870s. The above-mentioned William Ashton Ellis translated all our texts as part of his larger Wagner project, while his translation of *Über das Dirigieren* had already been preceded by that of Edward Dannreuther and by piecemeal versions by two other men. The most recent translations of *Über das Dirigieren* and of the 1873 essay on conducting Beethoven's Ninth are by Robert L. Jacobs. Since two of the texts in this volume were extracted by Wagner from his memoir *Mein Leben*, the original passages are also found in English translation in the first, anonymous translation of 1911 and in Andrew Gray's more recent English edition of that work.[3] The bibliography below offers more details on the different editions and translations that have been published.

As explained in my accompanying essay, Wagner's own obsession with achieving "clarity" seems to have been inversely proportional to his ability to achieve it in his prose. Like several of my predecessors, I too have resorted to paraphrasing Wagner where this seemed necessary to achieve some inkling of the clarity to which he claimed to aspire, though I have endeavored to remain as faithful as possible to what I believe is the content of the original (this excuse, perhaps ironically, is not unlike Wagner's own when explaining his alterations to Beethoven; see p. 131 on Wagner's efforts to realize his predecessor's "true intentions"). For example, if Wagner writes of something stretching almost to the point of impossibility, I prefer instead to simplify and say that it is "almost impossible." One might justifiably claim that such acts of clarification and simplification constitute a falsification. The more Wagner's bile rises as he writes of enemies real and imagined, the more his prose ties itself in knots. If we untie them all, then we risk making the odious seem palatable. Wagner's insistence on stringing together negatives, for example, can offer a fascinating window onto his own insecurities and his need to create adversaries and barriers to be overcome in the (to him)

---

3   See Wagner, trans. Anon. (1911) and Wagner, trans. Gray (1983).

inevitable, ultimate victory of his art. But reducing their number can also help to unclutter his style without doing undue violence to his content (for example, my translation of *Über das Dirigieren* has reduced instances of the word "not"—"nicht"—to about a quarter compared to the original German). I have preferred to err on the side of simplicity; those who delight for whatever reason in the complex side of Wagner will still find enough of him here. One area in which I have had to add, instead of take away, is indirect speech. German uses the subjunctive for this, but in English one has to add "they said" or the like to convey the correct meaning. I have generally retained Wagner's use of emphasis. He does this by using different fonts or spacings; all such instances are given here in italics, which I also use for work titles etc., as is the common practice today. I have also kept Wagner's habit of preceding a new thought with a dash, and adhered to his paragraph divisions except in one or two cases where he digresses from his topic within a particularly long paragraph, and starting a new paragraph seemed to the benefit of his text (these instances are few and are not otherwise indicated).

Each new translator owes a debt to those who have gone before him (as Jacobs also freely admitted).[4] The same naturally applies to me. However, I took care to consult my direct predecessors only after having made my first draft, both to avoid undue influence and in an effort to ensure that I did not plagiarize them, however unintentionally. There were occasions when they proved a real boon, and I am indebted to them all in many ways. If, upon consulting them, I found that they had here or there chosen a word more fitting to the context than my own, I adopted it without comment (I believe it would be absurd to provide footnotes for individual words that are themselves in common currency). It also happened that on consulting my predecessors about a particularly convoluted passage, I found that they had either paraphrased heavily to avoid the problem (in which I wholeheartedly sympathize), or had each alighted on a very different solution—almost as if we had all been translating quite different source texts. On other occasions, I found that my chosen wording was remarkably close to one or other of them—such as in Wagner's description, late in *Über das Dirigieren*, of the talented young conductors whose fate is that of the "heretics of old." It is also possible that some phrases might have stuck in my mind after earlier perusals of the translations in question (Ashton Ellis in particular has been a staple of English-speaking students for many years, and I consulted him often at university, nearly forty years ago). But some stock turns of phrase will also

---

4   Wagner, trans. Jacobs (1979): vii.

suggest themselves to any translator in the present context. I was amused to find, after having already translated a particular passage, that "Kraut und Rüben" (literally: cabbage and turnips) was already considered equivalent to "higgledy-piggledy" in Ashton Ellis's day. So if the observant reader finds unacknowledged similarities between my offerings and those of my predecessors, my excuse is one whose wording I shamelessly pilfer from Heinrich Böll: these are neither intentional nor accidental, but unavoidable.[5]

I have also benefitted from the work of recent Wagner translators who have worked on texts other than those I offer here. Roger Allen's translation of *Beethoven*[6] is a model of its kind, while reading any translation by Stewart Spencer leaves me astonished at his linguistic virtuosity and clarity, and wishing that I possessed either. Any errors or misunderstandings in the present translations are naturally the fault of the present writer alone.

While I was working on this book, Egon Voss published an excellent new edition of the original German text of *Über das Dirigieren*.[7] I only read Voss when I was already deep into my own work on the present volume, and in fact our approach is very different (Voss's is a critical edition that details the genesis of that text and its assorted versions, whereas the present book is focused on the context and reception of Wagner's several writings on the art of conducting). I did find that some of Voss's annotations coincided with what I needed to add here in order to make Wagner more easily comprehensible, and there are inevitable overlaps (mostly where we each felt a need to identify historical figures with dates of birth and death and a designation of their professional function). While I did not read Voss's annotations until I had made my own, I have acknowledged his precedence in my footnotes whenever we offer similar solutions. I am also grateful to Voss—a colleague of over twenty years' standing with a knowledge of Wagner far surpassing my own—for kindly providing me with information on numerous issues, and for taking the time to meet and discuss Wagner (and much else) more than once during my work on this volume.

---

5   Heinrich Böll: *Die verlorene Ehre der Katharina Blum oder Wie Gewalt entstehen und wohin sie führen kann*. Cologne: Kiepenheuer & Witsch, 2008, no page number.

6   Wagner, trans. Allen (2014).

7   Voss (2015).

Music Examples

As explained in my accompanying essay, Wagner's music examples are oddly cursory and abrupt (they often end at a bar line in the middle of a phrase, without regard for the musical flow). When Robert L. Jacobs made his abridged translation of Wagner's writings on conducting in 1979, he considerably expanded the original examples (though without specifying his changes in each case).[8] I have retained Wagner's examples wherever possible, abruptness and all, though I have had to concur with Jacobs on occasions where expansion seemed a prerequisite for ensuring comprehension on the part of the reader. I have also occasionally adjusted the order in which these examples occur in the text, so as to keep to a clear musical chronology (Wagner sometimes jumps back and forth in a score). In each case where I have amended the substance or the placing of the original example, this is specified in a footnote. Two things have been changed without comment, however: C clefs have been replaced by treble and bass clefs (except for viola parts), and all transposing instruments are here given in C. Wagner occasionally gives a reference for his source, though merely by pointing the reader to the relevant page in the scores published by Breitkopf & Härtel. I here give measure numbers throughout instead.

---

8   Wagner, trans. Jacobs (1979).

Part I

Richard Wagner's Writings on Conducting

Chapter One

Reminiscences of Spontini

Gaspare Spontini (1774–1851) was one of the most celebrated opera composers of his time. He studied in Naples, then in 1803 moved to Paris where he
enjoyed the patronage of the Empress Joséphine. His opera *La vestale*, first
performed at the Paris Opera in 1807, brought him international fame and
was admired and imitated by many others. In 1820 he was made the director
of the Berlin Opera on the invitation of King Friedrich Wilhelm III of Prussia,
where he played a major part in consolidating the importance of the conductor at roughly the same time that Weber was exerting a similar influence from
the podium at the Court Opera in Dresden. Spontini remained in Berlin for
twenty years, by which time his star had waned, and he was finally released
from his duties in 1841. Of all his operatic forbears, Spontini was one of those
whom Wagner most admired. He almost certainly met Spontini in Berlin in
1836, and eight years later, having himself assumed a position of power in the
operatic world, he was able to invite Spontini to conduct his masterpiece *La
vestale* in Dresden. As was typical of Wagner, his published praise of the man
and his work was generally tempered by criticism either explicit or implicit,[1]
and the expressions of admiration for the "immortal" composer in his later
correspondence with the man's family are not without ulterior motive (Spontini's wife was the sister of the piano manufacturer Erard, whose widow gifted
Wagner a lovely new grand piano). Nevertheless, a genuine admiration and
affection for the man and his work seems to shine through all the ifs and buts
of his essays and the flowery clichés of his correspondence.[2]

Wagner's essay on Spontini is a mash-up made in 1872 of two earlier texts.
It begins with a slightly truncated version of the obituary that Wagner had published in the *Eidgenössische Zeitung* in Zurich on February 11, 1851, just over
a fortnight after Spontini's death on January 24 (Wagner's admiration for the
man was made further apparent when he included the overture to Spontini's

---

1   See, for example, his discussion of Spontini in *Opera and Drama*, SSD 3: 240.
2   See Wagner's letter to Camille Erard of February 15, 1858, in SB 9: 193–94.
     His Erard piano is held today by the Wagner Museum in Tribschen, Lucerne.

opera *La vestale* in his next concert with the Zurich orchestra on February 25, 1851). The second, anecdotal part of this essay, about Spontini in Dresden, dates from roughly 1866 and was extracted from *Mein Leben*, Wagner's last and biggest autobiography. The resultant text, now entitled simply "Reminiscences of Spontini," was published in the fifth volume of Wagner's collected writings in the summer of 1872, amidst reprints of smaller essays from the 1850s and the libretto to *Das Rheingold*. Wagner dealt in similar fashion with his report on conducting Beethoven's Ninth Symphony in Dresden in 1846, which was also taken from *Mein Leben*, but similarly coupled with a much earlier text and placed in the second volume of his collected writings, alongside essays actually written in the 1840s and the libretto to *Lohengrin*. The second volume of *Mein Leben*, containing the original versions of his recollections of Spontini in Dresden and of performing Beethoven's Ninth in that city, was published in late 1872 in a limited private edition; the full text of this autobiography would not be made publicly available for another nine decades.

Anno Mungen revealed several years ago how Wagner's reminiscences of Spontini play fast and loose with the truth, being clearly couched with a view to a neat dramatic trajectory that enhances Wagner's reputation at the cost of Spontini's.[3] To give one such example: Wagner writes how Spontini insisted in advance that he would expect "le tout garni de douze bonnes contre-basses" (the full complement of 12 good double basses) for his performance, the financial consequences of which—thus Wagner—caused such horror among the management of the Dresden opera house that they tried to rescind their invitation as tactfully as possible. Spontini nevertheless turned up for the dress rehearsal, and all proceeded swimmingly since Wagner the supreme diplomat was at hand to solve any problems. In fact, Spontini had only asked for six or seven double basses, and Wagner had offered five; the rest was Wagner's invention.[4] Our purpose here, however, is not to tease out fact from fiction, but to observe Wagner's descriptions of Spontini as a conductor and of the changes to the orchestral set-up that supposedly resulted from the latter's visit to Dresden. As Mungen points out, Wagner deals in cavalier fashion with who was responsible for what innovations. But the very fact that "Spontini" is here a kind of Wagnerian construct (at times almost the dummy to Wagner's ventriloquist) means that we get a clear idea of what *Wagner* wanted from his orchestra—or at least, what Wagner in *circa* 1866 imagined that his earlier self must have wanted, or should have wanted. In fact, the blending of orchestral timbres that Wagner says here was his goal in 1844 was more relevant to the Wagner who composed his Prelude to *Lohengrin* a few years later.

Unlike the other texts translated in this volume, I here include only those passages that deal directly with our topic—conducting—and have excised the largely anecdotal sections.

---

3   Mungen (1995).
4   See Mungen (1995): 273.

[…] When I asked [Gaspare Spontini] to conduct the next day's rehearsal himself [in late 1844], he suddenly became very apprehensive, apparently in contemplation of the various difficulties that might present themselves. But in his highly flustered state he did not give any clear opinion about anything, so it became difficult to ask him what I might do to induce him to direct the rehearsal. After pondering for a while, he asked me what kind of baton we conducted with. I used my hands to explain the rough size and thickness of our average baton, which was made of normal wood, covered in white paper, and was always served up fresh to us by the orchestra attendant. He sighed and asked if I thought it might be possible by tomorrow to have a baton of black ebony made for him, of very considerable length and thickness (which he now explained using his arm and open hand), and at both ends of which a rather large white knob of ivory should be affixed. I promised both to procure him an instrument very similar to this for the next rehearsal, and that I would arrange for another to be made, of the required materials and to his complete specifications, in time for the performance itself. Noticeably reassured, he wiped his brow and told me I could announce that he would direct the next day's rehearsal. After insisting on describing his requirements for his baton once more, he travelled to his hotel.
[…]

I gave the theater's carpenter the most precise instructions for the baton, which turned out very well. It had the right length and thickness, was black, and had large white knobs at each end. Then we came to the rehearsal. Spontini was conspicuously embarrassed when he took his place in the orchestra. His main request was for the oboes to be placed behind him.[5] Because moving them in isolation like this would have caused much confusion to the orchestral set-up, I promised him that it would be done after the rehearsal. He said nothing more, and now took up his baton. I immediately understood why its form was so important to him, because he did not hold it at its end such as we other conductors did, but instead grasped it with his whole fist more or less in its

---

5   The arrangement of the orchestra in the opera pit varied from theater to theater at that time; the seating plan generally employed today only became established towards the end of the 19th century. The plan for the pit in the Dresden Opera House published by Gassner (1844): Beilage 2 puts the conductor next to the stage with the orchestra behind him, the strings to the left, the winds to the right. The plans given by Gassner (1844): Beilage 10 and 11 for the opera pits in Vienna and Darmstadt have a similar division between strings and wind. Spontini clearly preferred an arrangement closer to what we know today, with the strings spread across the pit (see below), though placing the oboes behind him seems as odd today as it clearly did to Wagner.

middle, moving it in such a way that we clearly understood he regarded it as a marshal's baton. He didn't use it to beat time, but to command the orchestra. Over the course of the first scenes, a sense of confusion spread that was all the more calamitous because the Master spoke to the orchestra and singers in an incoherent German that proved highly detrimental to establishing any general understanding. But we soon noticed that his prime concern was to dissuade us that this should be the dress rehearsal. Instead, he had in mind to begin studying the opera completely anew. Up to this point, my dear old chorus director and stage director Fischer[6] had been highly enthusiastic about the invitation to Spontini. But when he realized the unavoidable disruption that Spontini was going to make to the program of the house, he fell into a state of desperation that ultimately turned into open anger. In his blindness, he now felt that everything Spontini said was intended to harass him even more, so he began to respond bluntly in the coarsest possible language. On one occasion, Spontini gestured for me to join him so that he could whisper his praise of a chorus that had just ended: "Mais savez-vous, vos choeurs ne chantent pas mal" (but you know, your chorus doesn't sing badly). But Fischer eyed him suspiciously and asked me furiously: "What did the old ...[7] want now?" His former enthusiasm had swiftly disappeared, and I was barely able to calm him down. —

[Wagner then describes how the opera house acquiesced in Spontini's desire for more rehearsals. He also mentions Spontini's enthusiasm for the bass tuba, with which he had supposedly been unfamiliar (claims Wagner) until he first heard it in Wagner's *Rienzi*. Wagner then returns to the matter of the orchestral set-up.]

I also demonstrated my particular devotion to him by my zeal in completely reorganizing the set-up of the orchestra's instruments in accordance

---

6   Christian Wilhelm Fischer (1789–1859), German operatic bass and choral conductor, director of the chorus in Dresden from 1832 to 1857. Wagner had a high opinion of him, and included a laudatory account of their relationship in the fifth volume of his collected writings: "Nachruf an L. Spohr und Chordirektor W. Fischer," SSD 5: 105–10; Wagner claimed there that Fischer had been "the first to recognize me and to nudge me towards success" (SSD 5: 107).

7   This word is omitted in the published version of this article, but it features in Wagner's autobiography *Mein Leben*, from which he extracted these reminiscences: "Schweinehund." This passage is discussed in Gray (1988): 28; Gray gives "buzzard" in the Cambridge University Press translation of *Mein Leben* (Wagner, trans. Gray (1983): 280) but prefers "son of a bitch," which I agree to be much closer to the original.

with his wishes. This was not so much a reflection of any system on his part than a matter of habit. He explained that his manner of directing an orchestra made it vital for us to comply with his request without the slightest alteration. He conducted—so he said—only with his eyes. "My left eye is the first violins, my right eye the seconds; if you want to have the required effect with your eyes, then you can't wear glasses like the bad conductors do, even if you're short-sighted."[8] — He now admitted in confidence that "I can't see a single step in front of me, and yet I use my eyes to ensure that everything proceeds according to my will." The orchestral set-up to which he was accustomed was highly irrational in its details, however. His habit of having the two oboists directly behind him came from one of the earliest Parisian orchestras he had known. These two musicians thus had the bells of their instruments turned away from the ears of the audience, and our excellent oboist was so indignant at this imposition that I was only able to pacify him for the moment by treating it all in a particularly jocular manner. This custom of Spontini's was also founded on a system that was highly judicious, but which I am sad to say was completely unknown among most German orchestras. Under his system, the different sections of the string instruments were spread evenly across the two flanks of the orchestra, with the brass and percussion concentrated between them, and the softer wind instruments serving as a bridge between the violins. In Germany, by contrast, even the biggest, most famous orchestras have the usual division of the instrumental sections in two halves, with the strings together and the winds together.[9] This reflects a rough, insensitive attitude to what ought to be a beautiful, uniform sound in the orchestra that should coalesce intimately. I was delighted to be able to use this occasion to impose this happy innovation in Dresden. Thanks to Spontini's demands, it was now easy to get the king to insist on keeping the changes that had been made.[10] After Spontini left, it remained

---

8   Wagner, it seems, was himself short-sighted, and at least in later years conducted while wearing glasses. See the section "Wagner in the Picture" in the critical essay below.

9   This was apparently the custom in opera pits in Germany; see also fn. 5 above.

10   According to Schubert (1864): 48, the Dresden orchestra was still seated as given by Gassner several years after Spontini's visit, with the strings to the left, the winds to the right. However, as Koury (2010): 250 suggests, Schubert might well have copied Gassner's old plan of 1844 and was thus providing out-of-date information. It may be significant that Schubert's description of the orchestral seating plan in the Odeon in Munich on p. 49 also reads like a description of the plan given in Gassner (1844): Beilage 13.

for me only to balance out and correct a few peculiarities and haphazard aspects of his set-up. From now on I was able to achieve a satisfactory, highly effective seating arrangement for the orchestral musicians. [...]

Chapter Two

Report on the Performance of Beethoven's Ninth Symphony in Dresden in 1846

The date of this essay is often given as 1846 in the literature, though it is in fact an extract from Wagner's autobiography *Mein Leben* and was probably dictated to Cosima in early 1867. It was first published in the second volume of his collected writings in 1871. For more information on both this text and its overall context, see the section on "Wagner and Beethoven's Ninth" in the critical essay below.

In the winter [of 1845-46], my main task was to invest great care in preparing a performance of Beethoven's Ninth Symphony for Palm Sunday [April 5, 1846]. This performance caused intense struggles, and provided me with experiences that proved of great importance for the whole of my further development. This is what happened. Every year, the Royal Orchestra had just one performing opportunity independent of the opera house and the church. On Palm Sunday, the orchestra was given the use of the so-called old opera house for a large-scale performance in aid of its pension fund for widows and orphans. These occasions used to be restricted to giving an oratorio. In order to make the event more attractive, it had become customary to perform a symphony in the same program. We two capellmeisters, Reissiger[1] and I, were entitled to alternate in conducting this concert. For Palm Sunday

---

1   Carl Gottlieb Reissiger (1798–1859), German composer and conductor, royal capellmeister in Dresden from 1828 until his death.

1846 I was assigned the "symphony." I truly yearned to perform the Ninth Symphony, and was emboldened in choosing this work for our concert by the fact that it was almost unknown in Dresden. When word of this reached the orchestra's representatives who had to manage and enlarge the pension fund, they were so horrified that they arranged an audience with our General Director von Lüttichau[2] and asked him to exercise his high authority to deter me from my plan. They explained that performing this symphony would be detrimental to the pension fund because the work was in disrepute in Dresden and the audience would stay away from the concert. Many years before, Reissiger had conducted the Ninth Symphony in a concert for the benefit of the poor, and he himself had confirmed that it had been a complete flop.[3] So I needed all my passion and eloquence to overcome our director's initial reservations. As for the orchestral representatives, I heard that they were complaining throughout the city about my recklessness. This left

---

2   Wolf Adolf August von Lüttichau (1786–1863), General Director of the Court Theater and Orchestra in Dresden from 1824 to 1862, and thus Wagner's boss.

3   Reissiger performed the Ninth in Dresden on August 27, 1838. The *Allgemeiner musikalischer Anzeiger* of Vienna, 10/41 (October 11, 1838), 162 mentioned only that "the two middle movements seemed to please the most," though the anonymous correspondent of the *Wiener Zeitschrift für Kunst, Literatur, Theater und Mode* was openly enthusiastic, writing that the work, heard now for the first time in Dresden, "was performed with enthusiasm and clarity and delighted all true connoisseurs and lovers of music. May we now hear it more often so that we can become completely familiar with it! One would have liked the solo voices to sound more powerfully above all the instruments, and for the magnificent hall to have had a somewhat bigger audience. But it is the fate of this concert, which is merely an annual occurrence, that it is never very full" (No. 132, Saturday November 3, 1838, 1056). Given Wagner's tendency to denigrate others in order to heighten his own importance, it seems reasonable to suppose that Reissiger's performance in 1838 was not the disaster that Wagner here claims; nor does it seem likely that Reissiger would have spoken about it thus to his junior colleague. In his reminiscences, Wagner's friend, the sculptor Gustav Adolph Kietz (1824–1908), claimed that Reissiger's performance of 1838 had been a "complete fiasco" that had turned the Ninth Symphony into "carnival music, the product of a madman's brain": Kietz (1905): 46. However, Kietz would have been 14 at the time (and thus hardly able to offer an informed opinion), and it seems in any case that he was not even present at the concert. He began his studies in Dresden in 1841. He did, however, have the opportunity to observe Wagner at close hand in Dresden and claimed to have sat in on all of Wagner's main rehearsals in 1846.

me no other choice for the moment than to break off relations with them. In order to make them ashamed of their opinion, I decided to prepare the public for the work and my performance of it in a manner that would create a furor, attract an especially large audience, and ensure the work's success at the box office—the very thing that was feared to be under threat. The Ninth Symphony thus became a matter of honor to me in every possible respect, and I had to invest all my energies into making it a success. The committee expressed reservations about the cost of procuring the orchestral parts, so I borrowed them from the Leipzig Concert Society.

In my earliest years of youth, I had spent my nights copying out that score, and its pages prompted me to mystic rapture. My feelings were indescribable when I now saw those mysterious pages again and studied them carefully! Back in my darker days in Paris, hearing a rehearsal of the first three movements played by the incomparable orchestra of the Conservatoire had touched me deeply, transporting me away from all my years of confusion and alienation back to those days of early youth.[4] As if by some magic power, hearing it had inspired me to chart a new course for my inner strivings. When I first studied the score, it had been merely an optical mystery to me. But now my aural memory of that rehearsal in Paris brought the score alive as I read through it, and it acquired a strange power over me. Since those days, I had experienced many things that had remained unspoken inside me. But now they coalesced within me, inspiring me to ask urgent questions about my own destiny. What I dared not utter aloud was a recognition that my artistic, professional, and societal existence was without any real foundation; instead, I was proceeding along a career path on which I had to acknowledge I was a stranger, and devoid of real prospects. I endeavored to hide this sense of despair from my friends, but that despair was now transformed into utter enthusiasm as I grappled with this symphony. No work by any master could ever have seized the heart of a student with the ecstatic force I felt when faced with the first movement of this work. The score lay open before me as I pondered the means of its execution, and if anyone had come upon me and witnessed my convulsive sobs and tears as I worked on it, they would have asked themselves in astonishment whether this was how a Royal Saxon Capellmeister ought to behave! Luckily, I was on those occasions spared any

---

4   See Wagner's longer discussion of Habeneck's Paris performance in *Über das Dirigieren*, pp. 35–38 below; and see the first section of my critical essay on the uncertainty surrounding how many movements Wagner actually heard Habeneck conduct.

visits by either our orchestral representatives, their worthy first capellmeister [Reissiger], or any other gentlemen well-trodden in the paths of classical
music.

As was customary, a textbook for the chorus part was to be published.
With this as my starting point, I sketched out a program that offered an
introduction to a better understanding of the work. This was in order to
appeal not to the critical faculties, but to the feelings of the listeners.[5]
Goethe's *Faust* proved an effective aid in formulating the main points of this
program, which thereafter attracted gratifying attention not just in Dresden
at the time, but later in other cities too. I also wrote anonymously in the
Dresdner Anzeiger, publishing all kinds of brief, enthusiastic outpourings to
inspire the Dresden public and bring this hitherto "disreputable" work to
their attention.[6] My outward efforts in this regard were such a complete success that the income generated by the concert was far higher than it had been
in all previous years. What's more, our orchestral representatives regularly
used further performances of this symphony to ensure similarly high takings
in the subsequent years of my Dresden career.

As for the artistic aspects of this concert, I notated everything in the
orchestral parts myself and worked with the orchestra to ensure an expressive performance and to achieve a rigorous precision in the nuances of my
desired interpretation.[7] It had hitherto been usual to employ double wind,
but I took a far more subtle approach. Up to now, a simple solution had

---

5   Wagner remained fond of inventing such programs for audiences until his
early years in Zurich; the works he thus described ranged from Beethoven's
Eroica Symphony and *Coriolanus* to his own Overture to *Tannhäuser* and more
besides. See the section "Berlioz the Catalyst?" in my essay below.

6   Nicholas Vazsonyi describes Wagner's publicity and self-branding campaign in
detail in Vazsonyi (2010): 62–77.

7   These orchestral parts have not survived. Gustav Kietz (1905): 50, reports that
Wagner rehearsed from memory, a practice that is confirmed by other, later
reports about Wagner's conducting, such as Adolf Wallnöfer's recollections of
his 1872 performance in Bayreuth (Wallnöfer (n.d.): 17). Kietz's reminiscences
of 1846 sometimes paraphrase Wagner's *Report* to the point of plagiarism (without mentioning their source), but the greater detail he frequently offers—and
the undoubted fact that he was one of Wagner's close Dresden friends—means
his account should not be disregarded. Conducting from memory was the
norm for Hans Richter, who presumably modeled himself in this, as in other
matters, on his mentor Wagner. In 1876, Ferdinand Hiller, one of Wagner's
open critics, poured scorn on those who conducted from memory; when he

been applied: single wind were used in passages marked "*piano*," but double wind in those marked "*forte*." There is a passage in the second movement of the symphony that I can use to elucidate the precision I achieved in my performance. Here all the string instruments play the main rhythmic motif for the first time in C major, over three octaves.[8] They function as an accompaniment to the second theme, which is here assigned only to the weaker woodwind instruments. At every performance, because the whole orchestra is marked "*fortissimo*," the melody in the woodwind is obscured completely by the strings that are only supposed to be accompanying them. As a result, the wind cannot really be heard at all. No reverence to the letter of the law could prevent me from realizing what the Master had clearly intended, so I had the string instruments play only at a moderate *forte* up to the point where they continue this new theme in alternation with the wind instruments. This second motif, played with all their might by the double wind, could now be heard with utter clarity—surely for the first-ever time since the symphony was composed.[9] I acted similarly throughout the work in order to ensure the correct dynamics in the orchestra. When passages seemed rather difficult to grasp, I had them played so that they made a decisive impact on the emotions. The fugato in § in the "*alla Marcia*" section of the Finale, after the verse "Froh wie seine Sonnen fliegen," has always been very puzzling. I decided to approach it as a serious but joyful fighting game, taking my cue from the preceding strophes that seem to prepare us for battle and victory. So I had this fugato played throughout at an extremely fiery tempo, and with the utmost power. On the day after the first performance, I was gratified to receive Music Director Anacker[10] from Freiberg at my home. He came to

---

specifically mocks a "certain conductor" who conducts Beethoven without the score, he presumably means Wagner. See Hiller (1876): 132.

8   Wagner discusses this problematic passage in greater detail in the essay on the Ninth Symphony that he published in 1873, which is given in chapter 4 of this volume.

9   Charles Gounod later claimed that Habeneck had done something similar to solve the same problem; perhaps Wagner was in fact following Habeneck's example, but felt it advantageous to claim the idea as his own. See fn. 24 in chapter 3 below, "About Conducting," and fn. 10 in chapter 4 below, "On Performing Beethoven's Ninth Symphony."

10 August Ferdinand Anacker (1790–1854), cathedral cantor in his hometown of Freiberg, personally acquainted with Beethoven, Mendelssohn and others, and teacher to Robert Volkmann and Franz Brendel (Wagner's ally and editor of the *Neue Zeitschrift für Musik*).

tell me penitently that he had up to now been one of my opponents, but that this performance had changed him into my unconditional friend. What had completely overwhelmed him—he said—was my grasp of this fugato and my interpretation of it. — I also devoted great care to the very unusual, recitative-like passage for the cellos and double basses at the beginning of the last movement,[11] which had once caused such humiliation for my old friend Pohlenz.[12] Given the excellence of our double bass players, I felt able to achieve the utmost perfection in this passage. Thanks to twelve special rehearsals with the double basses alone, I succeeded in achieving a performance that seemed almost utterly free and yet possessed the most poignant tenderness and the greatest possible energy. — Right from the start of my endeavor, I had recognized that achieving a rapturous, popular impact would depend on an ideal performance of the chorus part despite its extraordinary difficulties. I knew that the demands made by this work could be met only by a big, enthusiastic mass of singers, so I had to ensure the participation of an excellent, large chorus from the outset. Besides getting the somewhat bland Dreyssigsche Singakademie[13] to offer the usual reinforcements for our theater chorus, I also managed to overcome assorted laborious difficulties to draft in the choir of the Kreuzschule with its capable boys' voices, plus the choir of the Dresden Seminary, which was well-practiced in singing for the church. These three hundred singers came together for regular rehearsals, and I did my best to inspire them to true ecstasy after my own fashion. I succeeded, for example, in proving to the basses that you cannot sing the famous passages "Seid umschlungen Millionen" and "Brüder, über'm Sternenzelt muss ein guter [*recte*: lieber] Vater wohnen" in a common or garden manner. They can only be sung as if cried out in the greatest elation. I led the way in this, demonstrating such euphoria that I truly felt I had now transported all and sundry into an utterly exceptional state of mind. Up to now, my own voice had penetrated everything, but I did not let up until

11 For information on how Wagner conducted this passage in later performances, see, e.g., the excerpt from the score annotated by Adolf Wallnöfer in Figure 5.17 below.

12 Christian August Pohlenz (1790–1843), composer and conductor, director of the Gewandhaus concerts from 1827 to 1835 and the Leipzig Singakademie from 1827 to 1843. At the early Leipzig performances of the Ninth, the orchestra's leader, Heinrich August Matthäi, directed the first three movements, Pohlenz the last. See Cook (1993): 48–49.

13 Wagner writes "Dreissigsche," as do other sources; but it was named after its founder, Anton Dreyssig (1774–1815), Court Organist in Dresden.

I could not even hear myself any more, being instead submerged in their warm sea of music. —

The baritone recitative "Freunde, nicht diese Töne" is almost impossible to perform on account of its fantastical difficulties. But Mitterwurzer[14] and I were intimately accustomed to working together, and I was thrilled to be able to guide him through a collaborative process, at the end of which he sang his part with rapturous expression. I also planned a wholly new seating arrangement for the orchestra, and needed the venue to undergo extensive conversions in order to ensure the very best acoustic.[15] As one can imagine, finding the money for this proved particularly difficult. But I did not give in, and was able to have a completely new podium constructed that allowed us to concentrate the orchestra wholly in the middle, with the many singers around it on steeply tiered seats after the manner of an amphitheater. This was extraordinarily advantageous to the impact of the chorus, while the careful organization of the orchestral set-up meant we could achieve great precision and energy in the purely symphonic movements.[16]

The hall was already overflowing at the dress rehearsal. My colleague [Reissiger] committed the incredible idiocy of inciting members of the audience against the symphony, convincing them of the regrettable aberration that Beethoven had committed in composing it. By contrast, Mr. Gade,[17] who was visiting us from Leipzig where he was conducting the Gewandhaus concerts, assured me after the dress rehearsal that he would gladly have paid twice the amount for his ticket in order to hear the recitative of the basses once again. Mr. Hiller[18] found that I had gone too far in my tempo

---

14 Anton Mitterwurzer (1818–76), Austrian baritone and a member of the Dresden Court Opera; he sang Wolfram in the first run of *Tannhäuser* and was later Wagner's first Kurwenal in *Tristan und Isolde*.

15 Wagner had a lifelong fascination for acoustics; he also designed an acoustic "shell" above the stage for his "Wagner festival" in Zurich in May 1853, and seems to have conceived even smaller works (such as *Träume* in the version for chamber orchestra and the *Siegfried Idyll*) specifically to achieve the best acoustic effect in the spaces where they were first performed. See Walton (2012).

16 Wagner seems to have been the first to organize the seating of orchestra and chorus in this manner. See Holden (2011a): 5.

17 Niels Gade (1817–90), Danish composer and conductor, at this time the assistant conductor of the Gewandhaus Orchestra under Mendelssohn.

18 Ferdinand Hiller (1811–85), German composer, conductor, pianist and writer, who deputized for Mendelssohn as conductor of the Leipzig Gewandhaus concerts from autumn 1843 to early 1844. He then moved to Dresden, where he

modifications; I later learnt how he felt it should be done when I heard spirited orchestral works played under his own baton. But my overall success was indisputably beyond all expectations, even among non-musicians. As I recall, these included the philologist Dr. Köchly,[19] who on this occasion approached me to confess that he had now, for the first-ever time, been able to follow a symphonic work from beginning to end with complete comprehension.

This occasion strengthened me in the gratifying conviction that I possessed the ability and the strength to carry through to a successful conclusion whatever I seriously desired.

---

became firm friends with Robert and Clara Schumann and helped to set up a series of subscription concerts that featured the world premiere of Schumann's Piano Concerto in December 1845. See also Wagner's criticism of him (though without giving his name) on p. 47 below.

19   Hermann Köchly (1815–76), German philologist, translator from the Latin and Greek, and educational reformer. Like Wagner, he participated in the Dresden May Uprising in 1849 and then went into exile; he taught at Zurich University in the early 1850s, when Wagner was active in the city.

Chapter Three

About Conducting

Über das Dirigieren—About Conducting—was first published in nine install-ments in the *Neue Zeitschrift für Musik* between late November 1869 and mid-January 1870, then in book form in spring 1870 by Kahnt of Leipzig. Wagner included it in the eighth volume of his collected writings, published by Fritzsch of Leipzig in 1873. For a detailed account of its origins, publication, and impact, see "*Über das Dirigieren*—Early Impact" in my essay below.

Flies' noses and midges' snouts,
And all of your relations,
Frogs in the bushes and crickets in the grass,
You shall be my musicians![1]

In what follows here, I shall offer up my experiences and observations in a field of musical activity whose practice has hitherto been a matter of mere routine, and in which a lack of knowledge has made critical appraisal impos-sible. My assessment of things is not addressed to conductors themselves, but to musicians and singers, for they alone can sense properly whether they are being conducted either well or badly. To be sure, they can only judge this if they have at some point actually experienced good conducting, and this is something that happens extremely rarely. I do not intend to construct any

---

1   This is an amended quotation from the Walpurgisnacht scene in Goethe's *Faust I*. The last line in the original runs: "They are the musicians!" Wagner's cryptic motto is presumably intended to mock his opponents, though its use is some-what ironic, given that he later complains of others appropriating Goethe for their own, unjustified reasons. See p. 85 below.

system here,[2] but shall instead offer a series of observations, and reserve the right to expand on them later.[3]

How one's works are performed before the public is indubitably a matter of concern to a composer. An audience can only get a correct impression of a work if it is performed well, whereas a bad performance will give an incorrect impression, perhaps even leaving it unrecognizable.[4] If the reader can heed and understand my explanations of the different elements of performance given below, he will be in a position to realize the true state of most opera and concert performances in Germany today.

I shall reveal here how the weaknesses of German orchestras, both in their organization and in their actual performances, are primarily a result of the negative characteristics of their conductors, capellmeisters, and music directors etc. The managers of our artistic institutions appoint their conductors in a manner that demonstrates a degree of ignorance and carelessness that is directly proportional to the increasing difficulties faced by the orchestras themselves. Back when a score by Mozart constituted the highest demands made on an orchestra, the man in charge was typically a true German capellmeister: always a man of weighty reputation (at least at his place of work), secure and strict, though despotic and impolite. The last man of this type

---

2   Regarding Wagner's use of the word "system," see the section "*Über das Dirigieren*—Structure, Context, and Meta-Text" in the critical essay below.

3   Wagner implies here that he might continue the topic of his essay at a later date, though he did not (with the exception of his essay on conducting Beethoven's Ninth, published in 1873 and also given in translation in this volume). But this sentence already underlines the open-ended, essentially unstructured nature of this essay, as discussed in greater detail in the same section of the critical essay below.

4   "Composer" here presumably means Wagner, who was worried about his works being inadequately performed. He even spoke of this frustration at length when he first met Friedrich Nietzsche, on November 8, 1868, in Leipzig, and made an exception only for Hans von Bülow's performances in Munich. Nietzsche wrote the next day, November 9, 1868, to his friend Erwin Rohde in Hamburg that Wagner "utters terrible curses about all the performances of his operas, with the exception of the famous [performances] in Munich." See Nietzsche (2009–): www.nietzschesource.org/#eKGWB/BVN-1868,599.

whom I knew was *Friedrich Schneider*[5] in Dessau; *Guhr*[6] in Frankfurt was also one of them. These men, and others like them, were what one might call bewigged,[7] hoary relics in their attitude to new music. I myself experienced the extent of their ability some eight years ago in a performance of my *Lohengrin* in Karlsruhe, under old capellmeister Strauss.[8] This most worthy man clearly approached my score with timidity and a sense of alienation; but he also conveyed his concerns to his orchestra, which could not have performed my score more precisely or with greater vigor. One saw how all obeyed him: this was a man who brooked no nonsense and had his people fully in his grasp. Strangely, this old gentleman was also the only well-known conductor I came across who possessed true fire. His tempi did not drag and were often too fast, but his performances were always gritty and well executed. I got a similarly positive impression of *H. Esser* in Vienna,[9] whose performances were of the same quality.

---

5   Friedrich Schneider (1786–1853), a German composer, pianist, conductor, and teacher; organist at the Thomaskirche and music director at the city theater in Leipzig during Wagner's youth. From 1822 to his death he was capellmeister in Dessau. His oratorio *Das Weltgericht* (1819) became popular all over Europe. His pupils included both Eduard Bernsdorf, whose relationship with Wagner was one of mutual dislike (see p. 70 below), and Theodor Uhlig, Wagner's confidant in Dresden.

6   Carl Wilhelm Ferdinand Guhr (1787–1848), a German multi-instrumentalist, composer, and conductor; music director of the theater in Kassel from 1814 to 1821, then in Frankfurt am Main until his death. See Gollmick (1848).

7   Wagner writes "Zöpfe" (the plural of "Zopf"), which today generally means pigtails or braids; Ashton Ellis uses the former term in his translation of this essay (Wagner trans. Ellis (1895): 106), as had Dwight before him (Wagner trans. Dwight (1870): 257); Dannreuther paraphrases, using the phrase "old-fashioned" instead. Wagner uses "Zopf" (generally associated with Prussian military fashion in the 18th century) to signify the philistine, fuddy-duddy customs of the *ancien régime*, much as Berlioz mockingly used the word "perruques" (wigs/the bewigged); see Berlioz ed. Kolb (2015): 114.

8   Joseph Strauss (1793–1866), court capellmeister in Karlsruhe from 1824 to 1863. Wagner criticizes Strauss—albeit based on hearsay—in a letter to Eduard Devrient of April 30, 1856 from Zurich, specifically mentioning a performance that's planned of *Lohengrin* (see SB 8: 49–50). Further criticism of Strauss ensues in Wagner's subsequent correspondence with Devrient over the years.

9   Heinrich Esser (1818–72), capellmeister at the Vienna Court Opera from 1847 to 1869, who had impressed Wagner with his preparations for the

In cases where this old type of conductor was less talented than the two just mentioned, they ultimately and inevitably proved inadequate to the task of training an orchestra after the emergence of the more complicated, newer types of orchestral music. This was primarily because they had an ingrained habit of organizing their orchestral personnel only according to what they needed for the tasks before them. I know of no example anywhere in Germany where an orchestra has been fundamentally reorganized to make it fit for the demands of more modern orchestration. In the big orchestras, musicians are still promoted to leading positions according to the laws of seniority. Consequently, they only ever arrive at the front desks when their powers are waning. The younger, more industrious musicians have to take on subordinate positions, which is highly detrimental to the music, especially in the wind section. More recently, wise efforts have been made in this regard, which together with a modest degree of self-recognition on the part of the musicians themselves have led to constant improvements to this sorry state of affairs. However, another trend has resulted in a deterioration of the string section, namely a complete lack of attention both to the second violins, and to the violas in particular. The viola is overwhelmingly played by decrepit violinists, or even by the weaker wind players if these have ever played a little violin. At best, efforts are made to put a really good violist just on the first desk so that he can cope with the occasional solo passages. But I have also experienced how the leader of the violins has on occasion been drafted in to help out the violas in such cases. I was once told that only one out of the eight violists in a certain major orchestra[10] was able to play the difficult passages that often occur in my newer scores. This old practice of assigning lesser players to these parts was excusable in terms of human charity. It was also made possible by the way composers scored their music in earlier times, when the viola was mostly employed to fill out the accompaniment. It can even be justified to a certain degree in our own times by the unworthy orchestration employed by those Italian opera composers whose works remain such a popular mainstay of the German operatic repertoire. These are the favorite operas of the major theater intendants, who are in turn merely mimicking the laudable tastes of the aristocratic courts they serve. When it comes to the works that those gentlemen dislike, it should not surprise us that the demands posed can only be met if their capellmeister is a man of

---

aborted Vienna production of *Tristan*.

10   Voss (2015): 4 remarks that Wagner's autograph of this essay specifically names the Munich Court Orchestra here; he later removed this direct reference.

weight, possessed of a serious reputation, and properly aware of the needs of today's orchestra. Most of our older capellmeisters did not possess any such awareness. Nor did they realize the necessity of increasing the number of string instruments in our orchestras to counterbalance the larger number and increased use of the wind instruments. They might take emergency measures if this mismatch in forces became too obvious, but this never sufficed to bring the famous German orchestras onto the same level as those of France. When it comes to the number and ability of the violinists, and especially of the cellos, the German orchestras still lag very much behind in comparison.

Those capellmeisters of the old school might have failed to move with the times, but it ought to be the first, proper task of the conductors of our own style and time to acknowledge that things have changed and to act accordingly. Yet our intendants have made sure that these newer conductors cannot pose a threat to them, and have prevented them from inheriting the powerful authority of the industrious, bewigged capellmeisters of earlier times.

It is both important and instructive to recognize how this newer generation has achieved its current status, because it now represents the whole German music scene. Since we owe the maintenance of our orchestras to the court theaters both big and small—indeed, to our theaters in general—we must acknowledge that it is our theater directors who have been responsible for appointing those musicians who have had to represent the dignity and spirit of German music (and who have then remained in their posts for up to half a century at a time). Most of the musicians thus promoted must surely know how they arrived at their elevated position, because it is not immediately obvious what achievements of theirs would merit it. These typical German musicians have attained these "good positions" (which are regarded thus only by their patrons) mostly by the laws of inertia, ascending one step at a time. I believe that the great Berlin Court Orchestra has acquired most of its conductors in this manner.[11] On occasion, some "great man" or other might manage to jump a few rungs at a time, thanks to the protection of a lady-in-waiting of some princess or other. These men are devoid of authority, and we cannot begin to measure the negative impact that they have had on the maintenance and training of our greatest orchestras and opera houses. Being completely without merit, they have been able to remain in their

---

11   From 1820 to 1869, when Wagner wrote his essay, the main conductors of the Berlin Court Orchestra were, in chronological order: Gaspare Spontini, Giacomo Meyerbeer, Felix Mendelssohn, Otto Nicolai, Heinrich Dorn, and Wilhelm Taubert.

positions only by subservience to a boss who is himself ignorant, but usually assumes that he knows everything. At the same time, they have ingratiatingly endeared themselves to the sluggardly demands of their musicians, who are subservient to them in turn. By abandoning any notion of artistic discipline (which was in any case beyond their ability), and through acquiescence and obedience toward every senseless demand from above, these "masters" have even managed to attain general popularity. Every difficulty met in rehearsing a work has been overcome by unctuously referring to the "longstanding fame of the Court Orchestra of N.N." and by giving a knowing smile on all sides. Was no one able to realize that the standards of these renowned institutions were sinking lower and lower every year? Where were the real masters who might have been in a position to judge this? Certainly none of the critics were capable of noticing it, for they only bark when their mouths aren't muzzled, and everyone knew the importance of muzzling them.

In more recent times, these conducting posts have been filled by those with a special calling. According to the needs and mood of the director in charge, he will appoint some industrious veteran to come and inject a certain "active energy" to relieve the sluggishness of the typical capellmeister. These are conductors who can put on an opera in fourteen days, who know how to make heavy cuts in a work, and can compose new endings for the works of others to make them more effective for their lady singers. Such skills are found in one of the sprightliest conductors of the Dresden Court Orchestra.[12]

Sometimes there is a real call for "musical greats" to come and help out. The theaters have no such conductors, but the singing academies and concert organizations can apparently churn them out every two to three years, judging by the praise they get in the cultural pages of our great political newspapers. These are the "music bankers" of our time, such as have emerged from Mendelssohn's school,[13] or who have been recommended to the world as having been his protégés. They are a very different kind of person from

---

12   Presumably Julius Rietz (1812–77), German conductor, composer, and teacher, a friend of Mendelssohn (he was his successor as music director in Düsseldorf), a sometime teacher at the Leipzig Conservatory, and in 1860–77 court capellmeister in Dresden as successor to Carl Reissiger. Ashton Ellis was the first to suggest that Wagner here referred to Rietz (Wagner trans. Ellis (1895): 295). For further criticism of Rietz on Wagner's part—again without naming him—see p. 102 below.

13   This is presumably a sarcastic reference to Mendelssohn's father, who was a banker; see "Of 'Elegance' and Anti-Semitism" in my essay below.

the inept progeny of our old bewigged capellmeisters. They are musicians who haven't grown up in the orchestra or in the theater, but have received a respectable education in the newly founded conservatories, composing oratorios and psalms and attending the rehearsals of subscription concerts.[14] They have also been given tuition in conducting, and have been educated elegantly[15] such as had never before been the case among musicians. There would be no more hint of uncouthness; the anxious modesty and lack of self-confidence among our poor, native-born capellmeisters was now replaced by good manners, which was also an expression of their somewhat bashful attitude towards our old-fashioned, German, societal structures. I think that these people have in some ways had a good influence on our orchestras. A lot of roughness and doltishness has now disappeared, and since their arrival many details have been better observed and made audible thanks to their elegant art of performance. They were already much more accustomed to the newer type of orchestra, because in many respects they owed to their master, Mendelssohn, a particularly delicate and refined training along those very same paths upon which Carl Maria von Weber's brilliant genius had first embarked.[16]

For the moment, however, these gentlemen lacked one thing that was necessary if they were going to help reorganize our orchestras and the institutions associated with them: energy, of a kind that can only emerge from the self-confidence possessed by those with truly innate strength. Regrettably, everything about them—their reputation, talent, education, and indeed their faith, love, and hope—was artificial.[17] The difficulties that arose from

---

14 Wagner's obvious envy of those who have received a structured music training in an academic institution (such as the Leipzig Conservatory, founded by Mendelssohn in 1843) is discussed in the same section of my essay below. Jens Malte Fischer has noted how making disparaging references to Mendelssohn's psalm settings and oratorios was a general feature of anti-Semitic music criticism in Germany, even before the publication of Wagner's own anti-Semitic tract of 1850. See Fischer (2015): 22.

15 See my essay below regarding Wagner's use of the word "elegant."

16 In the first-ever French version of this essay, Wagner's translator Guy de Charnacé adds the footnote: "We do not know whether Wagner is mocking or expressing approval, for there is so much confusion here in both style and spirit." See Charnacé (1874): 276.

17 Supposed "artificiality" in art is one of Wagner's favorite anti-Semitic tropes (as found, for example, on the very first page of his *Jewishness in Music*; see SSD 5: 66–85, here 66). It is coupled here with a reference to the three "Christian"

the artificiality of their position was one reason why they were unable to pay any attention to more general issues, such as bringing together what belonged together, doing what was logical, or renewing what ought to have been renewed. But none of this really concerned them anyway, and rightly so. They had moved up into the positions formerly held by the old-school, heavy-duty German masters, but only because the latter group had stooped too low and had become incapable of recognizing the needs of our own time and of our current style of music. It seems that these newer gentlemen regard their current positions as merely transitional in nature: they cannot properly come to terms with the German artistic ideals that are the only goal of everything noble, because those ideals are foreign to them in the deepest recesses of their nature. So when they are confronted with the most difficult demands of modern music, they too resort only to superficial remedies. *Meyerbeer*, for example, was very tactful. When he needed a good flautist to play a particular passage well for him in Paris, he paid for one out of his own pocket. Since Meyerbeer understood what it takes to play something properly, and was also rich and independent, he could have been extraordinarily useful to the Berlin orchestra when the king of Prussia appointed him as its general music director. *Mendelssohn* had also been appointed to the orchestra at the same time, and he truly did not lack the most unusual knowledge and talents. To be sure, they were both faced with the same obstacles that have hitherto hindered everything good in Berlin, but they were the very men who might have swept aside those obstacles, being so richly endowed with every means to do so; no one after them would ever have the same opportunity again. Why did their strength desert them? It seems because they had none. They let things remain as they were. As the "famous" Berlin orchestra now stands before us, even the last traces of Spontini's former precision have faded. And that was

---

virtues of faith, hope, and love, the mention of which is something of a *non sequitur*, being of no relevance to his argument. It seems that this passage is overall yet another of Wagner's snide digs at Mendelssohn (the three virtues in question are listed in St. Paul's first letter to the Corinthians, 13:13; since Mendelssohn wrote an oratorio about St. Paul, this might also explain the reference to "oratorios" in Wagner's text). See, too, the insistence later in this paragraph on how "German artistic ideals" are "foreign" to Mendelssohn's protégés. Heinz-Klaus Metzger sums up Wagner's criticism of Mendelssohn's Beethoven interpretations with characteristic bluntness: "The 'affect' that led Wagner to his ceremoniously incorrect tempo specifications in Beethoven's symphonies was nothing other than murderous and anti-Semitic." See Metzger (1985): 69.

Meyerbeer and Mendelssohn! So what could their dainty imitators possibly achieve elsewhere?

When we ponder the characteristics of the capellmeisters and music directors of the older generation and the newest of their species, it becomes evident that we cannot expect much of any of them when it comes to reforming our orchestras. In fact, any progress made in this up to now has come about on the initiative of the musicians themselves. This is very understandable, given the improved technical, virtuoso training they have enjoyed. Virtuosos on different instruments have indisputably brought much good to our orchestras, and their success would have been complete if their conductors had been up to the task too. Naturally, these virtuosos swiftly outgrew them all: the hoary remnants among our old capellmeisters, those who had climbed the greasy pole and were ever fearful of losing their authority, and those piano-teachers-turned-music-directors who owed their positions to the grace and favor of chambermaids. In our orchestras, these virtuosos have now assumed the role occupied by prima donnas in the theater. The elegant capellmeisters of the newest type have also aligned themselves with them, which in some respects has not been detrimental. This alignment could even have resulted in a successful collaborative venture, if those gentlemen had understood the heart and soul of true German music-making.

But for the moment, we must emphasize that these conductors owed their position to the *theater*—just as the orchestras too owed their very existence to it. And since most of their pursuits and achievements were in *opera*, their main task was to understand this same genre. This in turn meant that they had to learn something new in their music-making. Just as astronomy requires the application of mathematics, so they had to learn how to apply music to the dramatic arts. If they had properly understood dramatic singing and dramatic expression, this could also have enlightened them as to how an orchestra should play the newer German instrumental works. I received the best guidance with regard to the tempo and the performance of Beethoven's music from the soulful, carefully accentuated singing of the great *Schröder-Devrient*;[18] it has been impossible for me since then to let the inspiring oboe cadenza in the first movement of the C minor Symphony

---

18 Wilhelmine Schröder-Devrient (1804–60), a German singer who was long Wagner's ideal dramatic soprano. She created the roles of Senta in his *Holländer* and Venus in *Tannhäuser*. Sister-in-law to the actor and director Eduard Devrient.

Example 3.1. Beethoven, Symphony no. 5, 1st movement, m. 268

be so embarrassingly blown in that same manner in which I have otherwise always heard it.[19] Indeed, it was only when I realized the right way to perform this passage that I also understood, in retrospect, the significance and manner of expression that should be given to the first violins' fermata in their earlier, corresponding passage:

Example 3.2. Beethoven, Symphony no. 5, 1st movement, m. 21

The touching, poignant impression that these two seemingly unremarkable passages made on me provided me with a fresh understanding of the whole

---

19 As explained in the section "*Über das Dirigieren*—Structure, Context, and Meta-Text" below, this passage overlaps with one in *Mein Leben*—written roughly concurrently—in which Wagner specifically names Philipp Joseph Fries (1815–90), the first oboist in the semi-professional Zurich orchestra, as having played this "cadenza" to his full satisfaction. Fries was a German immigrant who had settled in Zurich in 1844. Wagner also writes something similar in a letter to Theodor Uhlig, undated but clearly from late February 1852, though he here refers not to Beethoven's Fifth Symphony, which he had conducted just days before on February 17, 1852, but to the same composer's *Egmont* music, which he had conducted complete a month earlier, on January 20, 1852 (see Walton (2007): 178): "I rehearsed the Egmont entr'acte with the oboist in my room as if with a female singer: the man was overjoyed at how he finally accomplished it" (SB 4: 297–302, here 298). Wagner presumably means the oboe cadenza at the start of the third entr'acte, no. 5 in the *Egmont* music. Perhaps Wagner confused the works in his autobiography, or perhaps (as seems more likely) he actually rehearsed several such oboe solo passages with Fries in private, including those of the Fifth Symphony and the *Egmont* entr'acte. Fries's original oboe, as it happens, is held today by the Music Division of the Zentralbibliothek Zürich: see Walton (2002).

movement. — This is only by way of an aside. I merely wish to intimate that if a conductor could properly understand his function in the theater, this could complement the higher musical training he has received in the interpretive arts. After all, it is to the theater that he in fact owes his office and his rank. And yet he regards opera as an irksome day job, groaning as he does his tasks (though the miserable state of opera in the German theaters sadly makes this understandable). Instead, he sees his place of glory in the concert hall, which is where he started, and to which venue he felt called. As I have said above, as soon as a theater intendant wants to appoint a musician with a good reputation as a capellmeister, then he looks for him outside the theater.

In order to be able to assess what such a former concert-and-choral conductor might achieve in the theater, we first have to pay him a visit where he really feels at home, and where his reputation as a "solid" German musician is founded. We have to observe him at work in the concert hall.

※ ※ ※

From[20] my earliest youth, I felt a pronounced sense of dissatisfaction whenever I heard our classical instrumental music performed in orchestral concerts. And this impression has only been confirmed again in more recent times, whenever I have heard such a performance. Whatever seemed so passionately spirited in expression when I read the score or played it at the piano was barely recognizable to me in the ephemeral, unappreciated way it usually passed over the listeners. I was astonished at the dullness of Mozart's cantilenas, which had beforehand seemed to me so vital and full of emotion. The reasons for this only became clear to me later, and I have discussed them in greater depth in my *Report on a German Music School to be founded in Munich*, which is why I request those who seriously wish to follow my arguments to read the relevant passages there.[21] To be sure, these reasons lie first

---

20 This is the first paragraph in the second installment of Wagner's essay as published on December 3, 1869 in the *Neue Zeitschrift für Musik* 65/49.

21 *Bericht an Seine Majestät den König Ludwig II. von Bayern über eine in München zu errichtende deutsche Musikschule*. Munich: Christian Kaiser, 1865, also SSD 8: 125–76. Wagner's remarks on Mozart are as follows (see SSD 8: 145–46): "In order to stay with the simplest examples, namely Mozart's instrumental works (which are really by no means that master's main works—those are his operas), we can observe two things here: The significant necessity of performing them *cantabile*, and the sparse markings provided to this end in the extant scores. … When compared with Haydn, almost the only major difference in Mozart's

and foremost in the complete absence of any truly German music conservatory in the strictest sense of the word: a place where the precise tradition of
performing our classical music authentically, after the manner of the masters
themselves, would be kept constantly, vibrantly alive and preserved. But this
in turn would naturally presuppose that those masters had themselves managed to have their works performed in accordance with their original intentions. Regrettably, the German cultural world failed to provide them with
any such opportunity. As a result, when we try to determine the spirit of a
classical work of music today, we are dependent on the individual whims of
our conductors with regard to its tempo and interpretation.

When I attended the famous concerts in the Leipzig Gewandhaus in my
youth, those works were not conducted at all. Instead, they were simply played

---

symphonies is the extraordinarily soulful, songlike character of his instrumental
themes. Herein lies expressed what made Mozart so great and inventive in this
branch of music. If there had existed in Germany an institution as authoritative
as the Paris Conservatoire in France, if Mozart had performed his works there,
and if he had been able to supervise the spirit in which they were performed,
then a valid tradition for their performance might have come down to us, after
the fashion of the Paris Conservatoire ... In order to describe this more precisely
with a specific example, one should play, for example, the first eight bars of the
second movement of the famous E-flat major Symphony [K. 543] by Mozart,
doing so in the glib manner that their expression marks seem to require, and then
comparing this with how a sensitive musician would spontaneously play this
wonderful theme. How would we experience Mozart if we only ever heard him
performed in a manner so devoid of color and life? It would be a soulless, black-
on-white music, nothing else." The opening of the slow movement of Mozart's
K. 543 seems to have occupied Wagner time and again. On March 13, 1868, he
wrote to Hans von Bülow from Tribschen about it, calling it (for what reason we
know not) the "swan andante": "I recall only that the main matter was to perform the principal theme correctly, and that it's a matter of singing the motifs, as
almost always with Mozart. Here, the difficulty is to find an overall tempo that
doesn't drag, while still allowing the first measure its due rights. Because if it's
simply brushed off at an unassuming tempo, just as it is, without any nuances (as
every orchestra plays it), then all its magic is lost." Wagner recommended playing
the first measure *rallentando*, with a *crescendo* to the last eighth-note in the measure, then with a *diminuendo* to the second measure, which should be a *subito
piano*. See SB 20: 81–82, here 82. Also regarding this movement, see fns 38 and
95 in this chapter, and p. 159 in the critical essay.

through under the auspices of Matthäi[22] the concert master, as if they were overtures or entr'actes in the spoken theater. So there was no hint of any troubling individuality on the part of a conductor. The principal works of our classical instrumental repertoire in themselves offer no great technical difficulties, and were regularly played every winter. The orchestra knew these works very well, so they proceeded smoothly and precisely. You could see how pleased the musicians were about playing their favorite works again each year.

It was only with *Beethoven's Ninth Symphony* that this practice just wasn't enough, though as a matter of honor they had to perform this work every year, too. — I copied out the score of this symphony myself, and made a piano solo arrangement of it. But when I heard this work in the Gewandhaus, I was astonished that its performance made only the most confused impression on me.[23] In fact, I felt so completely disheartened by it that I began to doubt Beethoven utterly, and for a while turned away outright from studying him. As for Mozart's instrumental works, it is highly instructive that I only found true delight in them when I later had the opportunity to conduct them myself, and so was able to obey my own feelings when interpreting his cantilenas. But I learnt the most fundamental lesson of all when I finally heard the so-called Conservatoire Orchestra in Paris in 1839[24] play that same Ninth Symphony that I had come to doubt so much. Now it was as if scales fell from my eyes. I immediately understood the secret to performing it properly, for that orchestra had learnt to recognize Beethoven's *melody* in every measure—something that had clearly been completely missed by our dutiful Leipzig musicians—and the orchestra *sang* this melody.

This was the secret. And they had by no means been taught it by a conductor of any especial brilliance. *Habeneck*, to whom was due the great credit

---

22   Heinrich August Matthäi (1781–1835), concert master of the Leipzig Gewandhaus Orchestra, who was responsible for directing instrumental music from the first desk in its concerts; vocal works were directed by Christian August Pohlenz (see chapter 2, fn. 12). Matthäi was succeeded by Mendelssohn, who was at the same time appointed to conduct the orchestra's vocal concerts, thus becoming its first music director in a modern sense.

23   As Egon Voss notes (2015): 11–12, Wagner's chronology is inverted here; he heard the Ninth Symphony in the Gewandhaus on April 14, 1830, and in his enthusiasm he afterwards copied out the score and made a piano solo arrangement of it.

24   Voss writes that Wagner probably only heard Habeneck conduct this symphony on March 8, 1840, not already in 1839. See Voss (2015): 12. On Habeneck's possible changes to the dynamics, see fn. 9 in chapter 2, and fn. 10 in chapter 4.

for this performance, had rehearsed this symphony throughout a whole winter, and had found it incomprehensible and ineffective—though it is difficult
to say whether any German conductor would have taken the trouble to feel
even that much. But he then had his musicians study the symphony in a second and a third year, and refused to give up until every musician had grasped
the new Beethovenian *melos*.[25] And since these musicians had meanwhile
acquired the right feeling for these melodies, they also played them properly.
Habeneck was in fact another one of those old-school music directors: he
was the master, and everyone obeyed him.

The beauty of this performance of the Ninth Symphony to this day
remains quite impossible for me to describe. But in order to offer an inti-
mation of it, I shall here consider one particular passage (though any other
passage would also suffice) to demonstrate both the difficulty of performing
Beethoven, and the German orchestras' lack of success in doing so. I have
never been able to get even the best orchestras to play the following passage
from the first movement as utterly smoothly as I heard it from the musicians
of the Paris Conservatoire Orchestra thirty years ago:[26]

Example 3.3. Beethoven, Symphony no. 9, 1st movement, mm. 116–22

---

25   For extensive information on Wagner's use of the word "melos," see the sec-
      tion "Melos and the Body" in the essay below. I follow previous translators in
      retaining Wagner's chosen term throughout.

26   This same music example from Beethoven's Ninth Symphony hereafter threads
      its way through the literature on conducting for over a hundred years. In both
      his editions of his booklet *Über das Dirigieren*, Josef Pembaur gives the first
      four bars of this quotation as an example of an ascending figure to be per-
      formed without *crescendo*. He does not, however, mention Wagner as a source:
      Pembaur (1892): 32; Pembaur (1907): 57. The same example is given in
      Rovaart (1928?): 131 and Schuller (1997): 96, with Wagner each time named
      as the source; Hermann Scherchen gives the parallel passage from the recapitu-
      lation in his *Lehrbuch des Dirigierens* (Scherchen (1929): 48).

It is this passage that often reminded me so clearly in later life what it takes to achieve a good orchestral performance. This is because it combines *movement* with a *legato sound* at the same time as encompassing the laws of *dynamics*. The Parisians demonstrated their mastery by being able to play this passage *exactly* as the score stipulates. Neither in Dresden nor in London—two cities where I later performed this symphony—was I able to get the strings to play the changes of bow and string so imperceptibly in this rising, repeated figure. Much less still was I able to suppress their involuntary accentuation as this passage rises, because ordinary musicians always tend to increase their volume as they ascend, just as they get softer when a passage descends. By the fourth measure of the above passage, we inevitably entered into a *crescendo*, meaning that the sustained G-flat in the fifth measure was instinctively and inevitably given a harsh accent that is highly detrimental to the unusual, tonal significance of this note. It is difficult to get those of a coarse nature to both recognize and reject the type of expression that is accorded this passage when it is played in this common-or-garden fashion, though it is contrary to the express instructions of the Master, which he has made clear enough to us. To be sure, this passage expresses dissatisfaction, disquiet, and desire; but *the manner* of it is something we only experience when we hear this passage played as the Master had himself intended. Up to now, I have only ever heard it played thus by those Parisian musicians back in 1839 [*recte*: 1840]. I recall the impression of dynamic monotony (if I may be forgiven this seemingly absurd expression for a phenomenon that is very difficult to describe!) in the incredibly, even eccentrically varied intervallic movement of the rising figure, with its climax on the long G-flat. This note was sung with infinite tenderness, and the G-natural [two measures later] sang just as tenderly in answer to it. All this opened up to me the incomparable mysteries of the spirit—a spirit that now spoke to me directly, openly, clearly, and intelligibly.

But let us leave this sublime revelation for now without further comment. When I consider my other practical experiences, I can only ask: by what means were those Parisian musicians able to solve this difficult task so unerringly? It became evident to them through the most conscientious diligence, such as is characteristic only of musicians who do not content themselves with mutual compliments, who do not fancy that they know everything by themselves, but who feel shy and anxious about what they initially do not understand. They therefore approach difficult things from a perspective where they feel comfortable, namely from the aspect of technique. To start with, the French musician essentially belongs to the Italian school, and he has been so admirably influenced by it that he can comprehend music only through song. To him, playing an instrument well means being able to sing well on it. And—as I already mentioned at the outset—that marvelous orchestra *sang* this symphony. In order to be able to "sing" it properly, however, the *correct tempo* also has to be found everywhere, and this was the second thing that impressed me on that occasion. To be sure, old Habeneck had no abstract, aesthetic inspiration for this. He was devoid of all "genius," but *he found the right tempo by applying persistent hard work that led his orchestra to grasp the melos of the symphony.*

Only by properly recognizing the melos can one achieve the correct tempo: these two are indivisible; the one determines the other. I shall not shy away here from expressing my opinion on the majority of our performances of classical instrumental works, for I regard them as insufficient to an alarming degree. And I believe I can prove it by pointing out that *our conductors are incapable of setting the correct tempo because they understand nothing of singing.* I have never yet come across any German capellmeister or conductor who has truly been able to *sing* a melody (regardless of whether his voice be good or bad). Instead, music is for them a peculiarly abstract thing, something hovering halfway between grammar, arithmetic, and gymnastics. A student of this music might well be good enough to become a decent teacher at a conservatory or a musical gymnastics association; but we cannot see how he might be able to breathe life and soul into a musical performance.

In this regard, I shall now offer further information about my own experiences.

If[27] one wished to sum up everything that a conductor needs in order to perform a composition correctly, it is that he always has to choose the right *tempo*, because setting the tempo enables us to recognize immediately whether or not he has understood the piece of music before him. When they have become more precisely acquainted with a composition, good musicians will find the right interpretation of it almost of their own accord, as long as they are given the right tempo. When a conductor has understood the tempo, then the right interpretation is inherent in it.[28] But conversely, it is also always true that you can find the right tempo only when you interpret a work correctly.

---

27   This is the first paragraph in the third installment of Wagner's essay, as published on December 10, 1869 in the *Neue Zeitschrift für Musik* 65/50.

28   Among the later tracts to emphasize this is Schroeder (1921): 33, whose second chapter begins: "A prime necessity when conducting a work of music is *gauging the tempi correctly.*"

In this, the instincts of the old masters like Haydn and Mozart were quite right when they offered only very general tempo markings. Their *Andante* was an intermediate step between an *Allegro* and an *Adagio*, and this simplest of categorizations encompassed everything that they considered necessary. [Johann] S[ebastian] Bach usually gives no tempo markings at all, which in a truly musical sense is actually the best thing to do. For he said to himself: If someone doesn't understand my theme or my figurations and can't sense their character and expression, then what use would an Italian tempo marking be to them? — And if I may speak from my very own experience: I gave eloquent tempo markings to my early operas, even providing them with metronome markings that were unerringly exact (or so I believed). Whenever I heard a performance at a ludicrous tempo (of my *Tannhäuser*, for example), those in charge defended themselves every time against my objections by saying that they had followed my metronome markings in the most conscientious way possible. I then realized that applying math to music is an uncertain business. So from then on, I both omitted all metronome indications and also denoted the main tempo only by means of very general markings. I devoted my care instead to the *modifications* of these tempi, because our conductors know next to nothing of them.[29] But lately, I hear, my general manner of indicating the tempo has annoyed and confused our conductors, especially because my markings are given in German. These gentlemen are accustomed to the old Italian manner and so are driven to distraction trying to determine what might be meant, for example, by "mässig" [moderate]. I recently heard this complaint from the entourage of a capellmeister who had expanded my *Rheingold* in performance to a length of three hours (thus the report printed in the *Allgemeine Zeitung* in Augsburg), whereas it had taken just two and a half hours in rehearsal with a conductor working according to my instructions.[30] I was once told similar reports about a

---

29   Wagner here takes a different stance from Berlioz, who in his *Le chef d'orchestre* recommends following a composer's metronome markings, and complains that composers who omit these often give tempo markings that are insufficient in their stead. See Berlioz (1855): 300. It is possible that Wagner's rejection of metronome markings here was an intentional, if implicit, rejection of Berlioz's approach.

30   Wagner refers here to the world premiere of *Das Rheingold* in Munich on September 22, 1869, which took place without his permission. His acolyte Hans Richter had rehearsed the work (taking the two and a half hours to which Wagner refers here), but pulled out at Wagner's insistence. The premiere was then conducted by Franz Wüllner (1832–1902), who had experience of the theater from his early years in Aachen, but who in the late 1860s was the

performance of my *Tannhäuser*.[31] I had conducted its overture in Dresden in twelve minutes, but in the performance in question it took twenty. These bunglers are so incredibly timid about the *alla breve* meter that they always beat four quarter-notes to a measure, just to remind themselves that they are actually conducting, and that they are there for some purpose. God knows how many of these four-footed musicians have left their village church and erred into in our opera houses.[32]

Dragging, on the other hand, is not really characteristic of the truly elegant conductors of more recent times. Instead, they have a fatal attachment to rushing. There is a reason for this—and since it can help to explain almost all the newest musical trends that are so popular everywhere, I shall now go into greater detail about it.[33]

Robert Schumann once complained to me in Dresden that *Mendelssohn's* concerts in Leipzig had ruined all his pleasure in the Ninth Symphony on account of the tempo being too fast in the first movement.[34] I myself only

---

conductor at the court church in Munich. He accordingly had to bear Wagner's considerable wrath (the fact that Wüllner was a friend of Brahms probably did not endear him to Wagner either).

31 Voss here refers to the autograph of the essay to explain that Wagner is writing of a performance in Prague, presumably that of November 25, 1854: see Voss (2015): 17.

32 This mention of church conductors venturing into the opera house is probably another dig at Wüllner.

33 In his personal copy of this volume of Wagner's writings, Arnold Schoenberg drew a single pencil line along the left-hand side of this paragraph, and underlined the second half of its first sentence (here split into two), also in pencil, from "truly" to "rushing" (held by the Arnold Schoenberg Center, Vienna, shelfmark W1v8, 276).

34 Wagner might be exaggerating here, as Hinrichsen (2016): 91 points out. Nevertheless, despite Wagner's obviously polemical intent, it does seem—as Hinrichsen (1999): 277 has observed—that Wagner and his circle regarded fast tempi as characteristic of the Leipzig Gewandhaus orchestra. In a letter of February 12, 1865 to Wendelin Weissheimer (a former pupil of Liszt and an acquaintance of Wagner's), Hans von Bülow added at the end, apparently in haste: written "at an oiled-up [*geschmiert*] Gewandhaus tempo." See Weissheimer (1898): 337 (this letter is also given in facsimile between pp. 336 and 337). It is worth noting here, however, that when Wagner conducted Mendelssohn's A major Symphony (the *Italian*) in London in 1855, one unnamed reviewer criticized him for displaying "contemptuous unconcern" by performing it too quickly, suggesting that Wagner's motto here had been "*Get*

ever heard Mendelssohn perform a Beethoven symphony on one occasion, at a rehearsal in Berlin: it was of the Eighth Symphony (in F major). I noticed that he here and there honed in on a particular detail, almost as if on a whim, and would work at it obstinately so as to articulate it clearly in performance. The result was such excellence in playing this detail that I could not properly comprehend why he did not devote the same attention to other passages too. All the same, this incomparably cheerful symphony ran extraordinarily smoothly and entertainingly. Mendelssohn told me several times in person that the greatest damage was done by taking the tempo too slowly when conducting. That was why he always recommended taking things a little too quickly instead. A truly good performance is something rare at any time, he said, but you can hoodwink your listeners so that they don't notice too much. The best way to do this is not to dawdle unduly, and to skim through everything quickly.[35] Mendelssohn's own students must have learned several tips about this, and in greater detail. It cannot have been a casual opinion expressed only to me, because I have since had ample opportunity to hear the consequences of his maxim. And I ultimately also learned the reasons behind it.

I had a vivid experience of those consequences with the orchestra of the Philharmonic Society in *London*. Mendelssohn had conducted that orchestra for a prolonged period, and they had thereafter doggedly kept to the Mendelssohnian tradition of performance.[36] That tradition aligned so snugly with the habits and peculiarities of the society itself that it seemed quite plausible that it was in fact they who had imparted this style to Mendelssohn. My concerts ate up[37] a tremendous amount of instrumental music, but they only allowed one rehearsal per performance, which meant I was often compelled to let the orchestra play according to its own traditions. In so doing, I was reminded vividly of Mendelssohn's remarks to me. Everything flowed like

---

    to the end of it as quick [sic] as possible." See Anon.: "Philharmonic society," *The Musical World* 33/16 (April 21, 1855), 251 (italics in the original).

35   In his review of this essay for the *Neue Freie Presse* after its publication in book form, Hanslick wrote of his disbelief that Mendelssohn would ever have expressed such an opinion. And if true, suggests Hanslick, then Mendelssohn probably said it in jest—perhaps even as a "malicious" means of putting an end to Wagner's constant, didactic chattering; see Hanslick (1870).

36   By the time Wagner conducted the Philharmonic, eight years had elapsed since Mendelssohn had last worked with them, and over a decade since he had done so on a regular basis. Their "Mendelssohnian" tradition thus presumably existed more in Wagner's imagination than in actual fact.

37   Wagner writes "verbrauchen," literally to consume.

water out of a town fountain. There could be no thought of holding back, and every *Allegro* ended in an undeniable *Presto*. The effort needed to intervene in this was embarrassing enough, because only when the orchestra played at the correct, carefully modified tempo did the detrimental aspects of their performance emerge that had hitherto been hidden by the overall flow. For the orchestra only ever played *mezzoforte*. It never reached a real *forte*, nor ever any real *piano*. In the most important passages, I tried as much as possible to keep to the interpretation that seemed correct to me, including the appropriate tempo. My musicians were capable, did not object, and were sincerely happy about it. It clearly also pleased the audience. Only the critics were furious, and even managed to bully the men running the society into urging me to rush through the second movement of Mozart's E-flat major Symphony [no. 39, K. 543] in the manner to which they had been accustomed, just as Mendelssohn had been wont to do it.[38]

This fatal maxim of haste was given precise verbal expression in a request made to me by a very jovial, elderly contrapuntist, Mr. Potter[39] (if I am not mistaken), whose symphony I had to conduct, and who sincerely asked me to take the *Andante* movement of it rather quickly, as he was very much afraid that it might bore people. I then proved to him that, however short it might be, his *Andante* would inevitably be boring if it were performed

---

38 By "critics," Wagner presumably means James Davison of *The Times* and Henry Chorley of *The Athenaeum*, who found his tempi in general erratic, and the *Andante* of this symphony far too slow. See the section "Wagner in Review" below. Mendelssohn had conducted the orchestra of the Philharmonic Society in this symphony on May 13, 1844. Since rehearsal time was meager back then too, and his program huge (it included his own *Scottish* Symphony, a piano concerto by Sterndale Bennett, a violin concerto by August Friedrich Pott, and assorted other pieces by Weber, Bellini, Meyerbeer etc.), the likelihood that Mendelssohn's performance of Mozart's Symphony in E-flat had been so notable as to imprint itself on the common mind of the orchestra in a manner still palpable eleven years later is absurd; Wagner is just being polemical again (see Eatock (2009): 84). Oddly, Wagner here draws on the same passage from his *Report to His Majesty* of 1865 to which he already referred his reader—see fn. 21 above—where he complained about those who play through this slow movement "glibly." See also fn. 95 in this chapter and p. 159 below.

39 Philip Cipriani Hambly Potter (1792–1871) was a noted British pianist and conductor who had studied with Thomas Attwood (Mozart's former pupil). Potter had met Beethoven, performed with Mendelssohn, and was Principal of the Royal Academy of Music in London at the time of Wagner's concerts.

glibly and devoid of expression. But if its truly pretty, naïve theme were played by the orchestra as I now sang it to him, then it could actually sound captivating. After all, I said, this was surely how he had intended it. Mr. Potter was noticeably touched, told me I was right, and apologized by saying that he was no longer accustomed to expect such a manner of orchestral performance. On the evening, after his *Andante*, he joyfully clasped my hands. —

I have been truly astonished at just how little our modern musicians can comprehend what I here describe as the correct interpretation and tempo of a work. Regrettably, I have had this same experience among the supposed luminaries of our music world today. For example, it was impossible for me to convince Mendelssohn of what I felt to be the right tempo for the *third movement* of Beethoven's F major Symphony (no. 8), as opposed to the appallingly negligent tempo generally chosen. This is just one of many cases that I shall choose here in order to demonstrate a matter of terrible gravity.

We know how *Haydn* took the form of the *minuet* and turned it into a refreshing, transitional movement between the *Adagio* and the *Finale* of his last symphonies by noticeably accelerating its tempo in a manner contrary to the original character of the dance. He also obviously took the "Ländler" of his time to form the Trio of these movements. The designation "minuet" thus no longer applied to the tempo, but was retained as a title merely as an indication of its origins. This notwithstanding, I believe that even Haydn's minuets are usually taken too quickly, and this is certainly the case in [the minuets in] Mozart's symphonies. We can clearly recognize this if, for example, we play the minuet of his G minor Symphony [K. 550] or that of the C major Symphony [K. 551] in a more measured tempo. The latter movement is usually rushed through almost as if it were *Presto*. But if it is played as I suggest, then it acquires a very different, graceful, yet festive, hearty expression. At a faster tempo, the Trio's pensive

Example 3.4. Mozart, Symphony no. 41, K. 551, 3rd movement, Trio, mm. 1–2

becomes a meaningless mumbling.[40]

---

40   In his recording of the *Jupiter*, Richard Strauss slows down the tempo for this dotted half-note chord each time, then resumes his normal tempo for the

But Beethoven, as elsewhere in his oeuvre, intended to write a real minuet for his F major Symphony [no. 8, op. 93]. He wanted it to complement the contrasting *Allegretto scherzando* movement that preceded it, and sandwiched these two movements between two larger-scale, main movements that are both *Allegro*.[41] In order for there to be no doubt about his intentions for the tempo, he did not call this third movement a "menuetto," but marked it "Tempo di menuetto." The innovative character of these two middle movements has been almost completely overlooked. People have assumed that the *Allegretto scherzando* (the second movement) had to be the usual andante, while the *Tempo di Menuetto* (the third movement) similarly had to be the usual "scherzo."[42]

---

eighth-note passage that follows. I am grateful to Raymond Holden for alerting me to this.

41 To be precise: *Allegro vivace e con brio* (1st movement) and *Allegro vivace* (4th movement).

42 In the list of metronome markings "determined by the composer himself" that were published in the *Allgemeine musikalische Zeitung* in Leipzig in 1817, the third movement of the Eighth Symphony is given as quarter-note = 126 (see Riehn (1985): 79); we also have Beethoven's own metronome marking for another "tempo di menuetto," namely that of the Septet, op. 20, which he gives as something similar, namely quarter-note = 120 (see Riehn (1985): 89). For a discussion of the problems surrounding Beethoven's metronome markings, see Metzger and Riehn (1985). Wagner had clearly been performing this "Tempo di menuetto" for several years at his preferred slower tempo. James Davison of *The Times* wrote as follows about Wagner's performance with the Philharmonic Society of June 11, 1855: "The only fault we could find was with the extreme slowness of the minuet—which, though 'tempo di menuetto' is indicated in the score, being in style entirely opposed to the stately old dance-minuet, should not be played with such a bag-wig [*sic*] gravity of measure." See Davison: "Philharmonic concerts," *The Times* (June 12, 1855). Wagner was not the only conductor of his day to insist on performing this movement at the tempo of a minuet, not a scherzo. In his discussion of Beethoven's symphonies in *À travers chants* of 1862, Berlioz specifically states that this movement should be played at the tempo of a minuet by Haydn, not as a Beethovenian scherzo. See Berlioz (1862): 48. In his *Ratschläge für Aufführungen der Symphonien Beethovens*, Felix Weingartner (1906) mentions Wagner's "justified polemic" against taking this movement too fast, adding that this is "so well known" that he doesn't need to deal with it further. He warns, however, that there is now a tendency to play it too slowly, and recommends a tempo of roughly quarter-note = 108 (this is also the speed he takes it in his recording with the Vienna Philharmonic). In Richard Strauss's annotated score of this symphony, he writes at the outset: "Tempo di Menuetto: see

But such an approach to these two movements was beneficial to neither of them. No one was able to perform them adequately when they were played in the customary andante/scherzo mold that we expect of a symphony's middle movements. As a result, our musicians came to regard this wonderful symphony overall as an incidental by-product of Beethoven's muse—a kind of one-off, lighter entertainment as recuperation from the exertions of the A major Symphony [no. 7, op. 92]. So the *Allegretto scherzando* is always slightly dragged, and then the *Tempo di Menuetto* is everywhere played with unwavering determination as if it were an invigorating Ländler.[43] As a consequence, no one can really remember what they've just heard once it's over. Usually, people are simply relieved that the torture of the third movement's Trio is behind them. This is the most charming of all idylls, but when played at the quick tempo that is the norm, the triplet passages for the cello turn it into a true monstrosity. This accompanying figure is regarded as one of the most difficult

---

Rich. Wagner," and to indicate the minuet tempo, he quotes the onstage minuet from the masked ball of Mozart's *Don Giovanni*, m. 406 in Act I. Strauss changes the tempo marking printed in his Eulenburg score from a quarter-note = 126 to 92. No recording by Strauss has survived of this symphony. Klemperer's recordings with the Berlin Staatskapelle of 1924 and 1926 both take this movement at about 112. Opinions seem to have differed no less wildly since then, as a perusal of the available recordings on YouTube and elsewhere can confirm. Furtwängler's 88 with the Vienna Philharmonic after the Second World War was almost exactly contemporaneous with Toscanini's 120 with the NBC Orchestra; then there is Karajan's 92 in the 1960s, and, more recently, Norrington and Harnoncourt at about 118 and Thielemann at 108. In his booklet *Über das Dirigieren*, Josef Pembaur paraphrases Wagner's argument about the middle movements of the Eighth Symphony; he does, however, mention his source (see Pembaur (1907): 68–69). We naturally do not have any recordings of Beethoven by Mahler, but his tempo marking for the second movement of his own Symphony no. 3 is instructive. It is not just marked "Tempo di Menuetto"—which surely refers back to Beethoven—but has the additions "Sehr mässig. *Ja nicht eilen!* Grazioso. Zart" (Very moderate. *Do not hurry at all!* Gracefully. Tender), which suggests a rather Wagnerian insistence on holding back the tempo of his minuet.

43 Wagner differentiated between the two. In 1875, when a string quartet played a Beethoven program for the Wagners at home, Cosima noted that "R recommends that the young musicians take note of the difference between 'Tempo di Minuetto' and '*Minuetto*' [*sic*]; the first is slower, while the second was turned into the Ländler by Haydn." CWT 1: 945, October 27, 1875.

passages for cellists, who struggle through the rushed staccato without being able to offer anything but a highly embarrassing scratching.[44]

Example 3.5. Beethoven, Symphony no. 8, 3rd movement, mm. 45–6

But even these problems disappear of their own accord as soon as one plays at the right tempo, taking one's cue from the tender song of the horns and clarinets. This also removes all the difficulties for the clarinets themselves, for otherwise even the best clarinetist is here embarrassingly exposed to the "squeak"[45] characteristic of the instrument. I recall the palpable relief of all the musicians when I had them play this piece at the correct, moderate tempo, at which even the humoristic impact of the *sforzandi* in the double basses and bassoons[46]

Example 3.6. Beethoven, Symphony no. 8, 3rd movement, mm. 66ff.

now became immediately comprehensible. The brief *crescendi* became distinct,

---

44 This music example is not given by Wagner. In London in 1855, the critic James Davison praised Wagner for having the cello part for the Trio played solo. See Davison: "Philharmonic concerts," *The Times* (June 12, 1855).

45 Wagner probably means mm. 72 and 74 in the third movement of this symphony, which could indeed provoke a nasty clarinet squeak if a fast tempo were imposed.

46 Wagner here gives only the first measure of the double bass/bassoon part in m. 68 as his music example, though he replaces the original *cresc.* with *p*.

the tender *pp* with which the Trio ends was properly effective, and the main section of the movement also achieved the leisurely gravitas that is its true character.

I once attended a performance of this symphony in Dresden that was conducted by the late capellmeister *Reissiger*.[47] I was there with *Mendelssohn*, and spoke with him both about the tempo dilemma I have discussed here, and my solution to it. I further mentioned that I had come to an understanding with my colleague Reissiger (or rather, I thought I had), who had promised that he would play the third movement slower than usual. Mendelssohn agreed with me completely. So we listened to the performance. But when the third movement began, I was startled to hear the same old, [swift] Ländler tempo once again. Before I was able to express my displeasure, Mendelssohn smiled at me, swaying his head complacently, and said "It's good like that! Bravo!," at which my shock turned to astonishment. I afterwards realized that I should not complain unduly about Reissiger's lapse into the old tempo (for reasons I shall discuss below). But Mendelssohn's insensitivity to this peculiar artistic instance naturally awakened doubts in me as to whether he was able to distinguish any difference in tempo at all.[48] I felt that I was gazing into a true abyss of superficiality—into complete emptiness.

❧ ❧ ❧

With[49] regard to that same third movement of the Eighth Symphony, I soon afterwards encountered a case identical to that of Reissiger in the person of another well-known conductor. He was one of Mendelssohn's successors as director of the Leipzig concerts[50] and he, too, had agreed with me about

---

47 These passages about Reissiger, Mendelssohn and Beethoven's Eighth Symphony were published in French in 1878; see Deldevez (1878): 101–2.

48 Grove (1896): 295 writes: "The necessity for keeping down the pace of this movement is strongly insisted on by Wagner, who makes it the subject of a highly characteristic passage in his interesting pamphlet, *Ueber das Dirigiren*. The remarks are all aimed at Mendelssohn, of whom, as is well-known, Wagner had a poor opinion, and their effect is greatly interfered with by the personal bias which they betray. We should like to know Mendelssohn's reasons for the faster pace which he is said to have adopted and adhered to."

49 This is the first paragraph in the fourth installment of Wagner's essay, as published on December 17, 1869 in the *Neue Zeitschrift für Musik*, 65/51.

50 Both Ashton Ellis in Wagner trans. Ellis (1895): 310 and Voss (2015): 23 note that Wagner here means Ferdinand Hiller (1811–85), who conducted at the

this Tempo di Menuetto. He promised that he would perform this movement at the correct, slower tempo at a forthcoming concert, and invited me
to attend. He, too, failed to keep his word, but his excuse afterwards was an
odd one. He admitted to me, laughing, that he had been so distracted by all
kinds of directorial matters that he had only remembered his promise to me
after having begun the movement in question. Naturally, he couldn't suddenly alter the tempo again, having already started at the old, familiar speed.
By necessity, it had thereafter remained the same as ever. However awkward I
found his explanation, I was nevertheless satisfied this time that I had at least
found someone to confirm the difference I had grasped, and who at least did
not think that the piece would be the same, regardless of the tempo at which
it was played. I don't believe I could accuse this conductor of flippancy or
thoughtlessness in the same way that he blamed himself for his "forgetfulness." Instead, I think that the reason he did not take the tempo slower was
something of which he himself was unaware, but was in itself quite correct.
To change a tempo so drastically on the off-chance, between the rehearsal
and the concert, would have demonstrated an alarming recklessness, and
in this case, the conductor's fortunate "forgetfulness" saved him from the
ill effects that would have been the result.[51] The orchestra was accustomed
to playing this piece at the quicker pace, and if it had suddenly been confronted with a more moderate tempo, it would have been utterly confused.
After all, the slower tempo would *also have required a very different manner of
interpretation.*

Here is the decisive, important point, which one has to grasp very clearly
if we are going to be able to perform our classics properly. These works have
often suffered neglect and have been corrupted through bad habits that were
justified by the tempi adopted, which in turn were intended to conform
to the prevalent style of interpretation. On the one hand, this congruity of
tempo and interpretation served to hide the true root of the evil. But on the
other hand, it actually prevented things from getting even worse, because if
you change only the tempo without also changing the manner of interpretation, then the results are usually quite unbearable.

     Leipzig Gewandhaus from autumn 1842 to early 1844; see Wagner's earlier
     criticism of him in this chapter.

51   Wagner implies here that Hiller had already rehearsed the work at the "old"
     tempo before agreeing (but then forgetting) to play it slower in the actual
     concert.

In order to demonstrate this with the simplest example possible, let us consider the opening of the C minor Symphony:[52]

Example 3.7. Beethoven, Symphony no. 5, 1st movement, mm. 1–2

After briefly lingering here, our conductors rush away from the fermata in the second measure. They linger almost solely in order to concentrate the attention of their musicians on playing this opening motif precisely when it returns in the third measure. The E-flat on the half note is usually held no longer than a string player can play *forte* in a single bow. But let us imagine the voice of Beethoven, calling to a conductor from his grave: "Keep my fermatas long and terrible! I didn't write them for my pleasure or out of embarrassment, as if wondering what to do next. In my adagios I employ a wholly compelling tone to achieve a luxuriance of expression, and I also use this same tone in the midst of the vehement, quick figurations of my allegros when I need it to depict a moment of bliss or a terrible, persistent convulsion. In such cases, the life of the note should be wrung out, down to its last drops of blood; I part the waves of my sea to let you gaze into its abyss; or I stop the clouds from scudding, I dissipate the hazy mists and all at once let you look into the pure azure sky and the brilliant eye of the sun. This is why I write my fermatas—those long, held notes that appear suddenly in my allegros. If you take note of my very specific thematic intent with this long-held E-flat after the three short, stormy notes, you will grasp what I want to say with all the later notes that have to be held for a similar length of time."

Imagine if our conductor were to bear in mind this admonishment, and suddenly demand that his orchestra should hold onto that fermata, giving it weighty significance by prolonging it to the extent he deems necessary to comply with Beethoven's intentions. What success would he have? None. He would fail miserably. After the initial force of the string instruments has

---

52 On January 20, 1873, Cosima remarked after a rehearsal of this symphony in Dresden that "R. says he would like to beat the first movement in ¼, because beating time [in ²⁄₄] is so ungainly, and also achieving any nuance is difficult in this meter—too many accents arise—Beethoven surely thought people would go mad if he wrote ¼." CWT 1: 630.

frittered away, holding the note for any longer would make it ever thinner, and it would end in an embarrassed *piano*. Here we come to one of the worst effects of today's conducting habits. Nothing has become more foreign to our orchestras than *holding a note at a constant dynamic level*. I urge all conductors to demand a full, equally sustained *forte* from any instrument of the orchestra. His players will experience astonishment at such an unusual request, and only then will they comprehend how much persistent practice is needed to fulfil the task successfully.

Yet this consistent, powerfully sustained note is the basis of all dynamics—both in singing and in the orchestra. Only with this as a starting point can one achieve all those nuances whose diversity determines the character of an interpretation. Without this basis, an orchestra can make a lot of noise, but will have no strength. This is one of the reasons why most orchestral performances are weak. Today's conductors haven't grasped this fact, placing much emphasis instead on achieving *an overly soft piano*. That is something you can get quite effortlessly from the string instruments, but it takes a lot of effort with the wind instruments, especially the woodwind. It is barely possible to procure a tender, sustained *piano* from the woodwind, and the flautists are the worst of them. Their instruments used to be so gentle, but have today been transformed into veritable pipes of violence. An exception might be found among the French oboists (because they have always retained the pastoral character of their instrument), and among the clarinetists if you ask them to play an echo effect. This ill state of affairs in performances by our best orchestras prompts the following question: if the wind instruments are unable to play *piano*, shouldn't we at least endeavor to compensate for it, and restore a balance by getting the string instruments to play more opulently? They otherwise tend to play so softly that the contrast is ridiculous. Obviously, however, our conductors completely fail to notice this imbalance. The real problem lies in large part elsewhere, namely in the character of the *piano* played by the string instruments. Just as they cannot give us a *proper forte*, so too they lack a *proper piano*. Both *forte* and *piano* lack fullness of tone. In this, our string players could learn something from our wind players. Whereas the strings find it very easy to move their bow lightly over the strings to make them whisper, a wind instrument requires great artistic mastery to be able to produce a pure, constant, yet soft note with only a moderate outflow of breath. For this reason, our violinists should let the wind players teach them how to play a truly full-bodied *piano*, just as wind players should emulate excellent singers.

The quiet note and the powerful, sustained tone mentioned above form the two poles of an orchestra's dynamics, between which it must move in performance. But what can we expect of a performance if neither *piano* nor *forte* is cultivated properly? How can modifications of dynamics feature in a performance when neither of the two dynamic poles is distinct? The result will undoubtedly be so deficient that Mendelssohn's maxim of rushing through a work becomes a serendipitous solution. This is why our conductors have raised this maxim to the status of a veritable dogma, one adopted by their whole "church" and their retinue. As a result, any attempt to perform classical music correctly is denounced by them as being well-nigh heretical.

If I may stay with these conductors for a moment, I shall return to the matter of the *tempo*, because as I said before, this is where a conductor shows himself to be right or wrong.

Obviously, getting the right tempo depends on the character of the interpretation required by a piece of music. In order to determine this, we have to be in agreement about whether an interpretation will tend more to sustained, legato tones (as in song) or to rhythmic movement (figurations). This makes a conductor decide what kind of tempo he should favor.

Here, the *Adagio* stands in contrast to the *Allegro*, just as the sustained tone stands in contrast to animated figurations. The *sustained tone* provides the rules for the *tempo adagio*; here the rhythm melts away into a realm of pure sound that is sufficient in itself. In a certain, subtle sense, one can say of the pure *Adagio* that it cannot be taken slowly enough. A rapturous trust in the persuasive security of pure tone must dominate. Here, a languorous sentiment becomes delight; what is expressed in an *Allegro* by shifts in figurations is expressed in an *Adagio* by the unending diversity of the inflected tone. The slightest change in harmony becomes surprising, though our sensibility becomes so heightened that even the most remote harmonic progressions feel inevitable and right.

None of our conductors dares to acknowledge this characteristic of the *Adagio*. When they're at the beginning of an *Adagio*, they peer forwards to try and find some figurations in it whose motion might help them to determine the tempo. Perhaps I am the only conductor who has dared to adopt a tempo for the third movement of the Ninth Symphony that is in accordance with its character as a true adagio. In this movement, the [$\frac{4}{4}$] *Adagio* alternates with an *Andante* in $\frac{3}{4}$, as if in order to draw attention to its strikingly individual character. But this never stops our conductors from blurring the contrast between *Adagio* and *Andante* here, with nothing remaining to differentiate them except the shift between quadruple and triple time.[53] This movement is surely one of the most instructive in this particular respect. Its richly figured section in $\frac{12}{8}$ meter also offers the clearest example of how a pure *Adagio* can be broken up by means of a more focused rhythmization of its accompanying figurations. These are made autonomous, though without the movement's uninterrupted cantilena losing its characteristic breadth.[54]

Example 3.8. Beethoven, Symphony no. 9, 3rd movement, mm. 99–101, with the $\frac{4}{4}$ *Adagio* theme in the woodwind, now in 12/8, accompanied by sixteenth-note figurations in the first violins

The delicately fluctuating motion of the *Adagio* hitherto longed for unending expansion, offering unlimited freedom to satisfy the musical expression. But here, it is as if its image were fixed, because the ornamented figurations in its accompaniment now require it to be played in a strict meter. This in turn provides us with a new law of musical motion whose consequences will ultimately enable us to determine the tempo of an *Allegro*.

---

53   Deldevez (1878): 185 here remarks that Wagner was not, as he maintains, "the only conductor" to interpret this passage correctly, as he was (thus Deldevez) merely following the tradition of Habeneck. Wagner later described the *Andante* to Cosima as "a dance, a minuet." See CWT 2: 112 (June 8, 1878).

54   Wagner does not give this example.

Just as the sustained note, modified in its duration, is the basis of all musical performance, so does an *Adagio* such as this third movement of Beethoven's Ninth Symphony offer us a basis from which we may determine all musical tempi. If we look at it carefully, the *Allegro* can be regarded as the ultimate outcome when the pure *Adagio* is refracted by means of more animated figurations. Even in an *Allegro*, if we observe its constituent motifs carefully, it is always the cantilena derived from the *Adagio* that predominates. The most important *Allegro* movements in Beethoven are usually governed by a basic melody that in a deeper sense belongs to the character of the *Adagio*.[55] This is what affords them their *sentimental* significance that sets off these allegros so clearly from the earlier, *naïve* genre of *Allegro*. But even Mozart's

Example 3.9. Mozart, Symphony no. 41, K. 551, 1st movement, mm. 244–47

and his

Example 3.10. Mozart, Symphony no. 41, K. 551, 4th movement, mm. 1–4

are already not far removed from Beethoven's

---

55 Deldevez (1878): 188–89 was one of the first commentators to highlight the importance of this passage in which Wagner posits a "basic melody" behind both *Allegro* and *Adagio*. Nicholas Cook (1993): 59 remarks perceptively: "If Wagner's description of the song-like root melody underlying the figuration of the Allegro looks back to his account of Habeneck's orchestra 'singing' the Ninth Symphony, then equally it looks forward to the *Urlinie* of mature Schenkerian theory. It is hard to avoid the impression that Schenker derived some of his most basic concepts from Wagner's writings on the Ninth Symphony—even if he found the truth standing on its head in them, as Karl Marx did in Hegel." See also the discussion on the *Urlinie* and melos in the section "Melos and the Body" in part II.

Example 3.11. Beethoven, Symphony no. 3, 1st movement, mm. 3–11

and the exclusive character of the *Allegro* also emerges in Mozart, as in Beethoven, only when the figurations completely gain the upper hand over the lyrical element—in other words, when the rhythmic motion utterly dominates the sustained tone. This is usually the case in rondo finale movements, of which Mozart's E-flat major Symphony [no. 39] and Beethoven's A major Symphony [no. 7] offer notable examples.[56] Here, the rhythmic motion goes wild, as it were, which is why these *Allegro* movements cannot be performed precisely and quickly enough.[57] But what lies between these two extremes is determined by the *law of mutual relationships*. This law must be comprehended in all its subtlety and variety, because in a deep sense it is the same law that applies when modifying the sustained tone itself in all its conceivable nuances. I shall now turn more extensively to this *modification of the tempo*. This is not merely unfamiliar to our conductors: In fact, they doltishly spurn it and denounce it, precisely because of this unfamiliarity. Whoever has followed me attentively thus far will understand that modifying the tempo is in fact a principle that determines the life of our music. —

❧ ❧ ❧

In[58] my above considerations, I have differentiated between two genres of *Allegro*, attributing a *sentimental* character to the newer, truly Beethovenian type, in comparison with the older, primarily Mozartian type, which I described as being *naïve*. In using these designations, I had in mind the apt

---

56   In his personal copy of this essay, Richard Strauss has here underlined the words "finale" and "A major Symphony," drawn a pencil line in the right-hand margin alongside the next sentence ("Here, the rhythmic motion …") and placed a question mark next to it.

57   Richard Strauss considered the last movement of the *Jupiter* Symphony to be "one of those pieces to which Wagner's maxim 'as quick as possible' applies": Strauss ed. Schuh (1989): 58. His recording of it is very fast indeed.

58   This is the first paragraph in the fifth installment of Wagner's essay, as published on December 24, 1869 in the *Neue Zeitschrift für Musik* 65/52.

terminology that Schiller uses in his famous essay about sentimental and naïve poetry.[59]

I want to keep to my main purpose here, so I won't engage any further with the aesthetic matters that I have just touched upon. I would merely like to mention that the *naïve Allegro* to which I refer is to be found in its fullest form in most of Mozart's quick *alla breve* movements. The most perfect of this type are the allegros of his opera overtures, especially those of *Figaro* and *Don Giovanni*. We know that they couldn't be played quickly enough for Mozart. When he had finally driven his musicians to such desperation that to their own surprise they were able to achieve the *Presto* he wanted in his *Figaro* Overture, he called out to them in encouragement: "That was nice! This evening, let's play it just a little faster!"[60] — He was quite right! I have said of the pure *Adagio* that it ideally could not be performed too slowly. Similarly, this true, completely unalloyed, pure *Allegro* cannot be played quickly enough. Just as the voluptuousness of sound in the former provides the only limit to how slow one may play, in the latter it is the rapid figurations that provide the upper boundary for the tempo. The tempo that is actually attainable is determined solely by the laws of beauty. These laws provide the outer limits for the extreme opposites of an utterly inhibited, slow tempo on the one hand, and an utterly uninhibited, fast tempo on the other. Once we reach the limits of the one, we naturally feel a yearning to experience the other.[61] — Thus there is a deeper meaning in how the movements

---

59 Wagner means Friedrich Schiller's essay *Über naive und sentimentalische Dichtung* of 1795 (On Naïve and Sentimental Poetry), in which the poet differentiates between "naïve" writers who "imitate nature" and "sentimental" writers who "reflect upon the impression" that events and objects have made upon them. Wagner here uses these terms roughly as we would "Classical" and "Romantic," though with certain important differences; see the discussion of his aesthetic terminology in "Finding a Vocabulary for Conducting" below.

60 The source of this anecdote is unclear. It is possible that Wagner heard something along these lines from Dionys Weber (also Bedřich Diviš Weber, 1766–1842), the Bohemian composer and theorist and founding director of the Prague Conservatory. Weber met Mozart in Prague and became a lifelong devotee. In November 1832, Weber gave the first performance of Wagner's early Symphony in C in Prague, in the presence of the composer—though this did not stop Wagner from criticizing him later; see p. 64 below.

61 This passage seems oddly prescient of the Devil's description of hell in Thomas Mann's *Doktor Faustus*, where the damned veer from extreme heat to extreme cold and back. See Mann (1975): 247.

of a symphony by our masters progress from an *Allegro* to an *Adagio*, and thence—through the intermediary of a stricter dance form (the minuet or scherzo) to the quickest *Allegro* in the finale. It is also a sign of a deterioration in sensibility when composers today believe they can compensate for the tediousness of their inspiration by stuffing their music into the older form of the suite, with its thoughtless juxtaposition of dances that have actually long since evolved into other forms that are far more varied and richly mingled.[62]

We can recognize the Mozartian, *absolute Allegro* as belonging especially to the "naïve" genre in two ways: first, on account of its dynamics, in its simple shifts between *forte* and *piano*; and secondly, because of its formal structure—in the way it indiscriminately juxtaposes stable, rhythmic-melodic formulae, which are suitable for playing either *forte* or *piano*, and which the Master employs with a surprising degree of indifference (the same applies to his incessantly recurring, identical, bustling half-cadences).[63] However, all this can be explained by the character of this type of *Allegro* (even the heedless manner in which utterly banal forms are employed in it). This *Allegro* does not aim to captivate us with its cantilenas. Instead, its restless motion aims to intoxicate us. The *Allegro* of the *Don Giovanni* Overture ultimately takes an unmistakable turn to the sentimental. When it reaches the upper limit of its tempo as outlined above, the music desires to move away from this extreme, necessitating a modification of the tempo. The tempo slows down imperceptibly, reaching the more moderate tempo at which the opening of the opera proper is to be taken (this imperceptibility is extremely important when performing these transitional measures). This tempo is similarly *alla breve*, though it has to be taken less quickly than the main tempo of the overture.

This peculiarity of the *Don Giovanni* Overture is ignored by most of our conductors in their usual rough-and-ready fashion. But I won't dwell on this here. I just wish to establish one thing, namely that the character of this

---

62 Dannreuther (1887): 40 here adds a footnote, referring the reader to [Franz] Lachner's suites for orchestra. Voss (2015): 31 does likewise, remarking on the personal antipathy between Wagner and Lachner—the latter having been the General Music Director at the Munich Court Theater until 1868. On March 28, 1869, Cosima's diary has a pejorative remark about a suite by Lachner that Hans von Bülow had been unwilling to conduct in Munich (CWT 1: 77).

63 As early as his essay *Zukunftsmusik* from the year 1860, Wagner complains about Mozart's "banal phrase construction" and his "stable, recurring … half-cadences" in his symphonies, which he finds reminiscent of *Tafelmusik* and to him conjure up the noises of serving and clearing away the dishes at a princely table. See SSD 7: 126–27.

older, classical, or—as I call it—naïve *Allegro* is vastly different from that of the newer, sentimental, truly Beethovenian *Allegro*. Mozart learned *crescendo* and *diminuendo* in orchestral playing from the Mannheim orchestra, whose innovation it was. Up to then, the way the old masters scored their works proves that there was no expressive intent behind their differentiation between *forte* and *piano* in an *Allegro* movement.

But how does the true Beethovenian *Allegro* relate to this? Let us consider his incredible innovation by looking at his most audacious inspiration, namely the first movement of his Heroic Symphony [no. 3]. How would it fare if it were played in the strict tempo of a Mozart overture? Would it ever occur to one of our conductors to take this movement at anything but the same tempo from the first to the last measure? If we can even speak of them actually "understanding" the tempo at all, then we can be sure that they will primarily follow Mendelssohn's motto, "chi va presto, va sano,"[64] assuming that they belong among our elegant capellmeisters. If the orchestral musicians themselves possess any musicality, then they are left by themselves to cope as best they can with:[65]

Example 3.12. Beethoven, Symphony no. 3, 1st movement, mm. 83–86

or with the following lamentation:

Example 3.13. Beethoven, Symphony no. 3, 1st movement, mm. 284–87

---

64   Italian for "whoever goes quickly, goes healthily." As Voss (2015): 32 points out, this is presumably an intentional parody of the Italian saying "Chi va piano, va sano e va lontano," namely "Whoever goes slowly goes healthily and goes far." See Wagner's similar corruption of an English saying below.

65   This is the same example that is given by Anton Schindler on p. 239 of his Beethoven biography of 1840, to illustrate how Beethoven supposedly wanted his second subject to be taken at a slower pace. In recordings of the *Eroica* by Mengelberg, Furtwängler and others, this theme is taken at a noticeably slower tempo, as recommended by Wagner.

These conductors aren't bothered about any of this, because they're on "classical" ground. So off they go at *grande vitesse*, elegant and lucrative at the same time.[66] In English, they say: *Time is music.* —

We have here reached a decisive point in our assessment of the whole of today's music-making scene. As the reader will be aware, I have approached it in a somewhat careful, circuitous manner. It has been my intention here to lay bare the problem, making clear to everyone how, since Beethoven, a quite fundamental shift has occurred in the treatment of musical material and its performance when compared with earlier times. Elements that were once kept apart to lead their own separate lives in isolated, closed forms now have their principal motifs placed together in contrasting, all-encompassing forms and are then developed with and against each other.[67] Of course, the performance of the work should also do justice to this fact. Above all, the

---

66 "Grande vitesse," French for "high speed." Wagner's subsequent English quotation is presumably an intentional corruption of "time is money," which ties in with his use of "einbringlich" (lucrative, profitable) in the previous sentence. This paragraph is unusually packed with *non sequiturs*, enabling Wagner to proceed from Beethoven's *Eroica* to Mendelssohn and money within just a few lines. Assorted concepts and languages are here juxtaposed without any coherent sense of causality, which suggests that we are here dealing with yet another instance of Wagner's animosity towards his predecessor, one in which his negative emotions get the better of his intellect. In his own essay entitled *Über das Dirigieren*, Felix Weingartner took up Wagner's criticism of these swift, "elegant" conductors, contrasted it with the tempo modifications advocated by Wagner, and turned Wagner's argument somewhat on its head: "Wagner speaks of 'elegant' conductors … whom he accuses of taking the tempo as fast as possible in order to skim over difficult passages that at first glance seem unclear. The 'tempo rubato conductors' are the exact opposite; they seem to make the simplest passages unclear by emphasizing unimportant details." See Weingartner (1913): 24–25.

67 As is frequently the case with Wagner, he here writes ostensibly about Beethoven, but seems instead to be describing his own compositional technique. In his later essay *On the Application of Music to Drama* of 1879, he specifically discusses how a music drama must possess the same "unity as a symphonic movement." See SSD 10: 185.

tempo should be no less flexible[68] than the thematic web,[69] which reveals its nature through the very fluidity of its motion.

When it comes to applying the principle of *tempo modification* to classical works of the newer style, we have to acknowledge finding ourselves confronted with difficulties equal to those faced by anyone endeavoring to promote a general understanding of the manifestations of the true German genius. If I were to list all the minor cases that I have experienced, my descriptions would descend into chaotic detail. This is why, in what I have written above, I have instead paid particular attention to my experiences of several of the foremost musical luminaries of our time. I have not hesitated to use my examples to prove that the true Beethoven is a mere chimera today because of how he is performed in public. However, I now intend to substantiate this serious claim by contrasting these negative aspects with the positive proof of what I believe is the correct manner of performing both Beethoven and those composers related to him.

Because the object of my interest seems inexhaustible, I will endeavor once more to concentrate on a few drastic instances drawn from my own experiences. —

One of the principal means of musical form-building is to write a series of *variations* on a given theme. This inherently loose form of simply juxtaposing a succession of variants of a theme was raised to artistic significance

---

68 Wagner writes here "Zartlebigkeit" (possessed of fleeting life), a noun it seems he himself created from the adjective "zartlebig" that is found in assorted scientific tracts of the time, such as in Maximilian Perty's 1852 tract about microscopic organisms (Perty (1852): 150), where the author uses the word "zartlebig" to describe their fragility and brief lifespan. Wagner means flexible tempi or *rubato*. See the discussion of Wagner's vocabulary in the section "Freedom, Control, and the 'Two Cultures'" below.

69 Dannreuther and Ashton Ellis both use "tissue" for Wagner's "Gewebe"; see Wagner, trans. Dannreuther (1887): 43 and Wagner, trans. Ellis (1895): 320. In Wagner's day, as today, the word could mean a whole host of things from woven fabric to human tissue to the membrane of a leaf. I have chosen "web" instead, as it more directly conveys the notion of something woven, which seems Wagner's intention, and to speak of Wagner's "thematic web" has in any case achieved currency in the literature. It also happens that "Gewebe" was the word used to translate "web" in the German edition of Darwin's *Origin of Species* that we know Wagner owned, and which I posit below had an impact on his choice of vocabulary at this time; see Darwin (1860): 83, Darwin, trans. Bronn/Carus (1867): 95, and "Freedom, Control, and the 'Two Cultures'" below.

first by Haydn, then ultimately by Beethoven, thanks to both the brilliance of their musical invention and the manner in which they established *relationships* between these variants. This is most successful when they develop out of each other, with one type of variation leading into the next, be it by developing further what was only hinted at in the preceding variation, or by complementing it with what it had lacked. The real structural weakness of variation form is revealed when starkly contrasting sections are juxtaposed without any connection or transition between them. Yet Beethoven also knew how to turn this weakness to his advantage, and did so in a manner that completely avoided anything awkward or accidental. He acknowledges the limits described above, so that either the unending expansiveness of his adagios or the boundless motion of his allegros suddenly awakens in us an intense yearning for the redemption offered by its opposite, with this contrasting tempo seeming the only possible option. We can learn this from the Master's greatest works, of which the last movement of the *Eroica* Symphony offers one of the most superb, instructive examples. This is a variation movement of infinite expansion, employing the most multifarious motifs. In order to master this multifariousness and evade its adverse impact on our emotions (here and in all similar movements), we have to be all the more aware of the abovementioned weakness of variation form. Too often, individual variations are composed only in and for themselves, and are then lined up according to some utterly arbitrary convention. These thoughtless juxtapositions are at their worst when a calm, solemn theme is followed by a first variation that is incomprehensibly merry. The theme of the second movement of Beethoven's great A major Sonata for piano and violin [op. 47, *Kreutzer* Sonata] is incomparably beautiful, but I have never heard the first variation played by any virtuoso except as a typical "first variation" whose purpose is to provide a springboard for instrumental gymnastics. My indignation at this always made me unwilling to listen any further. Whenever I complained to anyone about it, they admitted that I was right "on the whole," but they still did not comprehend in detail what I wanted (just like my experience with the *Tempo di menuetto* of [Beethoven's] Eighth Symphony).

But let us remain with the abovementioned example of the *Kreutzer* Sonata. To be sure, the first variation on this wonderful, sustained theme is already strikingly animated in character. When the composer wrote it, he will not have intended it to follow immediately after the theme, directly connected to it. He will have been led, at least subconsciously, by the formal insularity that is typical of the individual sections of variation form. But these individual sections are of course still played one after the other. Other movements by the Master are also modeled after variation form, though they are conceived as a unified, continuous whole (such as the second movement of the Symphony in C Minor [no. 5], the *Adagio* of the great E-flat major Quartet [op. 127] and, above all, the wonderful second movement of the great C minor Piano Sonata op. 111). We also know how sensitively and delicately he composed the transitions between the individual variations in these works. So in a case such as the aforementioned *Kreutzer* Sonata, it is at the very least the duty of the performers to vindicate the Master completely by playing the opening of the first variation in a manner that can establish a gentle relation to the mood of the preceding theme. One can do this by holding back the tempo so as just to hint at the new character of this first variation, instead of plunging headlong into it as is the inevitable practice among our pianists and violinists. If this is done with the appropriate artistry, then the first section of this variation can itself offer a gradual, increasingly animated transition to the new, swifter mood. As a result, quite apart from the interest offered by this variation in itself, it would acquire the charm of an affably mellifluous, though fundamentally not insignificant transition away from the primary mood in which the theme itself was conceived. —

A similarly significant case, but more striking, is the entrance of the ⁶⁄₈ meter in the *Allegro* [second movement] after the long introductory *Adagio* of the C-sharp minor Quartet [op. 131] by Beethoven. This is marked "*molto vivace*," which is apt for the character of the movement as a whole. Quite exceptionally, however, Beethoven has the individual movements of this quartet follow on one after the other without the usual break between them in performance. In fact, if we take a closer, judicious look, we can see that they develop out of each other according to certain subtle principles. This *Allegro* movement thus follows directly on from an *Adagio* that is possessed of a dreamy melancholy such as we find in hardly any other movement by the Master. It is like a delightful memory, which upon coming back to mind is embraced and nurtured with an increasing intensity of emotion. Here, the issue at hand is clearly how the *Allegro* should emerge from the melancholy languor with which the preceding *Adagio* closes. It has to arise out of it if it is to draw us in, instead of wounding our sensibility by the brusqueness of its entrance. It is appropriate that this new theme should also begin in an uninterrupted *pp*, as if it were a tender, barely recognizable dream image, and it disappears at once, melting away in a *ritardando*, after which it gradually gains strength and manifests itself, entering into its true, animated sphere by means of a *crescendo*.[70] It is here the subtle duty

---

70 Wagner returns to his dream-image similes when he discusses this quartet, op. 131, at greater length in his essay *Beethoven*, written just a few months after *Über das Dirigieren*. See SSD 9: 96–97.

of the performer to modify his first entrance by means of the tempo, in accordance with the character of this *Allegro* as elucidated above. In other words, he should pay attention to the close of the *Adagio*:

Example 3.14. Beethoven, String Quartet in C-sharp minor, op. 131, 1st movement, mm. 120–21

in order to initiate the following

Example 3.15. Beethoven, String Quartet in C-sharp minor, op. 131, 2nd movement, m. 1

so imperceptibly in the ensuing *Allegro molto vivace* that no one will notice any tempo change at all at first:[71]

Example 3.16. Beethoven, String Quartet in C-sharp minor, op. 131, 1st movement, mm. 120–21, 2nd movement, mm. 1–10

---

71 This music example in score is not in Wagner's essay, but is given here to aid comprehension on the part of the reader.

And then, after the *ritardando*, the next measure's *crescendo* should coincide with an increasing vigor in performance so that the swifter tempo specified by the Master emerges as a rhythmic correlation to the dynamic intensification. — However, without exception, no one ever makes this tempo modification in performance. Instead, performers simply tumble into the cheeky [*Allegro molto*] *vivace* as if everything were a matter of fun, and things ought to proceed merrily. This is a great offence to our sense of artistic decency! And yet the gentlemen in question call this "classical."

I have offered these few examples to prove at some length the necessity of these tempo modifications. Since they are immeasurably important for performing our classical music, I now intend to move on to take a closer look at what is needed for a correct performance of such music. In so doing, I shall have to state several tough home truths to our musicians and capellmeisters who claim to be so concerned about our classical music, and are venerated for it.

❧ ❧ ❧

I[72] hope that I have now succeeded in explaining the difficulties involved in modifying the tempo in works of the newer, intrinsically German style. These difficulties can only be recognized and solved by initiates possessed of a discerning spirit. In what I call the *sentimental* genre of recent music, which was raised up to eternal validity by Beethoven, we find co-mingled all the characteristics of the earlier, primarily naïve genres, resulting in a body of material that the Master's creativity always had at its disposal.[73] No longer do legato and staccato or the sustained cantilena and rapid figurations exist independently as contrasting, formal aspects; no longer are diverse variations simply strung together alongside each other. No, they touch each other directly and move imperceptibly, one into the other. To be sure, however (as I have shown extensively by means of individual cases), this new, multifariously structured musical material can only be employed in a symphonic movement if it is also performed in the manner it requires, otherwise it risks appearing as a monstrosity. I remember in my youth hearing older musicians

---

72   This is the first paragraph in the sixth installment of Wagner's essay, as published on January 1, 1870 in the *Neue Zeitschrift für Musik* 66/1.

73   In his copy of this essay, Richard Strauss has drawn a pencil line in the right margin next to the passage beginning at "all the characteristics" down to "legato"; he further underlined the words "stets bereit liegenden" (always had at its disposal).

speak critically about the *Eroica* Symphony. *Dionys Weber* in Prague treated it point-blank as an absurdity. And quite rightly so—this man only knew what I referred to above as the Mozartian *Allegro*, and he had the students of his conservatory play me the *Allegro* of the *Eroica* in just such a strict, Mozartian tempo.[74] Anyone who heard such a performance would have agreed with Dionys about the work. But in fact, no one played it any differently anywhere, nor do they today, despite which this symphony is usually applauded by everyone. And while we might feel that this is ridiculous, the symphony's success has come about only because people have been studying its music at the piano for the past decades, outside the concert hall. This has enabled it to exert its compelling power in its own, irresistible manner, albeit in a roundabout way. If fate had not mapped out this escape route for it, but had left us instead dependent solely on our gentlemen capellmeisters and their ilk, then our noblest music would inevitably have perished.

In order to substantiate these bold allegations with examples from experience, I shall offer one from a work that is far more popular in Germany than any other.

How often haven't we heard the Overture to *Der Freischütz* performed by our orchestras?

There are only a few people today who are aware of how humdrum performances of this wonderful music have trivialized it, and who recoil in horror when they contemplate the innumerable times they have heard it thus before realizing the truth. What's more, they were only able to come to this realization because they were in my audience when I performed the *Freischütz* Overture at a concert I was kindly invited to conduct in Vienna in 1864 [*recte*: on December 27, 1863].[75] In our rehearsal, the orchestra of the Vienna Court Opera—indisputably one of the finest in the world—completely lost its composure because of how I insisted on performing this work. Right at the outset it transpired that they had hitherto played the *Adagio* introduction as a staid *Andante*, in the tempo of the "Alphorn" or some other homely piece.[76] This was not a purely Viennese tradition, but the general

---

74   Wagner and Weber met in Prague in November 1832, when Weber conducted Wagner's early Symphony in C. See also fn. 60 above.

75   Wagner here refers to a concert in Vienna on December 27, 1863, organized by Carl Tausig, in which he conducted the *Freischütz* Overture along with excerpts from *Tristan und Isolde* and *Die Meistersinger von Nürnberg*.

76   Dannreuther (1887): 51 adds a footnote here: "A sentimental song by Proch," presumably referring to "Das Alpenhorn," op. 18, a song for voice and piano

rule, as I had already discovered in Dresden when I stood on the very same podium where Weber had once conducted his work. When I first conducted the *Freischütz* in Dresden, eighteen years after the Master's death, I took the Overture's introduction at my own tempo, without any concern for the habits that had become ingrained under my older colleague Reissiger. At this, a veteran from Weber's time, the old cellist Dotzauer,[77] turned to me and said earnestly: "Yes, *that's* how Weber took it; this is the first time since then that I've heard it done properly." Weber's widow still lived in Dresden, and she confirmed that I had the right feeling for her long-deceased husband's music. She spoke to me with true affection, saying she hoped I would remain in Dresden and thrive in my position as capellmeister. She had long given up any thought of ever hearing her husband's music played correctly in Dresden again. But after all the distress she had endured, she now had reason to hope once again, she said. I mention her lovely, satisfying testimony about me because it has remained a comforting memory in the face of many contrary appraisals of my artistic activities, also as a conductor. — It was also her noble encouragement that made me so bold as to insist on thoroughly cleaning up the orchestra's interpretation of the *Freischütz* Overture for the abovementioned Viennese concert. This piece is well known to the point of satiety, but the orchestra now *studied it* with me as if it were completely new. The horns were undaunted and completely altered their approach under the

---

by Heinrich Proch (1809–78), a violinist, composer, and conductor who played in the Vienna Court Orchestra from 1834 to 1867. See also Harten (1983). Proch's composition is in the same key as Weber's overture (C major), and has an undulating accompaniment figure almost identical to that in measure 9ff. in Weber's overture. Proch's song, first published by Diabelli in Vienna in 1836, enjoyed numerous editions over the ensuing decades, appearing in assorted vocal anthologies and albums of piano arrangements (one of which, for piano duet, was by Franz Abt, one of Wagner's numerous *bêtes noires*; see "Fantaisie sur l'Air favori: Das Alpenhorn de H. Proch" in Abt's *Album musicale des jeunes Pianistes*, op. 33, no. 1, Leipzig: Hofmeister, 1841). Voss (2015): 39 alternatively suggests that Wagner might in fact be referring to Otto Thiesen's "Ein Alphorn hör' ich schallen," op. 23, for three women's voices and piano.

77 Justus Johann Friedrich Dotzauer (1783–1860), German cellist and composer, who played in the Meiningen Court Orchestra, then in the Gewandhaus Orchestra, and finally from 1811 to his retirement in 1850 in the Dresden Court Orchestra, where he worked under Carl Maria von Weber and, later, under Wagner.

sensitive artistic leadership of R[ichard] Lewy.[78] They had hitherto played the introduction's gentle woodland fantasy as a brilliant, ostentatious showpiece, but now they obeyed the score instead, pouring a magical scent into their cantilena above the *pianissimo* accompaniment of the strings. Just once—also in accordance with the score—did they rise to a *mezzoforte* to offer a tender inflection instead of the usual *sforzando*:

Example 3.17. Carl Maria von Weber, Overture to *Der Freischütz*, horn, m. 24

only to melt away smoothly thereafter. The celli, too, tempered what was usually played as a hard accent above the violins' tremolo:

Example 3.18. Weber, Overture to *Der Freischütz*, cello, m. 27

Instead, they offered the gentle sigh that the composer had wanted. This meant that the subsequent *crescendo* culminated in a *fortissimo* that was able to express its true sense of terror and despair. — After I had restored the introductory *Adagio* to its unearthly grandeur, I gave free rein to the wild motion of the passionate *Allegro*. I did not yet have to take into account the gentler, mellow nature of the subsequent, second theme, because I was fully confident of *moderating the tempo again* in good time and would be able to reach its true tempo imperceptibly.

Most *Allegro* movements of the newer, heterogeneous type obviously comprise two fundamentally different components. In comparison to the earlier, more naïve, homogeneous *Allegro* structure, they have been enriched by combining the pure *Allegro* type with the thematic characteristics of the songful *Adagio* in all its nuances. The second theme of the *Allegro* in Weber's Overture to *Oberon*:

---

78 Richard Lewy (1827–83), Viennese horn player, opera director, and singing teacher, for many years a member of the Vienna Court Orchestra. Among his singing students were Mathilde Mallinger and Emil Scaria (Wagner's first Eva in *Die Meistersinger* in 1868 and his first Gurnemanz in *Parsifal* in 1882 respectively).

Example 3.19. Weber, Overture to *Oberon*, mm. 65–68

demonstrates this contrary character at its most explicit, for it is in no way associated with the manner of a "true" *Allegro*. In formal terms, its contrasting character is conveyed naturally by interweaving it with the primary character of the piece in question. In fact, this theme had already been conceived with just such a union in mind. In other words, on the surface, this song-like theme seems to be wholly in line with the overall formal scheme of this *Allegro* movement. But as soon as it needs to let its true character speak, that same formal structure must be capable of [tempo] modification so that it serves equally well for both the primary and secondary characters of a movement.

I shall now continue the tale of my performance of the *Freischütz* Overture with the Viennese orchestra. After urging the tempo on to the height of excitement, I utilized the long, expansive song of the clarinet, which is *Adagio* in derivation,[79]

Example 3.20. Weber, Overture to *Der Freischütz*, clarinet, mm. 96–104

to rein in the tempo imperceptibly. Here, all rapid figurations are dissolved into a sustained, tremulous tone. As a result, despite the subsequent, rapid intermediary figure:

Example 3.21. Weber, Overture to *Der Freischütz*, m. 109

we were able to ease back into what was a very slightly modified version of the main tempo for the ensuing E-flat cantilena:[80]

---

79 This is a rare case of Wagner using an example already featured in Berlioz's treatise on orchestration. See Berlioz (1855): 140–41.

80 This same example—though with the slur stretching to the final B-flat, and with an accent on the penultimate note, C—is given in Mikorey (1917): 49.

Example 3.22. Weber, Overture to *Der Freischütz*, mm. 123–26

I insisted on this being played *piano* throughout, with uniform slurring—thus without the vulgar accentuation as it ascends that is otherwise customary. In other words, not

Example 3.23. Weber, Overture to *Der Freischütz*, mm. 123–26

I first had to discuss all this with my excellent musicians. But the success of this interpretation was so immediately striking that when it came to the imperceptible reinvigoration of the tempo with the pulsating figure

Example 3.24. Weber, Overture to *Der Freischütz*, mm. 145–46

I could rely on the sympathetic zeal of the whole orchestra, and only had to give the slightest indication of forward motion in order to reach the main tempo again (though this time a more energetically nuanced version of it). It was not so easy to interpret the more condensed return of the movement's two highly contrasting themes without losing the right feeling for the main tempo, because up to the moment when the desperate energy of the *Allegro* finds its culmination:

Example 3.25. Weber, Overture to *Der Freischütz*, mm. 249–53

the conflict between the two themes becomes concentrated in ever shorter periods. It was here that my constant modifications of the tempo proved most successful. After the magnificent, sustained C major triads and the long, significant rests between them, the second theme is played as an exalted song of joy; here, the musicians were very surprised when, contrary to their usual custom, I did not choose the more agitated tempo of the first *Allegro theme*, but the gentler, modified version of the tempo.

When our orchestras play this work, it is highly common for them to rush the main theme at the close. Often, we'd only need to hear the crack of a horse whip to complete the aural effect of a circus ring. The acceleration of tempo at the close of an overture is something composers often desire, and it comes of its own accord when a swift *Allegro* theme leads the field, as it were, to celebrate its ultimate apotheosis. One famous example of this is the great *Leonore* Overture[81] by Beethoven. In the *Freischütz* Overture, however, the impact of the heightened *Allegro* is utterly demolished because conductors have not understood how to modify the main tempo in order to meet the differing demands of the thematic combinations elsewhere in the work (including where to hold back the tempo at the right time). As a result, the main tempo is by this point usually so quick that it precludes the possibility of any further intensification through acceleration, unless the string instruments embark on an inordinately virtuoso assault. I had even had occasion to hear the Viennese orchestra do precisely this. It had astonished me, and gave me no pleasure, because this eccentric exertion was caused by a serious mistake—the fact that they had already attained a rampant tempo by this point. The result was an exaggeration to which no work of art should be subjected, even if it might be able to tolerate it in a crude sense.

If we can admit at least some sensitivity on the part of German conductors, then it remains utterly incomprehensible how the close of the *Freischütz* Overture can be rushed in this manner. But it becomes explicable when one considers how, even at its first occurrence, the second, song-like theme is carried away as booty at the pace of the main *Allegro*; it is like a feisty young girl captured with the spoils of war and tied to the tail of a soldier's horse as he wildly gallops off.[82] At the close, that second theme is raised up as a

---

81   Presumably *Leonore* no. 3.

82   Wagner commonly used gendered and sexualized metaphors and similes in his theoretical writings—see the section below, "Charles Darwin and the Imperceptible Art of Transition," and Walton (2020)—though a violent sexual simile such as this is unusual for him. He did, however, make use of such sexual imagery in connection with Berlioz in a letter to Liszt of September 1852. See p. 196 below.

song of jubilation; and now, in a kind of poetic justice, it is as if that maiden is placed upon the horse herself—presumably after its wicked rider has fallen off—and it's the capellmeister who charges off at a merry pace. This motif is in fact suffused with the fervent gratitude of a pious, loving girl's heart, but every public performance we hear of the *Freischütz* Overture—year in, year out— offers this extreme trivialization of it (to put it mildly), leaving an impression of indescribable repugnance. If anyone can still find such a performance good, and can write of our supposedly vibrant orchestral culture while adding his own special thoughts about the art of music—as does old, fun-loving Mr. *Lobe*—well, then he truly does well to warn us elsewhere of the "absurdities of wrongly understood idealism by pointing out what is aesthetically genuine, true and of eternal validity in the face of all kinds of dubious, semi-certifiable doctrines and maxims."[83] As I have said, however, my performance of this overture in Vienna meant a number of local music lovers were able to hear this poor, much-defiled overture played differently—though of course I more or less had to force it upon them. They are still talking of my success in this, and claimed never to have known the Overture properly before. They asked me what I had done to get my results, but could not grasp the means I had employed to achieve a rapturous, new effect in the final section. Hardly any of them wanted to believe that the cause was merely to be found in the more moderate tempo. The gentlemen in the orchestra, however, could have revealed more—something that was a true secret. It was this: in the fourth measure of the splendid, broadly played introduction to the return of the cantabile theme,

---

83   Wagner gives a footnote here: "See Eduard Bernsdorf, Signale für die musi-kalische Welt no. 67, 1869." He is referring to Eduard Bernsdorf's review of Johann Christian Lobe's book *Consonanzen und Dissonanzen. Gesammelte Schriften aus älterer und neuerer Zeit*, published in *Signale für die musikalische Welt* 27/67 (December 6, 1869), 1057–58, in which Bernsdorf praises Lobe, in particular his ironic treatment of Wagner's pamphlet *Jewishness in Music*. The first installments of Wagner's *Über das Dirigieren* had already been published in the *Neue Zeitschrift für Musik* when Wagner read Bernsdorf's implicit criticism of him in the *Signale*, a rival Leipzig journal. Wagner's reaction is unusually extreme and incoherent, given the mildness of Bernsdorf's remarks, which sug-gests that he is avenging himself for some more significant slight. Perhaps he had not forgotten that the initial, anonymous publication of his anti-Semitic article in 1850 had at the time prompted a scathing, public response from Bernsdorf himself ("K. Freigedank und das Judenthum in der Musik," in the *Neue Zeitschrift für Musik* 33/31, October 15, 1850).

Example 3.26. Weber, Overture to *Der Freischütz*, mm. 288–91

the sign > stands embarrassed and pointless in the score, seeming to signify an accent. But instead, I followed the composer's intention and interpreted it as a *diminuendo* sign, > thereby achieving a more moderate dynamic and a gentler inflection in the performance of the ensuing thematic idea [in m. 292].[84]

---

84   This *diminuendo* in m. 291 was disputed in the press at the time. In his review of Wagner's *Über das Dirigieren*, Heinrich Dorn called Wagner's idea "arbitrary" and pointed out that Weber's expansive orchestration at this point should preclude any notion of reducing the dynamic below the *fortissimo* already given (Dorn (1870b): 57). Nevertheless, this *diminuendo* was adopted by numerous conductors after Wagner. We can hear it on recordings by Nikisch with the London Symphony Orchestra in 1914 (he also slows down the tempo at the *diminuendo*), by Weingartner (in his 1932 film with the Paris Orchestra), by Furtwängler (e.g., in his 1944 Berlin recording, where he combines the *diminuendo* with a *decelerando* like Nikisch), and by Mengelberg (in his 1931 recording, though he does only a slight *diminuendo*). Nikisch, Furtwängler and Mengelberg do a rapid *accelerando* soon after the theme returns in m. 292, whereas Weingartner only picks up speed a little later (Nikisch's recording, by contrast, rushes toward the close at a pace beyond the ability of his musicians to keep up). Even Toscanini, in an NBC recording of 1945, does a slight *decrescendo* in m. 291. A hairpin *diminuendo* has also been added in m. 291 in a score of the Overture held by the archives of the New York Philharmonic that appears to contain markings in the hand of Gustav Mahler, who conducted it there on November 13, 1910 (see Martner (2010): 282–83); however, it is unclear just who added it, and when. Richard Strauss felt differently, however, writing "I am not of Richard Wagner's opinion that the great final C major of jubilant innocence should be played really *piano*; that is too contrary to Weber's intention! But Wagner is quite right that the *fortissimo* brass is too brutal for the beautiful poetic melody. So I have the strings play the melody *forte*, with all the wind accompanying them *piano*, and only towards the high A do I have the strings increase to *fortissimo*, the wind to *forte*" (Strauss (1989): 62). Today, it is generally accepted that Weber's marking indicated an accent, not a *diminuendo*; in Weber's manuscript, the sign given in m. 291 is identical in size and shape to many placed elsewhere by the composer in his score that clearly signify accents. See Brown (1999): 111–13.

Example 3.27. Weber, Overture to *Der Freischütz*, mm. 288–95

I was able to let this swell up quite naturally into the return of the *fortissimo*, which meant that the whole, supple motif was given an expression of bliss, supported as it was by its grandiose accompaniment.[85]

Our gentlemen capellmeisters don't like hearing of things like this, nor of the success that such ideas achieve. Mr. *Dessoff*,[86] who was soon due to conduct the *Freischütz* again in the [Vienna] Court Opera House, was nevertheless of the opinion that he should let his orchestra play the overture in the new manner that I had taught them. He said to them, smiling: "Well, let's take the overture *à la Wagner*."[87]

Indeed: *à la Wagner*! – I believe quite a few things could be taken *à la Wagner* without doing them any harm, gentlemen!

Nevertheless, this did seem to be a *great* concession on the part of this Viennese capellmeister. My former colleague Reissiger (since deceased) once made only *half* a concession in a similar case. Back in Dresden, I performed Beethoven's A major Symphony after it had been played several times under Reissiger. In the final movement, I came upon a *piano* written into the orchestral parts that he had added solely at his own discretion, just where the conclusion of this finale is so wonderfully prepared. After the repeated, hammering, dominant-seventh chords on A in m. 345ff.:[88]

85　This example is not given in full by Wagner; I expand it here, to better explain what he wants.

86　Felix Otto Dessoff (1835–92), German conductor and composer, studied at the Leipzig Conservatory, later a close friend of Brahms, active as conductor in Vienna from 1860 to 1875.

87　Anton Seidl recounts this same tale in his own essay "About Conducting," though without giving his source (Seidl (1895b): 208–9).

88　Wagner gives only the 3-measure excerpt from the violins, beginning in m. 349; for greater comprehensibility, I here quote the full texture in Liszt's piano

Example 3.28. Beethoven, Symphony no. 7, 4th movement, mm. 345–51

this motif

Example 3.29. Beethoven, Symphony no. 7, 4th movement, mm. 349–51

continues always *forte*, leading later on into an even more impetuous "*sempre più forte.*" This irritated Reissiger, so in measure 349 he had the orchestra suddenly play *piano*, only to embark on a noticeable *crescendo* thereafter. Of course I deleted this *piano*, restoring the *forte* most energetically, and thereby infringed Lobe/Bernsdorf's "eternal laws" of the genuine and the true, which were presumably also guarded over by Reissiger back then. After I had left Dresden, Reissiger once again performed this A major Symphony, but had meanwhile become doubtful about this passage. So he stopped here and recommended that his orchestra should now play *mezzo*forte.

Another time, not long ago in Munich, I happened to hear a public performance of the Overture to *Egmont*[89] that was no less instructive to me than the *Freischütz* Overture had been before, and for a similar reason. In the *Allegro* of this overture, the tremendous, heavy, *sostenuto* in the introduction:

Example 3.30. Beethoven, *Egmont* Overture, op. 84, mm. 2–3

arrangement of the symphony, including the 4 measures before Wagner's chosen example.

89 Wagner apparently conducted this overture just three times, in 1852, 1853, and 1854 in Zurich; see Walton (2007): 178.

is taken up again as the first section of the second theme, with its rhythm in diminution, and it is then answered by a mellow, cozy counter-motif:

Example 3.31. Beethoven, *Egmont* Overture, op. 84, mm. 82–85

Here, as elsewhere, this incredibly tightly knit motif—which combines a terrible seriousness with amiable self-assurance—was played in the usual, "classical" manner and was swept away like a withered leaf in the unhindered plunge of the *Allegro*. If one were able to follow it at all, then one could at best have perceived it as a dance step,[90] with the first two measures serving to prepare the dancing couple for a brief twirl in Ländler fashion in the ensuing measures. On one occasion, the celebrated older conductor[91] was absent, at which [Hans von] *Bülow* took his place.[92] I had him conduct this passage the right way, and it immediately had the impact intended by our laconic composer. The tempo up to here is passionate and agitated, but if it is firmly reined in—be it only slightly—then the orchestra will gain the space necessary to accentuate the thematic combination correctly, alternating swiftly as it does between great energy and tender felicity.[93] Towards the end of the

---

90   Wagner combines a German and a French noun here, "Tanz-Pas." His use of the latter is presumably intended to be pejorative, signifying a supposed trivialization of Beethoven's Germanic seriousness. See fn. 120 on his other, more obviously pejorative, use of "pas" later in this essay.

91   Ashton Ellis (Wagner, trans. Ellis (1895): 333) adds a footnote here identifying the conductor as Franz Lachner; Voss (2015): 47 is of the same opinion, as am I.

92   We do not know to which performance Wagner refers. Von Bülow conducted the *Egmont* music in November 1868, after Lachner's retirement, though Wagner too had left Munich by this time (see von Bülow's letter to Josef Rheinberger of November 8, 1868 in the Rheinberger Archive, Vaduz, https://www.e-archiv.li/textDetail.aspx?backurl=auto&etID=42867&eID=5, accessed September 2020).

93   Weingartner remarks that when he heard von Bülow conduct this work, he did not merely rein in the tempo here, but jumped "from the allegro directly into an 'andante grave.'" He suggests that the effect Wagner desires can be achieved without any tempo modification; the strings just have to play their rests and their upbeat eighth-note precisely, he says, instead of shortening the latter into a sixteenth-note as is so often the case (Weingartner (1896): 18–19). In his recording

triple-time section, this combination of motifs is accorded a broader treatment and assumes immense significance. Making this tempo modification enables us to achieve a new, legitimate reading for the whole Overture. As for the impact made by this correct performance, I learned only that the management of the Court Theater felt that the work had been "capsized"!

No such notions occurred to the audience of the famous Munich Odeon Concerts when I once attended a performance of Mozart's G minor Symphony [no. 40], conducted by the aforementioned, comfortably classical conductor [Franz Lachner]. The manner in which he performed that symphony's *Andante* was a success with the public, and this taught me something that I had hitherto regarded as impossible. Who has not in his youth heard this apprehensively[94] floating piece of music and in his rapturous pleasure wanted in some way to make it his own? But how? No matter. Where the expression marks do not suffice, the feelings inspired by the wonderful course of this piece do their work instead, and our imagination tells us how we might give expression to these feelings in our actual interpretation.[95] It seems as if the Master wished to leave this completely to us, for he offers only the scantest of binding expression marks. Thus we are free to luxuriate in the ominous shudderings of its gently swelling eighth-note motion, and we can rhapsodize with the rising violin that is like the light of the moon,[96]

---

of the *Egmont* Overture with the Vienna Philharmonic in the late 1930s, however, Weingartner indeed slows down marginally at m. 82. Furtwängler does so too in his 1947 recording with the Berlin Philharmonic, though he does a slight *rallentando* before it; Mengelberg does the same in his recordings, though far more drastically in his last two, from 1943 and 1944; Nikolai Golovanov's recording of 1951 with the Moscow Radio Symphony Orchestra is even more extreme, sounding rather like how Weingartner describes von Bülow.

94 Voss (2015): 48 notes that the printed editions give "schwungvoll" (spirited) here, though this is a misreading of Wagner's autograph "ahnungsvoll" (apprehensively); I follow Voss and the autograph here.

95 This passage in *Über das Dirigieren* is a paraphrase of Wagner's description of the opening of the slow movement to Mozart's Symphony no. 39, K. 543 in the *Report to His Majesty* of 1865, where he postulates what the "wonderful" theme would sound like if played in the "glib" manner that its lack of expression markings suggests (SSD 8: 146). Since that symphony is in E-flat major, like the slow movement of K. 550, did Wagner perhaps get his slow movements mixed up? See fn. 21, fn. 38 and also p. 159 in the critical essay below.

96 Pembaur (1892): 32 gives this same music example (though marked *sempre pp*) and uses the same simile, describing it as "a dream pianissimo like the moon

Example 3.32. Mozart, Symphony no. 40, K. 550, 2nd movement, m. 9

whose notes should be gently slurred together; the gentle whisperings of

Example 3.33. Mozart, Symphony no. 40, K. 550, 2nd movement, m. 32

let us waft upwards as if on the wings of angels, and we die away at the fate-
ful admonitions of the questioning passage

Example 3.34. Mozart, Symphony no. 40, K. 550, 2nd movement, mm. 53–55

(which we imagine played in a beautifully legato *crescendo*). In this manner, we would ultimately reach the promise of a blissful death through love,
which then embraces us kindly in the closing measures. — But any such
fantasies were swept aside in the face of a truly classical, strict performance
of this movement by the famous old master in the Odeon in Munich. This
was such serious stuff that we shuddered in our skin, as if we were about
to experience eternal damnation. The light, floating *Andante* in particular
became a brazen *Largo*, and each eighth-note was given its full value with
not a hundredth of it left out.[97] Stiff and dreadful, like iron pigtails, this

---

rising in the night sky." As Voss points out, however (2015): 48, this passage is
already marked with a long slur by Mozart, and he suggests that Wagner might
have been using a faulty edition without a slur, or that he had forgotten the slur
while writing out the passage from memory.

97　Weingartner refers to this passage in his booklet on conducting Mozart's last
three symphonies. He says that Wagner's criticism of a slow tempo in this
movement has led younger conductors to assume they were meant to beat it
in two, to which Weingartner says "this is naturally out of the question, for
technical reasons alone"; he goes on to say that he beats this movement slightly
slower than the A major Trio for the boys in the *Zauberflöte* ("Seid uns zum
zweiten Mal willkommen"), which itself should be beaten in six, not in two,
thus Weingartner. See Weingartner (1923): 4–5.

strictly beaten *Andante* went over our heads, and even the feathers of its angels' wings turned to brightly polished wire curls, like something from the time of the Seven Years' War.[98] I imagined myself transported back to 1740, being measured up as a recruit for the Prussian Guard and fearfully trying to buy my freedom.[99] Who can imagine my horror when the old master turned back his pages to play the first half of this larghettoized *Andante* once more, merely because he assumed the two dots before the double bar in the score couldn't have been engraved there without good reason. I looked around for aid—and experienced a second miracle. Everyone was listening patiently, believing that it was all perfectly in order. They were convinced that they had experienced a pure, innocent delight: a truly Mozartian feast for the ears. So I bowed my head and held my peace.

Just once, at a later date, did my patience desert me a little. In a rehearsal[100] for my *Tannhäuser* [under the same conductor, i.e., Franz Lachner again], I had already acquiesced in all kinds of things, including taking the chivalrous march of the second act[101] at a clerical tempo. But our indubitable old master could not even understand how to resolve the $\frac{4}{4}$ meter into the corresponding $\frac{6}{4}$, in other words, where two quarter-notes ♩♩ become a triplet

---

98   Wagner presumably means the Seven Years' War of 1756–63 between Britain, Prussia, and Portugal on the one side, and France, Austria, Spain, Russia etc. on the other.

99   Wagner writes of being placed under the recruits' measuring stick (the "Rekrutenmaaß"), used to enforce the height requirements of different regiments—more specifically, for the "lange Kerls" (literally: long fellows), the "Potsdam Giants" of the King of Prussia's personal regiment of grenadiers. Given that Wagner was diminutive in stature—apparently about one foot smaller than required for those grenadiers—it is not impossible that this is an instance of self-mockery (a trait not uncommon in Wagner in private, as seen in Köhler (2012), but rare in his published essays). This reference to 1740 is a double *non sequitur*. As Voss remarks, the regiment was formed by Friedrich I and was dissolved when he died in 1740; in any case, they have no connection to the Seven Years' War under his son Friedrich II. Either Wagner got all his dates wrong, or simply liked his metaphors too much to be concerned with historical exactitude.

100 Voss identifies this as being presumably the rehearsal of March 4, 1865. See Voss (2015): 50.

101 Wagner here means the march in *Tannhäuser*, Act 2, Scene 4.

as was revealed in Tannhäuser's Narration in the third act, where instead of ⁴⁄₄ [102]

Example 3.35. Wagner, *Tannhäuser*, Act 3, Scene 3, Tannhäuser's Narration

we have the following in ⁶⁄₄:

Example 3.36. Wagner: *Tannhäuser*, Act 3, Scene 3, Tannhäuser's Narration

The old master found it difficult to beat this shift. He was seriously accustomed to beating the four parts of a ⁴⁄₄ measure solemnly in right angles, but ⁶⁄₄ is always treated by this type of conductor after the manner of a ⁶⁄₈ measure, thus *alla breve*, as "one — two" (only in the *Andante* of [Mozart's] G-minor symphony did I experience him beating each part of the measure in a serious 1, 2, 3 — 4, 5, 6). But for my poor Narration of the visit to the Roman Pope, the conductor made do with a hesitant *alla breve* as if he wanted to leave it up to the orchestral musicians to figure out how to cope with the quarter-notes. The result was that the tempo was twice as fast as it should have been. Instead of the relationship between ⁴⁄₄ and ⁶⁄₄ being as given above, it turned out thus:

Example 3.37. [Wagner, *Tannhäuser*, Act 3, Scene 3, Tannhäuser's Narration, the lower staff is given as supposedly conducted by Franz Lachner]

This was in musical terms rather interesting, but it compelled the poor singer in the role of Tannhäuser to offer his painful memories of Rome in a highly

---

102   Wagner gives the next two examples in C; I follow Jacobs in giving them in the original, as in the accompaniment to Tannhäuser's Narration in the third act of that opera.

frivolous waltzing rhythm that skipped along merrily.[103] This reminded me of Lohengrin's Narration of the Grail[104] as I had heard it once in Wiesbaden, where it was performed *scherzando* (as if it were for Queen Mab).[105] Since on this occasion in Munich I had the wonderful singer L[udwig] Schnorr[106] for the role of Tannhäuser, in order to do him justice I had to intervene most respectfully with our old master and get him to beat the right tempo. This caused some offence. I believe that over time it even led to acts of martyrdom that a cold-blooded critic of the Gospels felt compelled to extol in two sonnets.[107] These days, our pure classical music has its martyrs, and I shall allow myself to take a closer look at them in what follows here. —

---

103 It is difficult to believe that a conductor as experienced as Franz Lachner would really conduct this $\frac{6}{4}$ passage at twice the proper speed, not least because the tenor would be unable to spit out his words at such a tempo (see the eighth-note passage "da läuteten die Glocken," at which the music would surely have broken down). So Wagner is probably exaggerating, though we have no proof either way.

104 *Lohengrin*, Act 3, Scene 3.

105 Wagner presumably has the "Queen Mab Scherzo" in mind, from Berlioz's *Roméo et Juliette*, op. 17. The Wiesbaden performance in question was conducted by Johann Baptist Hagen (1818–70) in the summer of 1862; Wagner claimed in *Mein Leben* to have left early in a rage (ML: 708).

106 Ludwig Schnorr von Carolsfeld (1836–65), Wagner's favorite tenor, who died just six weeks after singing in the world premiere of *Tristan und Isolde*.

107 Wagner here refers to two sonnets by the theologian David Strauss (1808–74) in which the latter defended his friend Franz Lachner against Wagner's attacks (though without naming Wagner directly). Wagner reacted in turn by writing *three* sonnets attacking Strauss. See SSD 12: 371f., Janz (1997) and Voss (2015): 51–52. David Strauss had come across Wagner's music when he mixed with Liszt and others in Weimar in the early 1850s. He had already developed an antipathy towards things Wagnerian by the time he published *Der Christus des Glaubens und der Jesus der Geschichte* in 1865, for in a footnote there he mentions the enthusiasts for St. Mark's Gospel as being a "waste of time, like the music of the future [*Zukunftsmusik*] or the agitators against cowpox vaccinations": Strauss (1865): 54. Wagner will probably also have known that Strauss had criticized Beethoven's introduction of voices in the last movement of his Ninth Symphony, because Hanslick specifically refers to this in the 1865 edition of his *Vom Musikalisch-Schönen* (see Hanslick (1865), 69–71); this will have been another reason for Wagner to dislike Strauss. Wagner's antipathy towards him was later taken up by Nietzsche. See Ziegler (1908): 714–15.

🙼 🙼 🙼

As[108] I have already often touched upon above, attempts to modify the tempo in performances of classical works, i.e., in music by Beethoven, have always been met with reluctance by the conductors' caucus of our time. I have shown here extensively that a one-sided modification of the tempo, without a corresponding modification of the dynamics of performance, would seem to justify such objections, though I have also revealed the deeper, underlying problem, for these objections are solely a result of the general incompetence and lack of vocation on the part of our conductors. While I regard my methods as essential in the abovementioned cases, there is nevertheless a perfectly valid reason for warning against them. Nothing could be more damaging to those pieces of music than to subject them to arbitrary modifications (also of tempo), because it could open them up to the fantastical discretion of any and every vain time-beater keen to achieve a mere effect. Over time, this would merely disfigure our classical repertoire to the point of complete unrecognizability. There is nothing one can say here except that we have reached a sad state of affairs if such fears can arise at all. It means that people in our world no longer have faith in that true artistic awareness that can swiftly dispel any such arbitrariness. As a result, those objections (which, although well founded, are rarely raised honestly) serve to confirm the general incompetence of our conductors. But if we are to prevent the bunglers from subjecting our music to their whims, why haven't our own excellent, highly esteemed musicians seen fit to put things right? Why have they, of all people, led the performance of classical music onto the paths of triviality and disfigurement to an extent that ought to dissatisfy any feeling musician, or even sicken them?

Their seemingly justified objections [to my suggestions] are mostly just a pretext for opposing every endeavor along the paths that I have laid out here. The reasons lie, as always, in incompetence and mental lethargy—a lethargy that sometimes intensifies to the point of aggression. This is because incompetent and lethargic men are in the majority by far.

Most classical works were without exception introduced to us only in the most imperfect manner (just think of the reports on the circumstances in

---

108 This is the first paragraph in the seventh installment of Wagner's essay, published on January 7, 1870 in the *Neue Zeitschrift für Musik* 66/2.

which Beethoven's most difficult symphonies were first performed!).[109] Many
of them were initially brought before the German public in completely disfigured form (in this regard, see my essay on *Gluck*'s Overture to *Iphigenie
in Aulis* in the fifth volume of these collected writings).[110] These examples
can help us to comprehend the incompetence and idleness with which these
works have been most assiduously performed—we only have to consider
how even a master such as *Mendelssohn* went about conducting them! To be
sure, we cannot expect far more minor musicians to reach a state of comprehension of their own accord, when even their true master was unable to
attain it. This is because there is only *one* way to help the less gifted to grasp
the right manner of doing things: *we have to provide them with an example.*
But they won't find any such example on the paths they have chosen. It is
depressing that this leaderless path is so well trodden that there is no more
space left on it for him who might indeed provide such an example. This is
why I shall now take a keener, more in-depth look at the devout opposition
to performing our great works of music correctly. My aim is to reveal the
true wretchedness of these intractable men, and above all to deprive them of
the halo with which they adorn themselves as the supposed "chaste spirits of
German art." Because it is they who hold back our music life where it would
otherwise soar up; it is they who deprive its ambiance of any draught of fresh
air; and it is they who, with time, will turn the glories of German music into
a bland, laughable wraith.

It seems important to me to look them straight in the eye and to tell them
to their face where they really come from—and they quite certainly do *not*
originate in the spirit of German music, which in itself we do not need to
investigate further here. It is not so easy to weigh up the positive aspects
of our newer, i.e., Beethovenian music, precisely because it is so weighty,
and we shall wait for a better moment than today before embarking on
such an undertaking. For now, let us suffice by proving the worthlessness of

109 Wagner is here presumably relying again on the testimony of Anton Schindler;
see the discussion of his possible influence on Wagner in the section "Tempo
Modification" below.

110 Wagner means his essay "Gluck's Ouvertüre zu 'Iphigenia in Aulis.' Eine
Mitteilung an den Redakteur der 'Neuen Zeitschrift für Musik,'" first published in that journal in 1854 and then reprinted, as he states here, in the fifth
volume of the first edition of his writings that he was busy editing and publishing with Fritzsch of Leipzig. That article includes expression markings that are
also found in orchestral parts and a score held today by the Zentralbibliothek
Zürich. See Figures 5.13–5.15 below.

that type of music-making that currently pretends to be truly classical and Beethovenian.

The opposition of which I speak is supported by utterly uneducated hacks who are extremely loud and vociferous when they write in the press; but when you actually come across them, they in fact express themselves in a manner that is merely obstinate and timid. ("See, he can't express himself properly," a lady once said to me with a meaningful glance, referring to one of those prim-and-proper musicians.) Through their utter carelessness, the administrative bodies of German art[111] have placed the leadership of our higher organs of music life into their hands, and thus the fate of German music rests with them too. They consequently feel secure in their rank and office. As I observed right at the start here, this Areopagus[112] comprises two fundamentally different tribes: that of the German musicians of the old style that is today falling into decline, and which has retained its prestige especially in the more naïve climes of southern Germany, and that of the up-and-coming, elegant musicians of the newer style who have emerged primarily in northern Germany from the school of Mendelssohn.[113] These two species once thought little of each other, though certain recent disruptions to their smooth-running operations have resulted in their uniting in mutual recognition. Thus Mendelssohn's school—and all that goes with it—now enjoys just as much appreciation and support in southern Germany as prototypical southern German unproductivity is now greeted with welcome respect in the north. A pity that *Lindpaintner*[114] of blessed memory was no longer able to experience this. Both trends have been united in a metaphorical handshake to ensure mutual peace. Perhaps the former, southern type of musician had to overcome a certain inner resistance to this alliance, but any

---

111 In his copy of this essay, Richard Strauss has underlined "Through their utter carelessness, the administrative bodies of German art" and placed an exclamation mark in the right-hand margin.

112 The Areopagus (literally the "rock of Ares") is a hill near the Acropolis and was the name given to the council of city elders in ancient Athens.

113 As Voss points out, Wagner's contemporaries also believed that there were considerable north–south differences among German musicians of their day. See Voss (2015): 54. In his own conducting treatise, Zopff (1881): 100 writes specifically of different attitudes to tempo among conductors from north and south Germany.

114 Peter Joseph von Lindpaintner (1791–1856), German conductor and composer, born in Koblenz but active mostly in southern Germany, whom Mendelssohn regarded highly.

embarrassment was mitigated by a mixture of envy and helplessness—which together constitute an uncommendable characteristic of the Germans that has already ruined one of the most important musicians of modern times[115] (as I have already explained elsewhere). That man went so far as to deny his own nature, even making himself subservient to the new laws of the elegant type of musician—laws that are so ruinous to what is truly German. As to the opposition from the more subordinate men whose nature was more that of craftsmen, they had little to say except: "we can't make any progress, we don't want anyone else to make any progress either, and we'd be annoyed if anyone else did." All this was honest narrow-mindedness, and it only turns dishonest out of resentment.

But things are different in the more modern camp, where the strangest ramifications of personal, social, and even national interests mean that all kinds of different attitudes have come together. Without going into further detail about these manifold interests, I shall here highlight only their principal maxim, namely that these men *endeavor to hide much, and try to ensure that much goes unnoticed.* In a certain sense, they are keen that people should not even notice that they are "musicians." And they have good reason to want this.

It used to be difficult to associate with true German musicians, back in the day. Just as in France and England, musicians in Germany had always been very neglected in society, even despised. Here, the princes and aristocrats almost only ever regarded musicians as human beings if they came from Italy. As we can see in Mozart's treatment by the Emperor's court in Vienna, Italian musicians were preferred to Germans in a humiliating manner. In our country, a musician remained ever a peculiar, half-wild, half-childish being, and he was treated thus by those who paid him his wages. Our greatest musical geniuses bore the marks of this exclusion from finer, more stimulating society—just think of Beethoven when he met Goethe in Teplitz.[116] Musicians were regarded as inherently incapable of any higher education. When H[einrich] Marschner saw my intense efforts to raise standards in the Dresden orchestra in 1848, he warned me against it in my own interest,

---

115 Wagner means Robert Schumann. In his copy of this essay, Richard Strauss has also written the name "R. Schumann" in the left-hand margin here.

116 Wagner is referring to the often told tale of Beethoven encountering Goethe at the spa resort of Teplitz in 1812, when Goethe supposedly bowed to passing aristocrats, while Beethoven refused to do so. See, for example, Schindler (1840): 82–83.

saying I should remember that musicians were simply incapable of understanding me. — To be sure, as I stated at the outset, even our highest musical posts are in most cases held by "musicians" who have moved up from below, though their sheer good craftsmanship means they have also brought with them many admirable qualities. A kind of family feeling accordingly emerged within this orchestral patriarchy. It did not lack a sense of familiarity, though it lacked that fresh breath of genius that can spark a fire in the intelligent heart of an orchestra, and be it only a fire that warms more than it illumines.

But just as our world of craftsmanship has remained foreign to the Jews, so did our newer music conductors fail to emerge from the ranks of our musical craftsmen. That world is anathema to our conductors, not least because they are averse to the real hard work it entails. Instead, this new type of conductor has planted himself straight at the top of our musical guild system, just like the banker sits atop our craftsmen's guilds. To this end he had to bring one thing with him from the outset that those musicians who had risen from below did not possess, or at least found it very difficult to acquire on those rare occasions when they succeeded in it. Just as the banker has his capital, so the new conductor brings *learnedness* with him. But this is mere superficial learnedness, not real *culture*, because whoever truly possesses the latter is not to be mocked. He is superior to everyone. But let us consider instead the possessor of that superficial kind.

Those who possess true culture enjoy real freedom of mind—true freedom altogether, in fact. But I know of no case in which even the happiest cultivation of superficial learning has resulted in that kind of freedom. Mendelssohn possessed many talents, and cultivated them with earnest diligence, but it was still obvious that he never achieved real freedom. He was never able to overcome those peculiar inhibitions that the serious observer realized kept him outside our German artistic life, despite all his well-earned successes. Perhaps this even became a nagging source of anguish to him, and was what consumed his life at such an unfathomably early age. There is nothing unselfconscious about this kind of desire to become cultured. It originates not in any urge to express oneself freely, but in a compulsion to hide something from one's own nature. The culture that emerges from this can thus only be a mendacious, pseudo-culture.[117] It can enable one to hone

---

117 Wagner uses the word "Afterbildung," literally "anal culture," which is a not uncommon intensification of "half-" or "pseudo"-culture, and does not have the same vulgar connotation as in English.

one's intellect along certain paths—but the place where all these paths come together can never be a place of true, clear-sighted intelligence. — While it is almost deeply distressing to observe this inner process at work in an especially talented, finely developed individual, it soon becomes nauseating to us when we observe the same process and its effects in less talented, more trivial natures. In them, everything grins at us in a trite, trifling manner. If we are unable to follow most of the superficial representatives of our cultural institutions by simply smiling back at the smirking sham that is their understanding of culture, then we become truly resentful at the sight of them. The true German musician has serious reason to feel resentful, because he has had to realize that these trivial pseudo-artists have the temerity to sit in judgement on the spirit and significance of our magnificent music.

In general, it is a prime characteristic of the representatives of this pseudo-culture that they linger long on nothing, they delve deeply into nothing, and—to put it another way—they make much of nothing. They regard the greatest, most sublime, and most profound thing as perfectly natural and self-evident, as something that is at the disposal of everyone at all times, available for them to learn and, no doubt, to mimic. They do not dwell on what is immense, divine or daemonic because they will not find anything there that they might copy successfully. This is why these pseudo-artists customarily speak of excrescences, exaggerations, and the like. Out of this, they have formulated a new aesthetic that pretends to model itself primarily on *Goethe*, because he is supposed to have been averse to all such monstrosities and instead upheld a beautiful, calm clarity. Then they praise the "harmlessness" of art, while they treat Schiller somewhat scornfully for having been occasionally too intense. And thus, in clever unanimity with the Philistines of our day, they create a whole new concept of classicism. To bolster their arguments in the broader regions of art, they also inevitably drag in the Greeks because they were home to a clear, transparent serenity. This shallow reconciliation with all that is serious and awe-inspiring in our existence is then raised up to the status of a completely new, ideological system[118] in which even our new musical heroes of pseudo-culture ultimately find an uncontested, comfortable place of honor.

I have already demonstrated in a few eloquent examples just how these pseudo-artists have dealt with our great German works of music. All that remains is for me to explain the supposedly serene, Greek meaning of

---

118 See my discussion of Wagner's use of the word "system" in the section "*Über das Dirigieren*—Structure, Context, and Meta-Text" below.

Mendelssohn's urgent exhortation to just "skim through" a work. We can see this most clearly in his adherents and successors. For Mendelssohn, it was about hiding the unavoidable weaknesses of a performance, perhaps in certain cases also the weakness of the performers themselves. In his followers, however, their pseudo-culture comes into play because their aim is to hide as much as possible, and thereby avoid any and all fuss. There is a reason for this that is almost wholly physiological, as became clear to me in a case that is not as far removed from my topic as it might seem. When my *Tannhäuser* was performed in Paris, I reworked the first scene in the Venusberg, making more of what before had been only fleetingly alluded to. I pointed out to the ballet master[119] how the pitiful, skipping little dance steps[120] of his Maenads and Bacchantes contrasted ridiculously to my music. I insisted that he should instead invent something more appropriate here—something bold, wild, and sublime, based on the processions of Bacchantes as depicted on famous Classical reliefs. That was what his corps de ballet should be dancing. The man whistled through his fingers and said to me: "Ah, I understand you very well, but for that I'd need a corps just of principal dancers. If I said a word of this to my people here and tried to demonstrate the kind of gestures you want, they'd promptly do a 'can-can' and we'd be lost." The same attitude that led my Parisian ballet master to retain the utterly vacuous dance steps of his Maenads and Bacchantes is what prevents the elegant leaders of our new music life from giving free rein to their sense of pseudo-culture—they know that it can only lead to a scandal *à la* Offenbach. *Meyerbeer* was a cautionary example for them. His work at the Paris Opera had already enticed him to

---

119 This was Lucien Petipa (1815–98), *maître de ballet* at the Opera in Paris at the time. When Cosima Wagner decided to perform *Tannhäuser* at Bayreuth, she liaised with Petipa (whom she consistently called "Petit-Pas") in 1887 through Wagner's friend and translator Charles Nuitter, to try and get details of the choreography and staging of the Paris production of 1861. When *Tannhäuser* was finally presented in Bayreuth in 1891, Cosima engaged the renowned Italian dancer Virginia Zucchi to do the choreography; Zucchi, as it happens, was a favorite of Petipa's brother Marius, who was the ballet master at the Mariinsky Ballet in St. Petersburg for three decades. See Wagner and Nuitter (2002): 157–58 and 162.

120 Wagner writes the French word "pas" here; see fn. 90 above on the other, also seemingly pejorative use of this French word. It is also possible that he intends a blunt play on the name of his ballet master Petipa (whom he calls "Petitpas"—literally, little step—in ML: 644).

adopt certain Semitic accents in his music that made even the representatives of "pseudo-culture" take fright.

Much of their learning has always comprised keeping a careful check on their behavior, just as someone with a natural speech impediment, like a stammer or lisp, has to avoid all ardency in his speech so that he does not lapse into an unseemly stuttering or spluttering. This custom of always keeping themselves in check has undoubtedly been pleasantly successful in that it has prevented much that is repugnant from seeing the glaring light of day, while the general mix of mankind has gone about its business far more unobtrusively. This has had a positive effect on us all, because it has loosened up much in our own nature that had developed in a pretty poor, stiff fashion. I have already mentioned above that the coarseness of our musicians was moderated, and a gracefulness in the execution of certain details in performance came to the fore. But it's a very different thing when this compulsive reticence and suppression of questionable personal traits is then turned into a principle for the performance of our art. The German is angular and awkward when he tries to be genteel. *But he is noble and superior to everything when he is inflamed with passion.* Should we then hold back in this, just out of consideration for Them?[121]

But in truth, that's how it seems to be these days. Whenever I used to meet a young musician[122] who had been in Mendelssohn's proximity, he would mention only how the master would admonish him never to think of creating any "impact" or "effect"[123] when composing, but to avoid everything

---

121 Wagner capitalizes this word ("Jenen").

122 Ashton Ellis suggests that Wagner here means Joachim Raff. Wagner, trans. Ellis (1895): 344.

123 Wagner writes here "Wirkung oder Effekt," which is superficially tautological, as they are generally used as synonyms, the former of German origin, the latter being derived from the Latin. But in *Opera and Drama* (SSD 3: 301), Wagner had already set up these two words in opposition, choosing the latter "as a foreign word removed from our natural feeling" to signify the "secret" of Meyerbeer's music; Wagner's own "translation" of this was "Wirkung ohne Ursache," effect without cause. "Effekt" thus seems to have signified for Wagner—at least in his Zurich writings—something foreign/French/Jewish and not "German." In *Über das Dirigieren* he clearly remembers using "Wirkung" and "Effekt" to mean opposite things, but seems unable or unwilling to pursue this binary opposition with any real consistency. Thus he later on here reverts to "Wirkung" (see fn. 133 in this chapter), but then returns to "Effekt" without keeping the two words and their newly assigned meanings

that could cause it. That sounded perfectly reasonable. And indeed, those students who have remained faithful to their master have never yet achieved any effect in their music at all. But this seemed to me to be far too negative a doctrine, and rather precluded exploiting the positive aspects of what they had learned. I believe that all the teachings of the Leipzig Conservatory are founded on this negative maxim. I have discovered that the young people there are utterly tortured by its warnings, while even their finest talents cannot win themselves any favor with their teachers until they have expunged everything from their music that isn't suited for setting psalms.[124]

With regard to our present topic, these negative maxims had their biggest impact on the art of performing our classical music, which has become dominated by a fear of lapsing into anything radical. I have never yet heard of adherents of their teachings being able to learn and perform the piano works of Beethoven in a manner that presents his style at its most characteristic and recognizable. For a long time it was my fervent desire to find someone who could let me hear the great B-flat major Sonata [op. 106, the *Hammerklavier*]. This wish was ultimately fulfilled, though by someone with a background very different from those men who had been drilled in the war camps where Mendelssohn's maxims were upheld. It was the *great Franz Liszt*, who also stilled my yearning to hear *Bach* performed properly. They liked to cultivate Bach over there too; since no one could claim that his music harbored any modern effects or the radicalism of a Beethoven, they found it all the easier to play it in their beatifically smooth, utterly flavorless manner.

In connection with the *Tempo di Menuetto* of [Beethoven's] Eighth Symphony, I have already mentioned a colleague of Mendelssohn's who was one of the most renowned musicians of the older generation.[125] I once asked him to play to me the eighth Prelude and Fugue from the first book of the *Well-Tempered Clavier* (in E-flat minor), because this piece had always magically attracted me. I have to confess that I have rarely experienced such a

---

separate. This is surely further confirmation that Wagner's crass binary oppositions (such as "German" and "foreign," i.e. French/Italian/Jewish/whatever) were the result of momentary emotional needs rather than a consequence of any endeavor to create some kind of consistent, logical, aesthetic vocabulary. Because Wagner does not keep them separate, I here generally write "effect" for both "Wirkung" and "Effekt," except in the present case, where it seems necessary to define them more precisely.

124 This is presumably another snide reference to Mendelssohn and his psalm settings.

125 Wagner clearly means Ferdinand Hiller.

fright as when he kindly honored my request. There was no more hint of any gloomy German Gothic or any such supposed nonsense—instead, the piece flowed across the piano under the hands of my friend with a "Greek serenity," such that I didn't know where to turn any more in the face of so much innocuousness.[126] I involuntarily felt as if transported into some neo-Hellenic synagogue from whose musical rites all Old Testament accents had been eradicated[127] so as to make everything sound as genteel as possible. That peculiar performance was still tingling in my ears when I finally asked Liszt to purify my musical soul from that embarrassing experience. He played the fourth Prelude and Fugue for me (in C-sharp minor). I already knew what I might expect from Liszt at the piano, but what I now heard was something I would never have anticipated from Bach, regardless of how well I had studied him. Here I learnt the difference between any amount of studying and an act of revelation. For Liszt revealed Bach to me by playing just this one fugue. As a result, I now know unmistakably what he is, and can from this standpoint appreciate him in all his aspects. If ever I might feel in danger of going astray and doubting him, I can dispel all doubts through the strength of my robust faith.[128] But I also know that Those[129] who guard him as if he belonged to them in fact know *nothing* of him. And if anyone should doubt this, I shall say unto him: have them play Bach to you!

I also call on the best of that Pietistic musical temperance society (which I shall consider in greater detail below) to confess whether they have really known and understood Beethoven's great B-flat major Sonata before having heard it played by *Liszt*. I can at least name one man who heard that

---

126 As explained in the essay below, Wagner himself had only modest skills at the piano.

127 Wagner writes "ausgemerzt," a word whose origins were in animal husbandry. While we must beware of inverting history, the anti-Semitic context in which Wagner employs this verb is striking. It later became a favorite word of the National Socialists when describing their policies for exterminating those fellow human beings whom they regarded as unworthy of life. See, e.g., Schmitz-Berning (2007): 79–81.

128 These sentences seem to play intentionally with (Christian) religious terminology, though with anti-Semitic intent: "Offenbarung" (revelation); "Irrewerden" (to go astray); and the opposition of "Zweifel" (doubt) and "gläubig" (faithful). This is presumably intended to underline Wagner's supposed distance from those who would purportedly play Bach as if—thus Wagner—they were partaking of a musical rite in a "genteel" synagogue.

129 Again, Wagner capitalizes "Jenen."

wonderful event and was so moved that he felt compelled to make just such a confession.[130] But there is another man who today plays Bach and the true Beethoven in public and so enraptures every audience that they, too, confess to having never understood this music properly before. Is he a student of that school of abstinence? No! It is the man most qualified to be Liszt's successor, *Hans von Bülow*.[131]

This will suffice for now on this topic.

Now we must consider how these fine revelations further apply to those gentlemen with whom we are dealing here.[132]

Their political successes, inasmuch as their aversion to "effect" enables them to assert themselves "effectively"[133] in the German musical community, should not bother us further. But the religious developments in their community are certainly of concern to us. In this regard, their maxim "avoid all effect!," which used to be more a result of anxious inhibition and selfish apprehension, has been raised from being a subtle, prudent rule into a truly aggressive dogma. Its adherents turn away their eyes with peevish timidity when they come across a real man in music, almost as if they perceived him to be something unchaste. This timidity originally served to conceal their own impotence, but it is now used to defame the potent, and their accusations gain active strength from suspicion and slander. The nourishing soil in which all this thrives is poor German Philistinism, whose squalid spirit we find in the pettiest of men, and which envelops our music life too, as we have already seen.

The main ingredient, however, remains a certain judicious wariness towards those things that they cannot themselves achieve, while slandering everything that they would *like* to achieve. It is beyond sad that a man as able as *Robert Schumann* should have become entangled in this dreadful state of affairs—and indeed, his name became posthumously inscribed on the church banner of this new community. It was unfortunate that Schumann

---

130 It is unclear to whom Wagner is referring here.

131 While contemporary reports leave no doubt that Wagner's praise for von Bülow was justified, it is also worth noting that Wagner needed von Bülow to agree to divorce Cosima so that she and Wagner might be married. The divorce came through in July 1870, thus half year after *Über das Dirigieren* was published. Cosima married Wagner just over a month later.

132 This is the first paragraph in the eighth installment of Wagner's essay, as published on January 14, 1870 in the *Neue Zeitschrift für Musik* 66/3.

133 In this sentence, Wagner writes "Wirkung" and "Wirksamkeit," not "Effekt"; but afterwards, it's "Effekt" again. See fn. 123 in this chapter.

attempted things in which he was out of his depth, though it was what he obviously lacked that made him the most apt figurehead for this newest guild in music. Schumann wrote works that were quite charming and endearing, and which were therefore cultivated more beautifully and more commendably by us[134] than by his own adherents (in this I am proud to count myself among *Liszt* and his companions). But they deliberately ignored them, precisely because those works offered proof of true productivity—or perhaps because they were unable to play them. On the other hand, those men diligently prefer those works in which Schumann revealed the limits of his talent, namely his bolder, larger-scale works. If the public does not properly warm to these pieces, his adherents use this as proof that Schumann's music commendably refuses any "effect." And ultimately, they find it useful to compare him with the late Beethoven (who remains incomprehensible to them on account of how they play him). They happily lump late Beethoven together with those works by Robert Schumann that are uninteresting and overblown, but which they find easy to master because they almost demand to be played glibly. They thereby insist that Schumann's works are compatible with the boldest, most tremendous, most profound utterances of the German spirit. The shallow bombast of Schumann is thus supposedly equal to the ineffability of Beethoven—though always with the proviso that Beethoven's radical eccentricity really ought not to be allowed, whereas indifferent triviality, like Schumann's, is fitting and proper. Seen from this angle, Schumann and Beethoven go perfectly well together as long as the former is performed correctly, and the latter is performed badly.

In their attitude towards our great, classical music, these peculiar guardians of musical chastity are like the eunuchs of the great harem. This is why our Philistines are also keen for them to monitor the worrisome influence of music on our family life, as they are confident that nothing objectionable could emerge from them.

But where is our great, ineffably splendid German music in all this? —

Ultimately, our sole concern must be what becomes of our music. Even if nothing special is composed during a certain period, we will get over it, and we can still be proud of having enjoyed a hundred glorious years of the most marvelous productivity. But the people we are dealing with here have

---

134 Wagner writes "unsererseits," though he made no attempt as a conductor to promote Schumann's works, and the two men never really got on. Liszt and Schumann, by contrast, had a high regard for each other; Liszt even dedicated his Piano Sonata in B minor to Schumann.

appointed themselves the guardians and keepers of the true "German" spirit of our magnificent heritage, and are keen to legitimize themselves as such. It is this that makes them seem dangerous to us.

Taken on their own, there's not much wrong with these musicians. Most of them compose quite well. Mr. *Johannes Brahms* was once so kind as to play me a series of serious variations[135] that he had composed, and it was clear from them that he wasn't prone to jokes. I thought them quite admirable. I also heard him play a piano recital with compositions by other men, though this pleased me less. It seemed to me impertinent that those around him were willing to admit that Liszt's school "at least [possessed] an extraordinary technique,"[136] but nothing more. By contrast, I found the brittleness and awkwardness of Mr. Brahms's performance highly embarrassing, and I would rather have seen his technique moistened with the oil of Liszt's school (though this seems not to flow from the keyboard itself, but is won in a more ethereal realm than that of mere "technique"). Altogether, however, [Brahms] was a highly respectable figure, even if it remains impossible to imagine how by merely natural means he might become, if not the Messiah,[137] then at least His most beloved disciple.[138] Unless, perhaps, a prim enthusiasm for medieval carvings has misled us into imagining those stiff wooden personages to be the ideal of sainthood. Either way, we would at least have to protest at having our great, living Beethoven presented to us in the robes of that sainthood, merely for this misunderstood man to be thus disfigured and placed alongside Schumann, who also remains incomprehensible, though for the most natural reasons. The aim of this is to pretend that no difference exists between these two, just because *those men* are unable to notice any.

I have already intimated how things stand with their "sanctity." If we take a closer look at their aspirations, we shall find that our investigations into conducting will take us into a new field. —

---

135   Brahms visited Wagner in Penzing near Vienna on February 6, 1864, when he played him his *Variations and Fugue on a theme of Handel*, op. 24. Wagner's wordplay is perhaps more obvious in the German in its contrast between "ernst" (serious) and "Spass" (jokes), though it still falls rather flat.

136   The source of this supposed quotation remains obscure.

137   Almost twenty years earlier, in *Opera and Drama* of 1850–51, Wagner had already mocked Berlioz as a false "Messiah" of the music world. See SSD 3: 283 and the section "Berlioz the Catalyst?" below.

138   Wagner is presumably referring to the disciple "whom Jesus loved" in St. John's Gospel, traditionally identified as St. John himself, and who bore the same Christian name as Brahms.

Some time ago, a southern German newspaper editor accused my artistic theories of having "hypocritical" tendencies.[139] The man clearly didn't know what he was saying, and simply wanted to use an angry word. But in my experience of the repugnant sect of hypocrisy, it has the strange tendency to seek out avidly what is stimulating and seductive, only so that it might practice its powers of resistance against those selfsame stimulants and seductions.

The real scandal here was a result of the supreme initiates of this sect having revealed their secret, namely that they had turned their aforementioned tenets on their head, and that their resistance against seduction was intended only to intensify their ultimate submission to its enjoyment. When applied to art, it would not be incorrect to accuse this musical temperance society, with their peculiar school of chastity, of being hypocritical. For it is the lower ranks of this school that enter into the cycle of stimulant (such as is offered by the musical arts) and abstinence (which is imposed upon them by a maxim turned into a dogma), whereas we can prove that the higher ranks long only for those pleasures that are forbidden to the lower ranks. The *Liebeslieder Waltzes* of Saint Johannes, regardless of the absurdity of their title alone, can be assigned to the category of exercises for the lower ranks.[140] However, the ardent yearning for "opera" in which all the religious devotions of the abstinent are ultimately subsumed is unmistakably a matter for the higher ranks, indeed for the highest of them. If they were for once able to enjoy the happy embrace of "opera," we might expect the whole school to explode. Only the fact that they never succeed in this is what still keeps this school together. Every failed attempt at it can time and again be claimed as an act of voluntary negation as if it were a ritualistic exercise of the lower ranks. Thus opera—which they never court successfully—can also figure repeatedly as a symbol of the stimulants that are ultimately to be rejected. In this manner, the author of a failed opera can be portrayed as being especially saintly. —

But let us now ask in all seriousness: what is the real attitude of these gentleman musicians towards "opera"? — Because now that we have visited

---

139 Egon Voss identifies this editor as Julius Fröbel (1805–93), who on January 3, 1869 had written in the *Süddeutsche Presse* of Wagner's ideology as that of a "sect" characterized by "tasteless, hypocritical cravings." See Voss (2015): 65.

140 Here, Dannreuther adds the footnote: "For a curious example of such exercises, see Ferdinand Hiller's *Oper ohne Text*: a set of pianoforte pieces, à quatre mains"; he presumably means Hiller's *Operette ohne Text*, op. 106 for piano duet. Leipzig: Rieter-Biedermann, 1864.

them in the concert hall, where they had their beginnings, we still have to investigate their art of conducting in the opera house. —

In his recently published "Reminiscences," Mr. Eduard Devrient[141] has explained the "yearning for opera" felt by his friend Mendelssohn. We also learn from him how that needy master was convinced that the opera he was destined to write would be properly "German." He just needed to be provided with the right topic. But in this he had no success. I suspect that the reasons for this were perfectly natural. All kinds of things can be realized by mutual agreement. But "Germanness" and a "noble, serene" opera, such as Mendelssohn's perfidiously delicate ambition desired, are not among them. This is because there is no recipe to be found for them in either the Old Testament or the New.[142] But while such things remained unattainable by the master, they were never properly abandoned by his journeymen and apprentices. Mr. *Hiller*[143] believed he could achieve such an opera by force, by simply setting about it serenely and undaunted, because ultimately, it seemed all he needed was to get a proper grip on it. Others had managed it, and he felt sure that *he'd* be bound to succeed too, if he just kept at it long enough—rather like in a game of chance. But no matter how hard he and others tried, they kept failing. No one had any success in opera—not even poor Schumann[144]—and however many of the higher and lower ranks of that temperance church held out their arms to try and grasp the true operatic

---

141 Eduard Devrient (1801–77), German singer, actor and theater director; the brother-in-law of the singer Wilhelmine Schröder-Devrient. He sang the part of Jesus in the first modern performance of Bach's *St. Matthew Passion* under Mendelssohn in 1829; he also wrote the libretto for Heinrich Marschner's *Hans Heiling* and sang the title role at the world premiere in 1833. He worked as an actor at the Dresden Court Theater from 1844 until 1852, when he was appointed Director of the Court Theater in Karlsruhe; he retired in 1869, the year he published the reminiscences mentioned by Wagner. For Mendelssohn's repeated desire to compose an opera with Devrient, see Devrient (1869): 123–24, 234–35, 274.

142 Voss notes that Wagner is here almost certainly alluding to Mendelssohn's two oratorios *Elijah* and *St. Paul*, based on topics from the Old and New Testaments respectively. See Voss (2015): 67.

143 Hiller composed six operas, two of which were given their first performances in Dresden during Wagner's time there.

144 Wagner means Schumann's *Genoveva*, first performed under the composer in Leipzig on June 25, 1850, but which enjoyed little success. Hermann Levi conducted a revival in Karlsruhe in 1867.

success they all yearned for so chastely and innocently, they enjoyed nothing but a brief, painful illusion of success before failing again and again.

Such experiences can embitter even the most innocent of men, and they are all the more irksome because the nature of the music world in Germany means that capellmeisters and music directors are primarily bound by their function to the theater. These gentlemen are thus compelled to serve in a field of musical activity where they are themselves utterly incapable of achieving anything. Nor can this incapacity of theirs to compose an opera make any of them suitable for directing one. It cannot make of them a good opera conductor. And yet, as I described at the outset above, it is the strange fate of our artistic life that these gentlemen, who can't even conduct our German concert music, have been assigned the highly complicated task of directing opera too. Any comprehending person can now imagine what the results of this must be! — —

I have gone into extensive detail to reveal the weaknesses of these gentle-man conductors in the field where they ought to be most at home (i.e., in the concert hall). In the realm of opera, however, I can deal swiftly with their supposed achievements, because here one can only say: "Lord, forgive them, for they know not what they do!"[145] In order to describe their ignominious impact in this field, I ought to provide proof of the significant, good things that could be achieved; but this would lead me too far from the goal I have set myself. For this reason, I shall reserve such proofs for another time. Here, I shall only offer the following remarks to sum up their efforts as opera con-ductors. —

In the field of concert music, which is their starting point, these gentle-men think it fitting to set to work with the most serious countenance pos-sible. In opera, however, they find it more appropriate from the outset to wear a flippantly skeptical, witty and frivolous expression. They smilingly admit that they are not really at home here, and they don't much understand those things that they don't much like. So they display a gallant complacency towards their singers, whom they are delighted to accommodate. They adopt the tempi the singers want, insert their fermatas, *ritardandi* and *accelerandi*, they transpose passages to suit them, and above all they are happy to make cuts wherever and however their singers desire. For how could they ever find proof that these unreasonable demands by their singers are in fact absurd? If a more pedantic conductor were ever to insist on something despite his singers, he would inevitably be deemed in the wrong, because their own

---

145 Wagner here paraphrases Christ's words on the Cross: see Luke 23:34.

frivolous attitude towards opera means it is the singers who are utterly at home in it. Only the singers know what they can do and how to do it. So if ever anything laudable comes about in opera, it's solely thanks to the singers and their keen instincts, just as whenever anything turns out right in the orchestra, it's almost solely thanks to the good sense of the musicians in it. But you only have to glance at an orchestral part—for [Bellini's] *Norma*, for example—to see how such a harmlessly written piece of music can turn into a strange, musical changeling. The sheer sequence of transpositions to which it is subjected offers us a truly horrifying picture of the music to which our esteemed capellmeister has to beat time blithely. First there might be the *Adagio* of an aria in F-sharp major, then an *Allegro* in F major, and between them a transition to E-flat major (because of the brass band).[146] It was not until I happened to experience the *Barber of Seville* in a theater on the outskirts of Turin in Italy that I heard it performed correct and complete,[147] because our own capellmeisters find it too irksome to conduct even such an innocent score properly. They haven't a clue that even the most insignificant opera can have a relatively beneficial effect on the educated mind if played perfectly correctly, simply because its correctness provides us with a sense of satisfaction. The shallowest theatrical concoctions in the smallest theaters of Paris can still have a pleasant, even aesthetically liberating impact on us, because they are always performed thoroughly correctly and reliably in all their aspects. It is a powerful artistic principle that when just one aspect is properly fulfilled and implemented, it has an immediate aesthetic impact on us. What we find here is true art, if only on a very low level. But in Germany we learn nothing of this impact, except perhaps in *ballet performances* in Vienna or Berlin. Because there, *everything is in the hands of the one man* who really understands what he's doing: the ballet master. Fortunately, it is also he who determines the laws of movement in the orchestra, both in matters of expression and of tempo. What's more, unlike the individual singer in an opera who decides things according to his individual taste, the ballet master does so for the good of the whole ensemble, so that all are in concordance. And then suddenly, we can hear that the orchestra is playing correctly. This is an extremely beneficial feeling that will please everyone who attends such a ballet after the torment of an opera performance. In opera,

---

146 "Because of the brass band" – since brass instruments are usually tuned in E-flat or B-flat, playing in flat keys (such as E-flat) is easier for brass bands.

147 Voss notes that Wagner attended this performance in Turin on August 30, 1853; see Voss (2015): 69 and SB 5: 416.

it is the producer who could conceivably bring about a similarly successful degree of consistency. But strangely enough, the fiction remains alive that opera belongs somehow to absolute music, despite all proofs of the ignorance of the conductor, and despite his ignorance being well known to every singer. As a result, when on occasion a performance is truly successful thanks to the right instincts of talented singers and to the enthusiasm for the work demonstrated by the musicians and other participants, we see that it's still the gentleman capellmeister—as the representative of the whole ensemble—who is called forward to receive applause and all the accolades. He must himself be surprised at how he has achieved this; and then he, too, will have occasion to pray: "Lord, forgive them, for they know not what they do!" —

But since I only desire to examine the art of conducting itself, and do not want to digress further about the general state of our opera scene, I here only wish to state that this chapter brings me to the close of my essay.[148] As far as the conducting skills are concerned of our capellmeisters in the opera, it's not for me to debate them. Our singers can do that, perhaps; they will complain about a conductor who does not yield enough to them, or about another because he doesn't take enough care when giving them their entries. In short, we could engage in such disputes about the most general tasks of the conductor's craft. But from the higher perspective of truly artistic achievement, such conducting is of no consequence. It is to me that the task has fallen to say something about this—and in this I am alone among all living Germans.[149] This is why I shall now take the trouble to investigate in greater detail the reasons for rejecting that type of conducting.

When[150] I consider my experience of hearing our conductors perform my own operas, I have to confess to remaining in the dark about their particular qualities. Are they acting in the spirit of our great concert music, or of how opera is performed in our theaters? I think that what's fatal for me is that these two types join hands when dealing with my operas, despite not complementing each other in a very happy manner. When a conductor accustomed to our classical concert music is given free rein in the introductory instrumental movements to my operas, I experience only the most

---

148 Not yet; we naturally do not know when Wagner decided to add another installment.

149 In his copy of this essay, Richard Strauss has underlined "to me ... alone among all living Germans" and drawn a vertical line in the left-hand margin.

150 This is the first paragraph in the ninth and final installment of Wagner's essay, as published on January 21, 1870 in the *Neue Zeitschrift für Musik* 66/4.

depressing consequences, such as I have already outlined above so extensively. In this regard, I shall only discuss the tempo, which is either taken
at an absurdly fast pace (such as when Mendelssohn once performed my
Tannhäuser Overture in a Leipzig concert in order to offer it up as a deter-
rent example), or utterly botched (as in my *Lohengrin* Prelude in Berlin and
just about everywhere else), or botched and dragged at the same time (as was
recently the case with the Prelude to my *Meistersinger* in Dresden and other
places). Nowhere is my music played with those meaningful modifications
that would facilitate a comprehensible interpretation of it. I ought to be able
to expect this, just as I expect the musicians to play the right notes.

In order to give the reader an inkling of the nuances of this pernicious
manner of performance, I shall explain how conductors usually treat the
Prelude to my Meistersinger. —

I specified the principal tempo of this work as "sehr mässig bewegt" [very
moderate]. According to the old formula, this means roughly *Allegro maes-
toso*. There is no tempo that is more in need of modification in a longer
piece, especially when the thematic content is treated in a highly episodic
fashion. It is a popular tempo for performing manifold combinations of heterogeneous motifs, because its broad divisions in a regular $\frac{4}{4}$ meter make it
ideal for tempo modifications, and these in turn make it easier to play its
motivic combinations. This moderate tempo in a $\frac{4}{4}$ meter is also ideally open
to all kinds of ambiguity. When beaten in powerful, animated quarter-notes
it can express a lively, true *Allegro*. This is the principal tempo I intend here,
which presents itself at its liveliest in the eight-measure transition leading
from the march proper to the E major second subject:

Example 3.38. Wagner, Prelude to *Die Meistersinger von Nürnberg*, mm. 89–90

This meter can also be treated as a half-period comprising two $\frac{2}{4}$ measures,
meaning that when the main theme enters in diminution

Example 3.39. Wagner, Prelude to *Die Meistersinger*, mm. 122–23

it can introduce a lively *scherzando* character;[151] it can even be interpreted as an *alla breve* (in ₂/₂ meter), where it expresses the older, leisurely *tempo andante* (as employed in church music) that is correctly beaten as two moderately slow beats. I employ it in this last sense from m. 158, the eighth measure after the return to C major, when the main march theme, now played by the basses, is combined with the second subject that is sung unhurriedly and broadly[152] by the violins and cellos in rhythmic augmentation (at twice the original note values):

Example 3.40. Wagner, Prelude to *Die Meistersinger*, mm. 158–61

I have already introduced this second theme earlier [in the exposition] in a pure ₄/₄ meter[153]

Example 3.41. Wagner, Prelude to *Die Meistersinger*, mm. 96–98, in the piano version by Hans von Bülow

---

151 In his booklet *Über das Dirigieren*, Josef Pembaur reproduces the preceding music example, marking it "Im Charakter eines lebhaften Scherzandos" (with the character of a lively scherzando), which is a direct, unacknowledged quotation from Wagner. See Pembaur (1892): 34.

152 In his *Über das Dirigieren*, Pembaur reproduces the bass line of the following music example, marking it "Gemächlich breit gesungen" (sung unhurriedly and broadly) which is another direct, unacknowledged quotation from Wagner's essay. See Pembaur (1892): 34.

153 Wagner's example comprises just the two measures of the first violin from "Etwas mässiger"; I give the harmonic context to aid comprehensibility (here in Hans von Bülow's vocal score), and I also include the preceding measure because Wagner refers to it at the close of the following paragraph (the "*poco rallentando*" measure).

When played with the greatest tenderness of expression, this theme has a passionate, almost hurried[154] character (rather like a declaration of love whispered in secret). In order to maintain this tenderness that is its principal characteristic, the tempo has to be held back slightly here. Its passionate precipitousness is already expressed sufficiently by its more rapid figurations, so it must be played here at the most extreme, [slower] nuance of the main tempo, as fitting the *gravitas* of the $\frac{4}{4}$ meter. In order to achieve this imperceptibly (i.e., without really distorting the main character of the basic tempo), this change is introduced by a measure designated "*poco rallentando*" (see above).

The more agitated aspect of this theme finally begins to dominate:

Example 3.42. Wagner, Prelude to *Die Meistersinger*, mm. 105–06

which I have especially marked "more passionate" in performance. Thanks to this increased agitation, I am easily able to lead the tempo back to its original, swifter course, where it ultimately serves as the above-mentioned *Andante alla breve* [in m. 158, see Example 3.40 above]. For this, I only had to return to a nuanced version of the main tempo that I had already introduced in the exposition of the piece. I had let my first development of the solemn march theme run into a coda of cantabile character that has to be played more broadly from the outset; this can only be played correctly if it is understood as being in the *Andante alla breve* tempo described above. This passage is preceded by a fanfare that is to be played in a weighty $\frac{4}{4}$:[155]

Example 3.43. Wagner, Prelude to *Die Meistersinger*, mm. 41–42

---

154 In his copy of this essay, Richard Strauss has underlined "almost hurried" and added a vertical line in the left-hand margin.

155 I have swapped the following two examples round in order to match their order in the Prelude, though, as the reader can see from the measure numbers I have added to all the examples, Wagner tends here to jump back and forth somewhat arbitrarily between the different sections of the work.

but the succeeding cantabile coda is to be played sonorously in the above-mentioned *alla breve* tempo:

Example 3.44. Wagner, Prelude to *Die Meistersinger*, mm. 59–62

The tempo change clearly has to be initiated when the pure $\frac{4}{4}$ motion ceases; in other words, it must begin with the sustained dominant chord in m. 58 that introduces the cantabile:[156]

Example 3.45. Wagner, Prelude to *Die Meistersinger*, mm. 57–61, in the piano version by Hans von Bülow

Since this broad tempo in half-notes is subjected to an extended, lively intensification (aided by the use of modulation), I believed that I could leave the conductor to determine the tempo here. After all, if one gives full rein to the natural feelings of the orchestral musicians when performing such passages, this results in a quickening of the tempo of its own accord. As an experienced conductor myself, I was sure that I could count on this, and so only deemed it necessary to specify the passage in which the tempo returns to its original $\frac{4}{4}$. This seems natural to anyone with musical feeling, because the harmonic rhythm now moves in quarter-notes. At the conclusion of the Prelude, this broader $\frac{4}{4}$ meter enters in an equally recognizable manner with the return of the abovementioned, weighty, march-like fanfare [Example 3.43]. This is joined by the rapid figurative ornaments, in order to close in the same tempo in which the piece had begun. —

I first conducted this Prelude at a private concert in Leipzig,[157] and did so exactly as described above. The very small audience comprised almost solely

---

156 Wagner does not give this music example.

157 The audience for this concert on November 1, 1862 included Edward Dannreuther; see "Wagner in Translation" below.

friends of my music from elsewhere. The orchestra played so excellently that the audience animatedly demanded a repeat of the Prelude straightaway. Since the musicians seemed to be of the same mind as the audience, they did so in a mood of joyful willingness. The impression made seemed so positive that it was decided to play my new Prelude for the Leipzig public proper in a Gewandhaus concert. Capellmeister *Reinecke*[158] had attended the performance of my piece under my direction and was assigned to conduct it this time. The same musicians performed it; but it was hissed at by the audience. Whether this success of conventionality was thanks to the participants alone—in other words, whether it was an intentional act of disfigurement— is something I shall not investigate further here, for the simple reason that the genuine incapacity of our conductors is so evident to me anyway. Highly capable ear-witnesses told me *what meter* the gentleman capellmeister had beaten in my Prelude, and so I knew enough.

If such a conductor desires to prove to his audience or his director how bad my *Meistersinger* is, then he just needs to beat my Prelude the same way he conducts Beethoven, Mozart and Bach (a manner of conducting that can even do justice to R. Schumann). Then it's easy for everyone to claim that this is pretty unpleasant music. If such a vibrant, infinitely delicate, sensitive object as my tempo for this Prelude is turned suddenly into a Procrustean bed by such a classical time-beater, then one can easily imagine what the results must be! In other words: "lie in here—if you're too long, we'll just chop bits off you, and if you're too short, we'll stretch you out!" And then they play music to drown out the cries of the martyr's agony!

I also got to know the *Dresden* public with such a truncated experience. It had already heard works of mine, not just this Prelude to the *Meistersinger*, but the whole work too, as I shall elucidate (the "whole" work except for what had been cut in advance). To speak in technical terms again: the merit of the conductor[159] this time lay in his extending across the whole piece what he assumed to be the main tempo, beating his square, stiff, ¼ meter throughout,

---

158 Carl Reinecke (1824–1910), German conductor, composer and teacher, in his early twenties a member of Mendelssohn's circle. In 1860 he was appointed to teach at the Leipzig Conservatory. He was the chief conductor of the Gewandhaus Orchestra from 1860 to 1895, when he was succeeded by Nikisch. In fact, Reinecke was not averse to making tempo modifications himself, as can be heard on piano rolls he made. See the section "Tempo Modification" in my essay.

159 Julius Rietz, court capellmeister in Dresden at this time. For more information, see fn. 12 above.

taking the broadest variant of that main tempo as his unchanging rule. This also resulted in the following. Uniting the two main themes by means of an ideal *Andante alla breve* tempo towards the close of the Prelude—as explained above—also enables me to end the whole opera in an aptly cheerful manner, rather like an old, popular refrain. I expand this combination of my themes more or less as an accompaniment to Hans Sachs's homely but serious panegyric to the Mastersingers themselves, with his words of comfort for German art.[160] Despite the seriousness of the content, this closing apostrophe should have a serene, comforting impact on the soul. I aim to achieve this primarily through the impression made by the cozy combination of my themes. The rhythmic movement should only assume a broader, more ceremonial character towards the close when the chorus enters. (Everyone who is aware of my other works and activities will understand why I shall prudently refrain here from delving further into the dramatic aspects of my oeuvre. Instead, for the sake of pure, naïve "opera," I shall remain with the topic of conducting and beating time.) The conductor had already completely ignored the necessity of modifying the initial tempo of the march-like, grandiose processional music into an *Andante alla breve* in the Prelude; and he ignored it equally in the closing scene of the opera, which has no direct link back to the original march any more. The inappropriate tempo that had been chosen in the Prelude now became a binding norm, with the conductor yoking the otherwise spirited Hans Sachs into the most turgid ¼, unrelentingly forcing him to sing through his closing address as stiffly and woodenly as possible. Highly sympathetic colleagues solicited me to abandon this close for Dresden and let it be "cut" because it was far too depressing. I refused, and soon the complaints fell silent. I finally found out why—the gentleman capellmeister had come to the aid of the stubborn composer, and had employed his own artistic judgment to *cut* the ending himself (naturally only so as to "help" the work).

"Cut! Cut!"—that's the last resort[161] of our gentlemen capellmeisters. With it, they create an infallible balance between their own incapacity and the impossibility of their proposed solutions to the artistic task before them. They think "what I don't know can't hurt me," and ultimately, this has to

---

160 Wagner presumably means Sachs's closing monologue in the final act, beginning with "Verachtet mir die Meister nicht" (Don't scorn the Masters), and ending with "zerging' in Dunst / das heil'ge röm'sche Reich, / uns bliebe gleich / die heil'ge deutsche Kunst!" (if the Holy Roman Empire were to melt away in mist, we'd still have holy German art).

161 Wagner uses the Latin "ultima ratio."

satisfy the audience too. It only remains for me to ponder what I should think of such a performance of my whole work, sandwiched as it was between the utter failure of alpha and the equal and utter failure of omega. Outwardly, everything seemed very nice. The audience was tremendously excited, at the close there were even curtain calls for the capellmeister, for which my own monarch[162] returned, applauding, to the balustrade of his box. But afterwards I heard fatal reports of cuts and changes having been made, and of new, additional cuts. Since I had been able to experience a production of the work in Munich that was not just completely uncut, but was also performed completely correctly,[163] there was no way that I could possibly agree with the actions of those mutilators in Dresden. This dire predicament seems impossible to change, because hardly anyone understands just how bad it is. Nevertheless, there is a silver lining in an oddly comforting realization: however uncomprehending those in charge of its production might be, they still can't ruin the strong impact that the work makes in performance. This is the fatal power of "effect," about which the Leipzig Conservatory warns so urgently, but which even those bent on its destruction cannot evade—and this is surely their punishment. This truly seems like a miracle to me, for even if I cannot bring myself to attend a performance of my works such as that of my *Meistersinger* in Dresden, nevertheless its almost incomprehensible effectiveness is strangely comforting, for it lets me draw certain conclusions about the fate of our great classical music in the hands of those same conductors. It is now clear to me why it continues to thrive, despite their maltreatment of it: they are simply unable to kill it off.[164] And this conviction may miraculously serve as a kind of comforting dogma to the genius of German art, bestowing on him the consolation of faith, and the ability to continue his work after his own fashion.

But what are we to think of the *musical* abilities of these wonderful conductors with their famous names? If we consider how alike they are in everything, one might reasonably conclude that, ultimately, they have understood things correctly, and their activities might even be "classical" after all, even though all our feeling rebels against this possibility. People are so convinced

---

162 "My own monarch" here does not refer to King Ludwig of Bavaria, but to the King of Saxony, Wagner's homeland, of which Dresden was the capital.

163 Wagner here means the world premiere in Munich under Hans von Bülow on June 21, 1868.

164 In his copy of this essay, Richard Strauss has drawn a vertical line in the left-hand margin from "conclusions " to "kill it off."

of their excellence that the whole musical citizenry of Germany never wavers when they conduct something, such as at the big music festivals. Only Messrs. *Hiller, Rietz* or *Lachner* can possibly oblige in such cases. We couldn't properly celebrate Beethoven's forthcoming 100th birthday if these three gentlemen all happened to sprain their wrists.[165] Regrettably, I don't know a single man whom I might trust to beat proper time in a single passage of any of my operas—at least, none from the general staff of our time-beating army. Now and then I have come across a poor devil in whom I recognized true ability and conducting talent. Yet they harm their own careers, because not only do they see through the incapacity of our great capellmeisters: they are careless enough to speak about it too. A conductor is hardly going to recommend himself if, for example, he finds and draws attention to awful mistakes in the orchestral parts for *Figaro* that one of these great generals has used umpteen times, but whose errors he has failed to notice. These poor, talented, competent men come to grief just as the heretics of old.

All this is apparently right and proper, and promises to remain so—which means we end up asking ourselves time and again: Why? We are tempted to despair about whether these gentlemen are *truly musicians*, because they clearly display no *musical feeling* at all. Nevertheless, they *hear* very precisely (mathematically speaking, if not in ideal terms—after all, not all of them would be guilty of that misfortune with the defective orchestral parts!). They have a keen sense of broad outlines, they can read and play at sight (at least very many of them can); in short, they have proved themselves to be true professionals. And their education—despite everything—is of a kind that we can expect only of a musician, so that if they were deprived of this musicianship, nothing else would remain, least of all a man of spirit and culture. No, no! Truly, they *are* musicians, and very competent ones at that, who know and can do everything that pertains to music. But what of that? Once it comes to making music, they throw everything together higgledy-piggledy, feeling themselves secure in nothing except a "happy ever after" or, if needs be, a "Lord God of Sebaoth." To be sure, the only aspects of our great music they muddle up are precisely what make it great, and which can be expressed in words as little as they can be expressed in numbers. But surely it remains music, only music? So whence does this dryness come, this frost, this complete inability to melt in the face of music, to forget all troubles, all envious sorrows, and any supposed ideas of one's own? — Would *Mozart* have been

---

165 Richard Strauss has drawn a vertical line in the left-hand margin alongside this
sentence about Beethoven's 100th birthday.

able to explain this to us, given his immense mathematical gifts? His nerves were so overly sensitive to any discords, and his heart beat with such over-flowing benevolence, that it seems the ideal extremes of music touched each other directly in him, complementing each other to form a wonderful whole. *Beethoven's* naïve habit of getting help to do his sums is also well known, though arithmetical problems surely never had any possible impact on how he composed. Compared to Mozart, he seems a *monstrum per excessum*[166] in matters of emotion. Since his emotional side was not counterbalanced intellectually by arithmetic gifts, he was only able to thrive and be protected from premature demise by means of his abnormally powerful, robust consti-tution. Nor can you measure anything about his music by means of num-bers, whereas in Mozart (as we have already outlined above), much that is regular to the point of banality can be explained as a naïve mixture of those two extremes of musical perception, the emotional and the arithmetical. The musicians who are the subject of our present considerations instead appear as monstrosities only in purely musical arithmetic, but since their nature is so contrary to that of Beethoven, they can get by nicely with a perfectly nor-mal set of nerves. So if our gentleman conductors, whether famous or not, should happen to have been born with only a mathematical gift for music,

---

166 A "monstrosity through excess"; as Voss (2015): 79–80 suggests, Wagner here presumably refers to Schopenhauer's "Psychological observations" in his *Parerga und Paralipomena*, where he claims that in order to survive and thrive, every animal being, including man, needs to achieve a balance between its will and its intellect. But the genius, thus Schopenhauer, is characterized by an imbalance that favors the intellect, and is thus a *monstrum per excessum*, as opposed to the man driven by passions alone and devoid of intellect, the *monstrum per defectum* (Schopenhauer (1874): 616–17). Schopenhauer in turn is probably referring back to *On the Generation of Animals* by Aristotle, who in his discussion of reproduction posited that an animal that deviates in appear-ance from its parents is a monstrosity and in some way contrary to nature (see Aristotle (1912): 767b). Wagner seems to be suggesting that Beethoven is the metaphorical progeny of Mozart, but his sensibility is so different from this parent that he is a "monstrosity through excess," nevertheless able to survive this imbalance through his "robust constitution." Wagner uses the same term, "Monstrum per excessum," to describe Liszt's partner, Princess Carolyne zu Sayn-Wittgenstein, in a letter to Hans von Bülow of November 29, 1856 (SB 8: 204), some two years after we know he was reading Schopenhauer's *Parerga*. It is perhaps noteworthy that Nietzsche—who admired *Über das Dirigieren*—wrote of the "Monstrosität per defectum" in his *Birth of Tragedy*, written shortly after Wagner's conducting essay. See Nietzsche (1886): 72.

then we can fervently hope that some new school would succeed in explaining to them the correct tempo of our music according to the *regula de tri*.[167] But we must doubt whether they could be brought to such comprehension by musical feeling alone, which is why I now come to my conclusion.

We can only hope that the school I describe above as being desirable is truly in the offing. I hear that the Royal Academy of the Arts and Sciences in Berlin has founded an "Academy of Music," whose direction has already been assigned to the famous violinist Mr. *Joachim*. To set up such an academy without Mr. Joachim, were he available, would have been a grave mistake. I am hopeful for this academy, because according to everything that I know and have heard about Mr. Joachim's playing, this virtuoso is both perfectly acquainted with the true art of interpretation that I require for our great music, and also actually attains it in performance. He is the only musician known to me, apart from *Liszt* and his school, to whom I can point as providing practical proof of all my above observations. It is irrelevant here whether or not it is irksome to Mr. Joachim to be placed in such company (as I have heard via other quarters), because ultimately it does not matter what we profess to be, but what we truly are. If it suits Mr. Joachim to claim that he learnt his art of interpretation from Mr. Hiller or R. Schumann, we can ignore this as long as he continues to play in a manner that confirms the success of his many years of intimate acquaintance with Liszt. It also seems a good idea that the people who thought of setting up an "academy of music" should have turned first to an excellent *performing* artist. If I had to explain to a theater capellmeister today how he should conduct, I would rather recommend him to ask Mrs. *Lucca* instead of the deceased cantor *Hauptmann* of Leipzig, even if he were still alive.[168] In this matter, I am at one with the most naïve audience, and even with the tastes of our noble operatic friends: I prefer to hold to him who is productive, and whom our ears and sensibilities can actually experience in performance. However, it would alarm me if Mr. Joachim, seated on the curule seat[169] of the academy, should rule only with

---

167 The "rule of three" in math, by which three numbers are used to calculate a fourth.

168 As Voss (2015): 81 points out, Wagner means that the Milanese publisher Giovannina Lucca (1814–94) knows more about music than the recently deceased composer Moritz Hauptmann (1792–1868), who had been cantor at the Thomasschule in Leipzig and a theory teacher at the conservatory there.

169 A chair used by the holders of high office in ancient Rome, later also by Napoleon.

his violin in his hand, because violinists remind me of the "beauties" whom Mephistopheles imagines only "in the plural."[170] The conductor's baton seems not to have agreed with him, while composing seems more a source of bitterness to him than of pleasure to anyone else. How this "higher school" should be conducted only from the high stool of its first violinist is something I don't quite comprehend. Socrates didn't believe that the state would be able to flourish under the leadership of Themistocles, Cimon or Pericles just because they were excellent generals and speakers. Sadly, their [lack of] success provided him with his proof that ruling the state was an ill move for all three of them. But perhaps things are different in music. — Just one thing worries me. Mr. Joachim's friend J. *Brahms* anticipates great things for himself from a return to Schubert's art of melody in song. I am now told that Mr. Joachim for his part is in expectation of a *new Messiah* in music. Should he not rather leave such expectations to those who have made him master of the academy? So I call unto him: Up and at them! If he should ultimately happen to be the Messiah himself, at least he can hope that the Jews won't crucify him! —

---

170 A reference to Goethe's *Faust II*, Act 4, where Mephistopheles says "I say women; because once and for all I think of those beauties in the plural."

Chapter Four

On Performing Beethoven's Ninth Symphony

On May 22, 1872, Wagner conducted Beethoven's Ninth Symphony in the Margravial Opera House in Bayreuth, to commemorate laying the foundation stone for the Festspielhaus (it was also Wagner's 59th birthday). He had not conducted the work for nearly twenty years, and it would be his last-ever performance of it. He published the following essay in April 1873. It reflects his experience of conducting the work, and explains what he would do differently in future. It was published over two issues of the *Musikalisches Wochenblatt*, the journal run by Fritzsch of Leipzig, the same publisher who was busy issuing Wagner's complete writings, edited by the composer himself. *On Performing Beethoven's Ninth Symphony* was included in the ninth volume of that complete edition later in 1873; this was the last volume to be published during Wagner's lifetime (a final, tenth volume was issued within several months of his death in 1883). For more information on the history and impact of this essay, see "The Bayreuth Performance of Beethoven's Ninth in 1872" in the critical essay below.

At a performance I recently directed of this wonderful work, I found I had misgivings about certain issues. Because I believe these to be essential to the clarity of the symphony's interpretation, they preoccupied me greatly—so much so that I afterwards decided to examine how to overcome the problems I saw. I am here placing the results of my deliberations at the disposal of seriously minded musicians. It is not my intention that others should simply emulate what I do, but I hope what I say will induce them to engage in meaningful reflection on the work.

As a general matter, I should like to draw attention to the unusual position in which Beethoven found himself when orchestrating his music. He made the exact same assumptions about his orchestra's abilities as had his predecessors Haydn and Mozart, though the character of his musical conception

soared inconceivably far beyond them. The art of separating and combining
the different instrumental groups of an orchestra is something we could very
well describe as *plastic*, though in the time of Mozart and Haydn, the character of their works matched the configuration of their instrumental forces and
the interpretive style of their orchestra. There can be nothing more appropriate than a Mozartian symphony played by a Mozartian orchestra. We
can assume that neither Haydn nor Mozart ever had a musical thought that
could not immediately have been expressed by the orchestra at their disposal.
There was utter congruence here.[1] There were the *tutti* with trumpets and
timpani (to be properly effective, the latter had to be used only in the tonic
key), the four-part string section, the wind section (whether solo winds or an
ensemble) and then the immutable duo of the French horns: all this formed
the basis both of their orchestra, and of how they conceived their orchestral
works. It is astonishing to consider that even Beethoven knew only this same
orchestra. Using it was completely natural for his manner of thinking.

We can only marvel at how the Master set about using that same orchestra to realize his works as best he could, despite the fact that they were far
more varied and diverse in their conception than anything known to Mozart
and Haydn. In this respect, his *Sinfonia Eroica* remains both a miracle of
design and a miracle of orchestration. However, Beethoven here requires a
style of performance that no orchestra to this day has managed to deliver.
The orchestra ought to be as brilliant as the Master's own conception. It was
in fact with the first performance of the *Eroica* that people began to find
his symphonies difficult to grasp, even to the point of being unable to like
them at all. The musicians of the older generation never really approved of
them. These works lack clarity in performance because achieving such clarity
was no longer inherent in the orchestral organism that Haydn and Mozart
had known. It can in fact only be achieved by musical brilliance on the part
of individual instrumentalists and their conductor—a brilliance that must
verge on the virtuosic.

Since the richness of his musical conception required far more varied
material and a concomitantly flexible organization, Beethoven saw himself

---

1   In January 1901, Heinrich Schenker published an article in which he criticized
Wagner's alterations to Beethoven's Ninth (ideas he expanded on in his long
essay on the Ninth in 1912); he quotes Wagner's mention of this "congruence"
in Mozart and Haydn, adding: "If only we could all at last accept that the
exact same congruence also dominates in Beethoven's orchestra!" See Schenker
(1901): 268. In fact, Beethoven clearly on occasion wanted more from his
instruments that they could give; see fn. 18 below.

compelled to demand from his instrumentalists an ability to perform abrupt changes in dynamics and expression such as would be regarded as a great achievement from even the finest virtuosos. This is true of that typically Beethovenian *crescendo* that climaxes not in a *forte*, but in a sudden *piano* instead.[2] This nuance occurs often, but is usually so foreign to our orchestral players that cautious conductors compel their musicians to reverse the *crescendo* and embark gingerly on a *diminuendo* instead, so as to ensure the timely entry of the *piano*. The problem with this sudden change in dynamics is that Beethoven expects a single body of instruments to play something that can only be utterly clear when it is played by different instruments alternating with each other. Modern composers are aware of this, because they have today's expanded orchestra at their disposal, and know how to use it. Today's composers could ensure that certain effects desired by Beethoven are realized with complete clarity, without having to make eccentric demands on the virtuosity of their orchestral musicians. They could simply redistribute the parts among different groups of instruments instead.

However, Beethoven expected his orchestra to perform with a virtuosity equal to his own on the piano. Great technical ability enabled the performer to free himself of all mechanical shackles; this in turn meant he could perform the most varied combinations of expressive nuances with utter clarity (for without this clarity, even the melody itself might seem to exist in a state of uncomprehending chaos). The Master's final piano compositions were conceived thus, and have become accessible to us only thanks to Liszt. Before him, they had remained almost completely misunderstood. This example may offer us sufficient proof of the truly difficult state of affairs with regard to performing Beethoven's late [piano] works properly. But the same applies to performing the Master's late quartets. Here, in a certain technical sense, the individual player often has to stand in for several players. As a result, when you hear an excellent performance of a quartet from this late period, you can often be deceived into believing that you are hearing more musicians playing together than are actually involved. Only in the most recent times has the virtuosity of our quartet players in Germany reached a level necessary to perform these wonderful

---

2   Adorno (2001): 57 makes the following remark: "The main proof for instrumental construction: Beethoven's $\prec p$ [can] only be realized through dividing the melody up between instruments (this is essentially already the principle of the Schoenberg School as mediated through Mahler, whose whole practice of orchestration is probably founded on Wagner's work on the IXth)."

pieces correctly. I recall having heard excellent virtuosi from the Dresden Orchestra—with Lipinski[3] at the head of them—who played these quartets so imprecisely that my then colleague Reissiger felt justified in declaring the music to be utter nonsense.

In my opinion, this precision can be achieved only by placing a drastic emphasis on the melody. I have already pointed out elsewhere how French musicians found it easier to discover the secret of performing these works properly, because they belong to the Italian school and so comprehend how melody alone—song—is the essence of all music.[4] This is the only correct solution. We must seek out and emphasize the pure melodic essence of this music. If truly gifted musicians proceed down this path, they can succeed in discovering the manner of interpretation necessary for those works by Beethoven that people used to consider incomprehensible. Just as Bülow has already so admirably succeeded in establishing this style of interpretation as the norm for Beethoven's piano sonatas, so we might hope that other musicians might do the same for his quartets. And then we might understand the great Master's creative compulsion to take the extant technical materials of his art—the piano, the quartet and ultimately also the orchestra—and drive them beyond their hitherto possibilities. He expanded sheer mechanical technique into the spiritual realm. This in turn served to promote an unprecedented, spiritual heightening of virtuosity such as performers had never before attained.

I shall now turn once more to Beethoven's orchestra and the need to ensure the primacy of the melody. But I believe that not even virtuosity of the most spiritual kind is capable of ensuring this primacy, nor can I discuss this properly without first shedding light on an ill state of affairs that is related to it, and that seems almost impossible to solve.

Beethoven's musical ideas themselves required a new way of handling the orchestra, and this in turn made it indispensable for him to be able to hear everything clearly. But after he went deaf, it is undeniable that Beethoven's aural image of the orchestra faded so much that he was no longer clearly aware of the dynamic relations within it. Mozart and Haydn

---

3   Karol Józef Lipiński (1790–1861), Polish violinist and composer, concert master in Dresden from 1839 onwards, friend of Liszt, dedicatee of Schumann's *Carnaval*, op. 9.

4   See my section on "Melos and the Body" below, and also the discussion in the section "Wagner in Review" of the Dresden critic of 1843 who declared Wagner's extreme tempi to be wrong because they were "French."

had been in complete formal command of their orchestra, and had never employed the tender woodwind instruments in a way that required them to produce a dynamic effect equal to a large body of strings. However, Beethoven often felt compelled to overlook this naturally occurring imbalance between the wind and the string sections. He alternates them as if they were equal in power, and at other times he uses them in combination. The varied expansion of the orchestra in our time has made it perfectly possible to implement such ideas to great effect. But it was illusory to try and achieve this in Beethoven's orchestra. To be sure, sometimes Beethoven succeeds in giving the necessary definition to the woodwind by adding brass instruments to them. However, he was lamentably restricted in this because he only had natural horns and trumpets at his disposal. As a result, using these instruments to reinforce the woodwind merely causes confusion; instead of ensuring the prominence of the melody, he merely obscures it in a manner that seems impossible to rectify. I don't need to explain these problems with Beethoven's orchestration to today's musicians (I have only touched upon them here), because they are easy to avoid, now that chromatic brass instruments have come into general use. I shall merely confirm that Beethoven found it necessary to have his brass instruments cease playing suddenly whenever he moved into distant keys, or otherwise had to let them play those garish single notes that were the only ones at their instrument's disposal, but which are completely disruptive and veer away from both the melody and the harmony.

I regard it as superfluous to illustrate this last, unsatisfactory state of affairs by offering numerous examples, and instead shall demonstrate how I endeavored to rectify things in those individual cases where the disruption of what the Master had actually intended ultimately became unbearable to me. One solution that came quite naturally was when the second horn—like the second trumpet—had passages such as this:

Example 4.1a.

or

Example 4.1b.

for I simply recommended replacing the high note with the note an octave below it, thus:[5]

Example 4.2.

This is easy with the chromatic instruments that are the only ones used today in our orchestras. I have found that this serves to correct the major problems. It is less easy, however, where the trumpets dominate the music but then suddenly break off because the music moves into a key in which the natural instruments don't have the right notes at their disposal—even when the music is intended to remain at the same, sustained level of volume. As an example of this, I here refer to a *forte* passage in the *Andante* of the C minor Symphony [no. 5]:[6]

---

5   In his book on performing Beethoven's symphonies, Felix Weingartner quotes Wagner's music example, but suggests that Beethoven in fact knew how to get what he wanted from the "imperfect" instruments at his disposal, and that he sometimes actually wanted the sound of natural tones on his brass instruments; consequently, Weingartner says he only transposes such notes where it seems absolutely necessary to him. See Weingartner (1906): viii.

6   Wagner gives a piano reduction of only the first measure; here the orchestral texture has been condensed, while retaining the trumpets and timpani on separate, inner staves, in order to illustrate Wagner's point. This music example is also found in Berlioz's treatise on orchestration, though—oddly—to demonstrate the capabilities of the Alexandre melodium. See Berlioz (1855): 292.

Example 4.3. Beethoven, Symphony no. 5, 2nd movement, mm. 114–20

For two measures, the trumpets and timpani fill the music with their mag-nificence. But then they suddenly cease for two whole measures. Then they enter again for a measure, only to fall silent once again for yet another measure. Given the character of these instruments, it is unavoidable that the listener's attention will be drawn spontaneously to how their timbre is turned alternately on and off for no good musical reason at all. This dis-tracts the listener from what is of prime importance, namely the melody in the bass. Until now, I have believed that I could only solve this problem by denying these intermittent instruments their splendor—in other words, by asking them not to play too forcefully.[7] This in itself proves advantageous to achieving greater clarity of the melody in the bass. — With regard to the highly disruptive involvement of the trumpets in the first *forte* of the sec-ond movement of the A major Symphony [no. 7], however, I finally

7   Toscanini solved this "problem" by having the trumpets and timpani play throughout the passage given in Example 4.3, filling out their rests with fur-ther sixteenth-notes appropriate to the harmony. See his annotated score in the New York Public Library, Shelf locator: JPB 90-1, folder A35 a. Other conduc-tors of his generation, however—such as Richard Strauss—followed Wagner by leaving the measures in question empty.

decided to try a more drastic solution. Beethoven was quite right to feel a need for the two trumpets to play here, though their simple construction at the time meant they were hindered from doing so in the manner that was truly necessary.[8]

Example 4.4. Beethoven, Symphony no. 7, 2nd movement, mm. 75–84

So I had the trumpets play the whole theme in unison with the clarinets. The impact of this was so excellent that none of the listeners felt any sense of loss, but instead felt that something had been gained. At the same time, no one noticed that anything new or different had been done.[9]

8　Wagner gives no music example here; I have placed the trumpets and clarinets on separate staves above a piano reduction in order to illustrate his point.

9　This idea does not seem to have caught on. Strauss left the trumpet parts as they were; Weingartner wrote that he regarded Wagner's solution as "inappropriate," though he did recommend doubling the woodwind and horns that play the melody here. See Weingartner (1906): 107.

I was not yet able to decide upon a similarly drastic solution to a comparable problem in the orchestration of the second movement of the Ninth Symphony, the great scherzo of that work. This was because I still hoped to solve it by purely dynamic means. The passage in question is the second theme of this movement, which appears in C the first time, in D the second:

Example 4.5. Beethoven, Symphony no. 9, 2nd movement, mm. 93–96

Here it is the weak woodwind—two flutes, two oboes, two clarinets and two bassoons—that have to assert themselves emphatically with their exuberant theme against the force of the following figure, played over four octaves in a continuous *fortissimo* by the accompanying string section:

Example 4.6. Beethoven, Symphony no. 9, 2nd movement, m. 93

The support that the woodwind receives from the brass instruments is similar to what we have already described. In other words, their intermittent natural tones interfere with the clarity of the theme far more than they can support it:

Example 4.7. Beethoven, Symphony no. 9, 2nd movement, mm. 93–96

I ask any musician whether he can claim, with a clear conscience, ever to have heard this melody distinctly in performance? And would he even recognize it, if he had not known of it first by studying the score or playing a piano arrangement? In our normal orchestral performances, people do not even seem to resort to the most natural means of achieving this, namely by heavily dampening the *fortissimo* of the string instruments.[10] Every time I have brought musicians together to play this symphony, they have all played this passage

---

10   In his article rejecting Wagner's changes to the score of the Ninth, Charles Gounod recalls a performance he attended under Habeneck (sadly without mentioning the date), in which the strings were reduced to *mezzoforte* to allow the woodwind theme to come to the fore (Gounod (1874): 189). Wagner's praise of Habeneck's interpretation of the Ninth in *Über das Dirigieren* does not include any mention of his having altered this passage thus. See fn. 9 in chapter 2 and fn. 24 in chapter 3.

ferociously. I too had always dampened the strings here, and I believed that it would guarantee success as long as I could also double the number of woodwind.[11] But I never achieved what I hoped, or at best only managed it to a highly dissatisfactory degree. This was because the woodwind instruments are here expected to play with a rousing energy, resulting in a sound that will always remain abhorrent to their real character. This incredibly energetic dance is thus in danger of a lack of clarity, even to a point where it simply disappears into inaudibility. So as soon as I plan another performance of this symphony,[12] I know that I will have no other solution than to employ the four horns in the thematic argument.[13] This could be done perhaps in the following manner:

---

11   This was apparently Wagner's own approach in Dresden in 1846. See p. 19 in chapter 2.

12   Wagner never conducted Beethoven's Ninth again, so was never able to put these ideas into practice.

13   Adolf Wallnöfer mentions these horn doublings in his reminiscences of the Bayreuth concert (Wallnöfer (n.d.): 17), though this might well be a slip of the memory, as it seems Wagner only proposed them after this performance. Wagner's recommendation to have the horns play with the woodwind was taken up by many later conductors, as is evident either from their marked-up scores, their recordings, or from the testimony of those who knew them, from Hans von Bülow to Gustav Mahler, Richard Strauss, Otto Klemperer, Clemens Krauss and Hermann Scherchen; even Toscanini did it. Some added trumpets too, as did Mahler in his marked-up score in the Austrian National Library; he also transposed the clarinets and bassoons up an octave for mm. 97–100 and 105–8, and did the same when the same passage is given later in the tonic. Klemperer was insistent that Beethoven "should never be modernized," though he added that "there are passages in the Ninth Symphony, as Wagner emphasized, in the Scherzo, where the main theme is completely obscured if it is played as it was written. Only in this case should a conductor made changes. In order to make the main theme clear and distinct" (Klemperer (1993): 54). According to von Bülow's student Walter Damrosch, who possessed a copy of the score annotated by his master (since lost), von Bülow added the horns, and also dampened the strings in every other bar of the accompaniment, because he found that merely adding the brass was insufficient to make the theme heard properly (see Damrosch (1927): 287). However, Bruno Walter wrote in his memoirs that "with all respect for Wagner and his exemplary, pure intentions … for me his alterations here seem to go too far: as an example, I refer to his using the horns to strengthen the woodwind theme in the Scherzo, which increases the sonority but alters the tone colors in an un-Beethovenian manner, whereas merely doubling the woodwind—while holding back the strings a

Example 4.8 Beethoven, Symphony no. 9, 2nd movement, mm. 93–101, Wagner's suggestion for the horns and woodwind

One could try this, to see if the above reinforcement of the theme suffices to let the strings play their accompanying figure *ff* as the Master indicated. This is important, because Beethoven here unmistakably intends to achieve that same boisterous exuberance that later returns with the movement's main theme in D minor, leading into a state of wild, excessive abandon such as could only be expressed by this unique, wonderful Master's imaginative

---

little and keeping the horns and trumpets as in the original—keeps the piercing sound and wild abandon intended by Beethoven" (Walter (1957): 164). Kirill Kondrashin was one of the many later conductors who opposed Wagner's use of the horns here, arguing (like Walter) that one can compensate for the larger string sections of today's orchestra by simply doubling the woodwind and lowering the dynamics in the strings. He further writes as follows: "Proof of the illogical nature of [adding the brass here] is the fact that the natural horns (in C and D) can actually play all the notes of this theme, and Beethoven could have himself increased the number of woodwind instruments here. He obviously wanted to achieve a very different character. When we lower the dynamics of the strings here to *mezzoforte*, keeping the original instrumentation—though with double woodwind—we straightaway get a jubilant sound: an exhilaration of elves. Using horns in this passage 'militarizes' the sound, as it were." Kondrashin (1989): 46–47.

invention. Just dampening the strings to allow the wind instruments to come to the fore seemed to me a very dissatisfactory solution, because this also cancels out the wild nature of the passage, making it almost unrecognizable. My final piece of advice is to reinforce the theme in the wind instruments—if necessary, even by the trumpets—until it emerges clearly and penetratingly, and dominates even the most energetic *fortissimo* in the string section. When the passage returns in D, the trumpets participate anyway, though once again, regrettably, they serve to obscure the theme in the wind. For this reason, I saw myself compelled once more to tell the trumpets (like the strings) to restrain themselves in a manner that went against their true character. When making such decisions, all that matters is whether the composer's intentions are temporarily obscured to the listener, or whether one prefers to use whatever means at one's disposal to do justice to them. However, our concert halls and opera houses are accustomed to the utter rejection of such means.

There is another passage in the orchestration of the Ninth Symphony that is problematic for the same reasons mentioned above. At the performance I recently conducted, I finally decided on a radical solution to it. The passage in question is the "terror fanfare"[14] in the wind instruments at the beginning of the last movement. Here, a chaotic outburst of wild despair pours out in screams and bluster that anyone will immediately understand who follows this woodwind passage at its swift tempo. Its impetuosity is such that the time signature is barely discernible. Fearful conductors usually want to keep to a cautious tempo so that they don't capsize things when they come to the subsequent recitative of the basses. But if they try to conduct this passage so that we can clearly hear its triple meter, it inevitably comes across as almost absurd. However, I found that even the most reckless tempo left the unison melodic line in the woodwind unclear, while also unable to fulfill the composer's intentions by completely casting off the shackles of its rhythmic

---

14   This is Wagner's first and seemingly only use of the word "Schreckensfanfare," which soon entered general currency to describe the opening of the last movement of Beethoven's Ninth, and was then adopted elsewhere (as a simple Google Ngram search can confirm). I translate it here as "terror fanfare" because "Schrecken" had long been the standard German term for the "Terror" in Revolutionary France. There is, interestingly, an echo of Wagner's infatuation with the Ninth Symphony in his libretto for his first opera, *Die Feen*, when Arindal sings early in the second act: "O hemmet dieses Jubels Töne, / mit Schreckensmahnung drängt er mich!" Wagner also quotes this phrase in a letter to his sister Rosalie of December 11, 1833. See SB 1: 136–42, here 138.

meter. The problem lay in the fragmentary participation of the trumpets; but nor can we omit them either, without contradicting the Master's intentions. These blaring instruments dominate the woodwind and interrupt their participation in the melodic line so that we can only hear the following rhythm:

Example 4.9. Beethoven, Symphony no. 9, 4th movement, mm. 1–7, trumpets

Emphasizing this rhythm is also completely contrary to the Master's intentions—as we can clearly see when this passage returns for the last time, reinforced by the strings. Once again, it was only the limitations of the natural trumpets that had prevented Beethoven from carrying out what he had really intended. So—with a sense of desperation that actually seems fitting for this passage—I decided to have the trumpets play along with the woodwind throughout, like this:[15]

Example 4.10. Beethoven, Symphony no. 9, 4th movement, mm. 1–7, Wagner's suggestion for the trumpet parts

[and:]

Example 4.11. Beethoven, Symphony no. 9, 4th movement, mm. 17–24, Wagner's suggestion for the trumpet parts

When this passage returns later, the trumpets again play as in the first example above.

---

15   Adolf Wallnöfer (n.d.): 17 mentions this use of the trumpets in his reminiscences of Wagner's 1872 performance of the Ninth in Bayreuth.

Now everything became as clear as day. The terror fanfare overwhelmed us in its rhythmic chaos, and we understood why "the word" had to enter.

But there were passages where it was more difficult than this to restore in full[16] the Master's intentions. In those cases, neither reinforcement nor completing what is fragmentary could rescue Beethoven's melodic intentions from imprecision and incomprehensibility. Instead, this can only be achieved by actually intervening in the fabric of the orchestration and in the part-writing.

Beethoven made no effort to expand his orchestra. But as he gradually became unable to hear an orchestra in performance, its limitations undeniably led him to an almost naïve disregard for the gap between his musical ideas and the practicalities of performing them. He kept to his old habit of never writing higher than

Example 4.12.

for the violins in his symphonies,[17] so whenever his melodic intentions extended beyond this point, he resorted to the timid, almost childlike solution of having his violins jump down to play the note in the lower octave. This not only interrupts the melodic line, but also falsifies its meaning. In the great *fortissimo* of the second movement of the Ninth Symphony, Beethoven writes the following merely out of an anxious desire to avoid the high B-flat:

Example 4.13. Beethoven, Symphony no. 9, 2nd movement, mm. 280–81

I hope that all our orchestras will readily agree that this passage should not be played thus by the violins and violas, but as the melody itself requires it, namely:

---

16   Wagner here writes "restitution in integrum."

17   Beethoven had no compunction about going beyond this in his chamber music, long before the Ninth Symphony; see, for example, the coda of the first movement of the String Quartet, op. 59 no. 1, with its long-held C three octaves above middle C.

Example 4.14. Beethoven, Symphony no. 9, 2nd movement, mm. 280–81, Wagner's proposed solution

I also assume that the first flute will not hesitate to play

Example 4.15. Beethoven, Symphony no. 9, 2nd movement, m. 280, Wagner's proposed solution

instead of

Example 4.16. Beethoven, Symphony no. 9, 2nd movement, m. 280, Beethoven's original

This solution is very simple, and applies both here and in many similar cases. But the trickiest instances require more drastic solutions. These occur in wind passages where the Master on principle avoids going beyond the accepted range of an instrument. Instead—as with the flute in the above instance—Beethoven either distorts the melodic line completely, or has it disrupted by giving an instrument notes that are not actually in the melody.[18] In this case, it is primarily the flute that attracts our attention as soon

---

18   The conductor Kirill Kondrashin was one of those who argued in favor of the original in all these cases, writing: "mechanically filling in these 'holes' would fundamentally alter the color of Beethoven's orchestration (for example, I mean removing the characteristic leaps of a ninth in the second horns and trumpets, or adding notes in the flutes)" (Kondrashin (1989): 46). But there were in fact cases where Beethoven did want the upper, unplayable note in the flute, such as in a parallel passage in this second movement of the Ninth, at m. 65, where the first flute was originally indeed assigned the same as given in Example 4.15 above, only for the top B-flat to be erased in a smudge and replaced by what I give here as Example 4.16 (though with the semi-erased upper B-flat still clearly visible). The autograph of the Eighth Symphony also features instances where Beethoven wrote b‴ flat for the flute, then replaced it with the lower octave after remembering that it was unplayable; see Beethoven ed. Herttrich (2019) for a complete list. Just because Wagner seems to have been right about

as it enters, because we expect it to play the uppermost line of the melody. And if it does not play all the notes of that melody, it is inevitably distracting. Over time, our Master seems to have completely ignored this problem. For example, when he has the oboe or the clarinet play the top line of the melody, but the flute in its upper register is unable to play the theme itself an octave higher, he gives the flute notes that deviate from the melody. This only confuses the listener, because the flute is still playing at a higher pitch than the real melody in the lower instruments. Today's instrumental composers have very different means for ensuring the absolute audibility of a principal motif that is assigned to the middle or lower registers underneath a higher, overlying superstructure. They can reinforce the lower sonority by assigning it to instruments whose timbre is so distinct from those playing above that there can be no confusion and no blending. In the Prelude to my *Lohengrin*, for example, this practice enabled me to keep the main theme prominent despite it being fully harmonized, and also let me lead it to a climax despite other instruments playing in the registers above it. This main theme was able to hold its ground against all movement in the upper voices.

Beethoven himself pointed the way to such developments, just as he did in the case of all other such innovations. However, it is quite impossible to achieve such an effect [in his own music], given the abovementioned barriers that need to be removed for us to hear the melody properly. In Beethoven, these non-melodic upper lines are a disturbance—like random ornaments we would prefer to see removed in order to lessen the damage they do. I cannot remember ever having heard the opening of his F major symphony [no. 8] without my enjoyment of the clarinet melody being disturbed by the non-thematic entry of the oboes and flute above it in the sixth, seventh and eighth measures respectively. By contrast, the non-thematic music for the flutes in the first four measures does not prevent us from hearing the main theme beneath it, because the melody is brought to vivid clarity by being played *forte* by the violin section.[19]

Beethoven wanting his flutes to play beyond the bounds of technical feasibility does not necessarily mean that he was similarly correct in his adjustments to Beethoven's brass and string parts; but it does bolster Wagner's case.

19 Wagner does not offer a music example here; it has been added to illustrate his point. In the copy of this score in the New York Philharmonic archives that was used by Gustav Mahler, the oboes and flute in mm. 6–8 are all marked "*pp*" in red crayon in a hand that seems to be Mahler's—which is presumably Wagner's own implied solution to the balance problem as he sees it. Unlike Wagner, Weingartner remarks that in some concert halls even the opening violin theme

Example 4.17. Beethoven, Symphony no. 8, 1st movement, mm. 1–8, omitting brass and timpani

Such problems only become evident in woodwind passages. There is one such disconcerting example in an important passage in the first movement of the Ninth Symphony. I shall use it here as my main example in order to explain my thoughts clearly.

This is the eight-measure *espressivo* passage for the woodwind towards the close of the first section of the first movement, which in the Breitkopf & Härtel edition begins with the third measure of page 19 [measure 138], and later returns similarly in the third measure of page 53 [measure 407], i.e.

---

cannot always be heard properly. In such cases—and also when the orchestra has few strings at its disposal—he recommends a *diminuendo* for all the wind and the timpani in the first measure, with *mf* at the start of the second and a subsequent *crescendo* to a renewed *forte* at the beginning of the fourth measure (Weingartner (1906): 121).

Example 4.18. Beethoven, Symphony no. 9, 1st movement, mm. 138–45

Who can claim to have ever heard the melodic content of this passage played clearly in any orchestral performance? Only Liszt, with his unique, brilliant insights has succeeded in properly revealing the melodic significance of this passage in his wonderful piano arrangement of the Ninth Symphony. The flute takes up the theme from the oboe in a higher octave, but its intervention here is usually disruptive. So Liszt shifts its part back into the lower register of the oboe, which actually carries the melody, thereby ensuring that the Master's original intentions are not misunderstood. Liszt transcribes these melodic lines as follows:

Example 4.19. Beethoven, Symphony no. 9, 1st movement, mm. 138–45

It would probably seem too bold a step to perform this passage completely without the flute, or only to employ it as a reinforcement of the oboe part at the unison. That would also be contrary to the character of Beethoven's orchestration (which has its own justifiable idiosyncrasies). So instead, I recommend keeping the main features of the flute part while remaining faithful to the actual melodic line; the flautist should be instructed to show a certain restraint towards the oboe in both volume and expression. Above all else, we have to be able to follow the oboe here, as it is the predominant instrument.

Thus after the fifth measure, in which the flute plays the oboe's melody an octave higher:

Example 4.20. Beethoven, Symphony no. 9, 1st movement, m. 142

it should not play the sixth measure as notated:

Example 4.21. Beethoven, Symphony no. 9, 1st movement, m. 143

but instead play these two measures thus:

Example 4.22. Beethoven, Symphony no. 9, 1st movement, mm. 142–43, Wagner's solution

This would make the melodic line more correct than Liszt was able to achieve, given that he was constrained by the limits of writing for the piano. If we alter the oboe in the second measure so that it continues the melodic line just as in the fourth measure, namely

Example 4.23. Beethoven, Symphony no. 9, 1st movement, m. 139, Wagner's solution

instead of

Example 4.24. Beethoven, Symphony no. 9, 1st movement, m. 139

then we could also give it the correct expression markings so that it comes properly to the fore. The tempo should be held back slightly, and the musicians should be told to play with the following expression markings (these are in any case merely a continuation of the Master's own):

Example 4.25. Beethoven, Symphony no. 9, 1st movement, mm. 138–43, Wagner's suggestion for the flute and oboe

In mm. 144 and 145, however, a nicely played *crescendo*—which should intensify considerably towards the end—can help the music to achieve the same kind of expression that we find in the ensuing, poignant, cadential passage.

It is far more difficult to bring the same degree of comprehensibility to the melodic content of the parallel passage in the recapitulation of this movement, where the music returns in a different key and at a different pitch. Here, the flute's higher register is needed. Beethoven employs it superbly, but its limited range prompts the composer to change the melodic line in a manner that hinders it from achieving the necessary clarity. The flute part in the score runs thus:

Example 4.26. Beethoven, Symphony no. 9, 1st movement, mm. 407–14, flute part

But if we were to keep to the melodic line that is clearly recognizable from the combination of the oboe, clarinet and flute so that it corresponds to the earlier shape of the phrase at the end of the first section, this would instead give us:

Example 4.27. Beethoven, Symphony no. 9, 1st movement, mm. 407–14, Wagner's condensed score for a proposed revision of the flute, oboe and clarinet parts

We must acknowledge that this passage in Beethoven offers a dubious disfigurement of the musical idea and distracts us from properly understanding the melody. Restoring that musical idea here would nevertheless be an overly daring move, because it would entail changing an interval on two occasions. In the third measure for the flute, it would mean writing

Example 4.28. Beethoven, Symphony no. 9, 1st movement, m. 409

instead of Beethoven's original

Example 4.29. Beethoven, Symphony no. 9, 1st movement, m. 409

and in the fifth measure

Example 4.30. Beethoven, Symphony no. 9, 1st movement, m. 411

instead of

Example 4.31. Beethoven, Symphony no. 9, 1st movement, m. 411

Even Liszt decided against taking such a bold step, but left this passage as the melodic monstrosity it is. And it indeed sounds monstrous in performance, for the eight measures in question have gaps in the melody whose intention is completely obscure. After having suffered repeatedly under the embarrassment of this passage, I would now prefer to have these eight measures played as follows by the flute and oboe:

Example 4.32. Beethoven, Symphony no. 9, 1st movement, mm. 407–14, Wagner's suggestion for the flute and oboe parts

Here, the second flute would have to rest in the fourth measure, but the second oboe would complement it by playing the following in measures 413 and 414:

Example 4.33. Beethoven, Symphony no. 9, 1st movement, mm. 413–14, Wagner's solution

The same, abovementioned *espressivo* nuances are necessary for this melodic line. But in order to do justice to the altered melody in measure 408, we would this time have to offer a more urgent ⋖; a particularly emphatic *molto crescendo* would then be necessary in m. 414 to provide the correct expression to the despairing leap of the flute from the G to the high F-sharp:

Example 4.34. Beethoven, Symphony no. 9, 1st movement, m. 414, Wagner's solution

I regard all this as in line with the Master's true intentions, and I believe that performing this passage thus will place those intentions in the most favorable light.

The most important thing in every musical work is that the melody should constantly captivate us, even if the composer frequently only offers us its tiniest fragments. Furthermore, the correctness of his melodic language may in no wise be inferior to the logically correct, conceptual flow of our spoken language. Otherwise, the music will confuse us by being just as inarticulate as an unintelligible spoken sentence. We must acknowledge that nothing is more worthy of our greatest care than trying to clarify a passage, a measure, even a note of a musical statement made by a genius such as Beethoven. This is because every new utterance by such an original man arises solely from his divine, consuming urge to reveal to us poor mortals the deepest secrets of his world-view in irrefutably lucid terms. We should never skip over a cryptic passage in the work of a great philosopher if we have not understood it clearly, because otherwise, as we read on, our lack of attention means we will understand him less and less. Similarly, we should not pass over any measure of a work by Beethoven without being explicitly aware of its content. Unless, of course, our only concern is to beat time throughout its performance, such as is the practice of our well-established, academic concert conductors. I fully expect them to accuse me of blasphemy towards the holy t-crossers and i-dotters on account of the suggestions I have made above.

Despite anticipating such attacks, I cannot refrain from offering several examples in an endeavor to prove how carefully considered alterations to the musical notation can here and there serve to promote a correct understanding of the Master's intentions.

In this regard I should like to mention a dynamic nuance whose intention is correct, but whose execution serves to obscure that very intention. In the following, gripping passage in the first movement of the Ninth Symphony (m. 92ff.):

Example 4.35. Beethoven, Symphony no. 9, 1st movement, mm. 92–94

this melodic idea is extended by repeating the first two measures three times in sequence in mm. 96–107. In mm. 96–97, the Master has these two measures played *piano* throughout by the clarinets and bassoons; he then writes *crescendo* from the beginning of the next statement in m. 98, where more woodwind enter; and then for the last two-measure sequence in mm. 100–101, he assigns the melodic idea to the strings. These then dominate, and increase in volume until the *fortissimo* arrives in m. 102 (ex. 4.36).[20]

The entry of the [second] flute in m. 98 and its accompanying string figuration in contrary motion are both marked *crescendo*; but in my experience,

---

20 The next three music examples in score are not given by Wagner.

Example 4.36. Beethoven, Symphony no. 9, 1st movement, mm. 96–102, reduced score

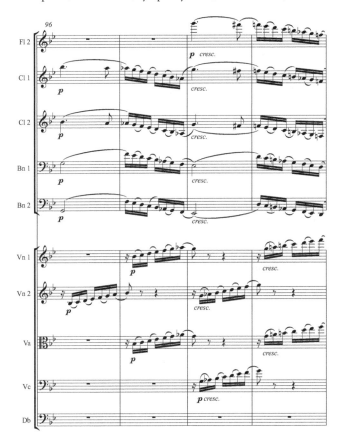

—(*continued*)

this is detrimental to the impact of the *più crescendo* of the violins in m. 100, because it distracts us too soon from the exquisite melodic idea heard in the wind instruments (and which is in fact too weakly scored for them). This *crescendo* for the flute and strings in m. 98 also impedes the thematic entry of the violins in m. 100 with their own characteristic *crescendo*. This is not a major problem, however. It can be resolved completely by adding *poco* to the first *crescendo*, in measure 98. But while *poco crescendo* is a necessary prerequisite for the subsequent *più crescendo* in m. 100, it is regrettably almost completely unknown to our orchestral players. This is why I recommend that conductors should explain this passage at length, and rehearse its dynamic nuances thoroughly.

Example 4.36—*concluded*

Even if the suggestions we have outlined here were carefully put into practice, this still would not solve the awful consequences of the Master's failure to realize his own intentions in certain passages towards the end of this
first movement. This is because the dynamic disparity between the alternating instrumental blocks makes it almost impossible to resolve problems by
means of dynamic subtlety. This is the case with the similar passage in mm.
363–69, where the first violins are accompanied by the rest of the strings, all
of them with a *crescendo* right from the start (ex. 4.37).

Example 4.37. Beethoven, Symphony no. 9, 1st movement, mm. 363–69, reduced score

—(continued)

When the clarinets enter with the same idea in m. 365, they are unable to play with the necessary power, nor can they perform their own *crescendo* adequately. So I decided to abandon the *crescendo* completely in mm. 363–64, recommending instead an urgent *crescendo* to the wind instruments in the subsequent two measures, mm. 365–66. Since this leads to a true *forte* in m. 367, the *crescendo* in the clarinets can also be supported wholeheartedly by the strings. It is because of a similar dynamic disparity between the different sections of the orchestra that when this passage returns again in m. 457, its first two measures should be played *piano* throughout, then in the next two measures the wind should play an intense *crescendo*, accompanied by a weaker *crescendo* in the strings, and then the last two measures before the

Example 4.37—*concluded*

forte in m. 463 should be played with an increasing intensification in volume (ex. 4.38).

I do not intend to discuss further the character of Beethoven's expressive markings nor how I believe they should be performed, as I think I have already offered my opinion to a sufficient degree, and have expressed with due diligence my motivation for making such nuances in these rare cases. But I should just like to stress that the purpose of these expression markings must be studied as carefully as Beethoven's themes themselves. This is because we can only properly understand the Master's intentions if we comprehend his concept of the musical motif. When I wrote in my earlier essay *Über das Dirigieren* about the true motivation of tempo in Beethoven, I certainly did not intend recommending the comical manner in which I am seriously

Example 4.38. Beethoven, Symphony no. 9, 1st movement, mm. 457–63, reduced score with dynamics by Beethoven; see the above text for Wagner's proposed changes

—(continued)

assured a chief capellmeister from Berlin has conducted these symphonies.[21] To spice up certain passages, he wants them played now *forte*, now *piano* in an echo effect; now slower, now quicker. When I offered my complex explanations about how to play Beethoven's music correctly, I had not imagined

21   Does he perhaps mean Robert Radecke (1830–1911) or Ludwig Deppe (1828–90), who both conducted in Berlin in the early 1870s, and included Beethoven symphonies in their programs?

Example 4.38—*concluded*

that a capellmeister in jovial mood would indulge in such jests as he might make in the *Fille du régiment* or *Martha*, for example.[22]

It is also in order to reveal the Master's intentions more clearly that I wish to close by discussing an extremely difficult passage for the solo quartet of singers in the Ninth Symphony. It was only after long experience that I discovered the reason for this problem. It is wonderful in its conception,

---

22   Gaetano Donizetti: *La fille du régiment* (first performed 1840); Friedrich von Flotow: *Martha, oder Der Markt zu Richmond* (first performed 1847), both staple comic operas in the 19th-century repertoire. Wagner had conducted both in the 1840s when a capellmeister in Dresden.

but every time I heard it, I felt that it was robbed of the positive impact it deserves. It is the last solo passage at the close of the symphony, the famous B major passage "wo dein sanfter Flügel weilt." This passage usually goes wrong—in fact, it always goes wrong. This is neither because of the soprano's rising line towards the end, nor because of the contralto's D natural [in m. 841], though this note is admittedly difficult to sing in tune. These difficulties can be solved to one's complete satisfaction if one has a soprano with a fine upper register, and a musical contralto who is also aware of the harmonic context. No, the hurdle to achieving a pure, beautiful result with this passage lies in the tenor part, and it can only be surmounted by radical means. The figurations in the tenor begin too soon, which is detrimental to the clarity of the overall performance. It would be an exhausting passage under any circumstances, because the tenor cannot take the breaths he needs without a dreadful struggle. Let us take a closer look at this passage. At the entrance of the six-four chord in B major in m. 836, the captivating melodic idea turns into soprano figurations that are continued in free imitation by the contralto, then the tenor and, finally, the bass in their respective registers. If we jettison for a moment the accompanying voices, we can clearly observe the imitation in the four parts:

Example 4.39. Beethoven, Symphony no. 9, 4th movement, mm. 836–39, omitting the tenor in m. 837

etc.

But when the contralto begins its own figurations in m. 837, it is already accompanied by the tenor in sixths and thirds. Since the tenor thereby becomes an object of our attention, his own imitative entry one measure later in m. 838 is deprived of its significance and impact:[23]

---

23 This music example is not given by Wagner, but is necessary for the reader to understand what he is explaining.

Example 4.40. Beethoven, Symphony no. 9, 4th movement, mm. 834–41, solo voice parts

We thus lose the charm of hearing the soprano's melisma repeated in the tenor. But the problem is not just that this makes the Master's melodic intentions indistinct. For while a tenor soloist can easily cope with one measure of figurations, he cannot manage two such measures with the same degree of security, one immediately after the other. This fact is similarly injurious to this wonderful passage. So, after much deliberation, I decided to spare the tenor the task of shadowing the contralto part in the measure before his own entry, assigning him instead only the most important harmony notes. So instead of singing:

Example 4.41. Beethoven, Symphony no. 9, 4th movement, mm. 834–39

he should sing just this:

Example 4.42. Beethoven, Symphony no. 9, 4th movement, mm. 834–39

I am convinced that every tenor who has until now struggled unsuccessfully with this passage will be grateful to me, because he can now sing the melodic idea that is his own, and can also master the correct expression of his phrase if he sings it with the dynamic markings I recommend:[24]

---

24   Wagner's proposed version proved controversial from the outset. It was rejected by certain early commentators: see, for example, Hollaender (1875): 1. Schenker was similarly opposed to it, interpreting it as further proof of Wagner's having misunderstood Beethoven's intentions (Schenker (1912): 358–61). As for conductors: Weingartner rejected it, though acknowledged the difficulty of this passage for the tenor and instead suggested a different text underlay that would allow the singer to breathe differently (Weingartner (1906): 194–96). However, we find Wagner's version written in Mahler's annotated score in the archives of the New York Philharmonic, though without the *decrescendo* in m. 839; instead, it has *p* above its first beat (Mahler's annotated score in Vienna, however, has no markings on these pages; nor can we be absolutely sure that it was Mahler who made the changes in the New York score). Schoenberg's score includes Wagner's notes in green ink in m. 837, but no changes in dynamics. Mengelberg similarly adopts Wagner's version, but holds the first syllable of "sanfter" for the whole of m. 838.

Example 4.43. Beethoven, Symphony no. 9, 4th movement, mm. 838–39

To close, I would just like to mention one more matter, though without wishing to offer any extensive motivation for its introduction. At my recent performance of the Ninth Symphony, the excellent Betz[25] took on the baritone solo with amicable zeal. I had no difficulty in convincing him to replace[26]

Example 4.44. Beethoven, Symphony no. 9, 4th movement, mm. 240–42

with

Example 4.45. Beethoven, Symphony no. 9, 4th movement, mm. 240–42

However, we shall leave it up to our academic singers of the venerable English oratorio school to decide whether or not they wish to follow the letter of the score in future, and dispose of their "joy" correctly in two quarter-notes instead.[27]

---

25 Franz Betz (1835–1900), German bass-baritone, sang in the Ninth under Wagner in Bayreuth in 1872 and was his first Wotan in 1876.

26 Wagner's own music example omits the first measure here; it has been added because it clarifies what he is saying.

27 This proposed alteration proved largely unpopular. Weingartner (1906): 189 found it "incomprehensible" and he mentions, too, how Betz had often sung the Ninth under his baton in Berlin (implying that Betz himself set no store by Wagner's changes). In Mahler's annotated copy of the Ninth in the archives of the New York Philharmonic, this "Freude" passage has been altered as Wagner suggests, though his Vienna score leaves this passage as is. Other conductors (including those who were otherwise influenced by Mahler, such as Schoenberg and Mengelberg) also left it unaltered.

Part II
Critical Essay

Chapter Five

Richard Wagner and the Art of Conducting

About Conducting

Studying Wagner's essay (*Über das Dirigieren*) ought to be a matter of course for every conductor.

—Karl Böhm, written in his working copy of the score to Beethoven's *Eroica*[1]

Richard Wagner published his essay on conducting over nine issues of the *Neue Zeitschrift für Musik* in late 1869 and early 1870. Karl Böhm was just one of many major conductors who held it in high regard. Bruno Walter called *Über das Dirigieren*[2] a "treasure trove" for him in his youth,[3] Richard Strauss referred to it as "monumental,"[4] for Hermann Scherchen it offered a "musical theory of tempo,"[5] while Felix Weingartner paid homage to it more daringly by writing an essay of his own with the same title.[6] There is barely a book or essay on conducting from the late 19th or 20th centuries that

---

1   See the catalogue of the fifty-fourth antiquarian book fair in Stuttgart, 2015.

2   I shall here use the German title of this essay throughout, partly because its opening preposition sounds awkward when discussing it (to write about *About Conducting*, for example, sounds tautological at best), but also because previous translations have rendered its title in different ways. Using the German original leaves no doubt as to the subject of our discussion.

3   Walter (1947): 59.

4   Strauss (1931): 7.

5   Scherchen (1929): 39.

6   Weingartner (1896).

does not draw on Wagner's *Über das Dirigieren*, either directly or indirectly. Some authors have even plagiarized it.[7] (One of the few conductors of note to ignore Wagner's essay in a tract on his art was Adrian Boult in his *A Handbook on the Technique of Conducting* of 1920, though it is admittedly only twenty pages long, was intended as a practical guide for students at the Royal College, and can serve as the exception that proves the rule).[8] I here present *Über das Dirigieren* in a new English translation, alongside its sister article of 1873 on performing Beethoven's Ninth Symphony, plus two other texts by Richard Wagner that deal with conducting. They were all written within the space of about eight years, but were the result of over three decades of experience on the conductor's podium, both in the opera house and in the concert hall. In this essay, I shall be investigating the history of Wagner's career, reception, and reputation as a conductor. I shall also consider how he went about ensuring that his art of interpretation would escape the ephemerality of the moment. As we shall see, his conducting aesthetic exerted a lasting impact on how music—not just his own—was thereafter played and conducted.

When Wagner embarked on his conducting career in 1832, the profession itself was barely older than he was. There is ample pictorial evidence that directing a musical performance by visibly beating time—whether with the hand alone or a roll of paper—had been a common practice since the late Renaissance, while in the 18th century it became customary for the lead violinist and/or the keyboard continuo player to take on the task of coordinating an ensemble in performance; the former could naturally use his violin bow as an extension of his hand when directing and not playing.[9] In some countries, most notably France and Italy, it remained common until well into the 19th century for performances to be directed by the principal violinist. It is generally accepted that "conducting" as we understand it today became established in the German-speaking world in the second decade of the 19th century, with Louis Spohr (1784–1859) and Carl Maria von Weber (1786–1826). Both men began conducting with a baton in about 1820, and this practice soon spread to Great Britain and elsewhere.[10]

---

7   See, for example, Josef Pembaur's own *Über das Dirigieren* (1892).

8   See Boult (1920).

9   Schünemann (1913) still provides one of the most detailed overviews of the evolution of time-beating.

10   For a detailed description of early conductors and the emergence of the baton, see, e.g., Siepmann (2003): 117–18 and Koury (2010): 72–76.

Numerous musical, social, economic, and technological factors played a role in the emergence of the conductor as an independent agent in musical performance. The increasing complexity of opera and symphonic music, not least the music composed by Spohr and Weber themselves, required more complex management structures for rehearsing and performing it. The boom in music publishing since the introduction of lithography in *circa* 1800 meant that more and more full scores were being published (conductors needed these if they were to be able to supervise all the instrumentalists under their baton). The increasing significance of the bourgeoisie in post-Napoleonic Europe also saw a growth in the number of orchestral and choral associations and opera companies (both amateur and professional), all of which needed a conductor to lead and coordinate their performances. There was a concomitant surge in constructing urban concert halls and opera houses for growing middle-class audiences. More and more music journals sprang up to discuss, criticize and praise what was heard and seen, and they played a role, too, in establishing the role of the conductor. Gaspare Spontini (1774–1851) dominated the conducting scene in Biedermeier Berlin for over twenty years after he took up his appointment there in 1820. Carl Maria von Weber ran the Dresden Court Opera from 1817 until his death in 1826, establishing a culture of orchestral excellence to which Wagner often referred enthusiastically in later life, even though he had only been a child on the few occasions he experienced Weber in the opera house.[11]

In Paris, the violinist and conductor François-Antoine Habeneck (1781–1849) founded a concert series in 1828 with an orchestra comprising professors and graduates from the Conservatoire, and their performances over the next two decades garnered praise from everyone on account of their precision and musicality. Habeneck's admirers included Felix Mendelssohn Bartholdy (1809–47), whose own supreme gifts were given ample space in which to flourish by his wealthy, doting parents. They provided his first experience of conducting an orchestra by simply engaging one to play under his direction at their home on Sundays. As music director in Düsseldorf (1833–35) and at the Gewandhaus in Leipzig (1835–47), and also as a regular guest conductor in Britain and elsewhere, Mendelssohn did more than anyone else to establish the role and status of the orchestral conductor. As the founding director of the Leipzig Conservatory in 1843, he also ushered in a new professionalism in the German music world that extended to the art of conducting. Many of

---

11   See, for example, CWT 2: 192 (October 6, 1878), and CWT 2: 255 (December 11, 1878).

the most important conductors of the ensuing decades would emerge from this institution—a fact about which Richard Wagner complained bitterly, as we can read in the texts given in this volume.

Richard Wagner's conducting career was very different from that of Mendelssohn, for whom he came to feel a complex mixture of emotions in which envy played the dominant role. They both came from talented families. Wagner's uncle Adolph was a scholar, his sister Rosalie a popular actress, his brother Albert an actor-singer, and Richard too enjoyed a privileged education, first at the Kreuzschule in Dresden, then at the Thomasschule in Leipzig. But unlike the upper-class Mendelssohn, Wagner had to begin his conducting career at the bottom, working his way slowly up the ranks of provincial German theaters. His first job, procured by his brother Albert, was as chorus director in Würzburg. In 1834 he was appointed the music director for Heinrich Bethmann's theater company in Magdeburg, where he got to know his future wife, Minna Planer, an actress with the same troupe. When she moved to Königsberg in 1836, Wagner followed her, married her, and was appointed music director at the local theater in spring 1837. A similar post at the opera house in Riga, yet further to the east, followed later that same year. These "galley years" meant conducting often inadequate singers and ad hoc ensembles in a rapid turnover of stock repertoire with little rehearsal time, and in a world where theatrical bankruptcies were a frequent occurrence. The operas that the public wanted and got—by Mozart, Bellini, Rossini, Donizetti, Auber, Weber and the like—all had an impact on Wagner's own stage works of these years, from his romantic–magical *Die Feen* (1833–34, not performed until several years after his death) to his Italianate comic opera *Das Liebesverbot* (1834–36) and his attempt at a *grand opéra* in the mold of Meyerbeer and Spontini, namely *Rienzi* (1837–1840).

Wagner also occasionally conducted concerts with the forces at his disposal, making sure to program the assorted concert overtures he was composing at the time. In Riga he even managed to set up a concert series in which a large number of amateur players joined the members of the theater orchestra. It was here that Wagner was able to conduct works of the symphonic repertoire on a regular basis for the first-ever time, including Mozart's symphony no. 40 in G minor and Beethoven's symphonies nos. 3, 4, 5, 7, and 8. Regrettably, we have little documentary evidence of these activities (the earliest surviving poster from his Riga concert series seems to be that of March 19, 1838, when he conducted a potpourri program including his own overtures *Columbus* and *Rule Britannia* and bits and bobs by Spohr, Weber and others).[12] For all Wagner might have groaned under the yoke, compelled as he was to invest his energies in the popular operatic repertoire under difficult conditions for little financial reward, the exigencies of conducting under such circumstances clearly honed both his organizational skills and his ability to communicate his instructions succinctly.

Always in debt wherever they went, the Wagners fled by ship from Riga to France in 1839, with Richard hoping to establish himself as a composer and conductor in Paris, the operatic Mecca of the day and home to a lively German expatriate community ("The capital city of Germany is Paris," remarked Heinrich Heine to Ferdinand Hiller in the mid-1830s).[13] But work proved hard to come by, and Wagner's debts accumulated again. He did, however, hear François-Antoine Habeneck conduct Beethoven's Ninth Symphony with the orchestra of the Conservatoire in early 1840—an experience that had a profound impact on him and that reverberates throughout his writings of the next three decades, as can be seen in the texts reproduced in this volume (though it remains a matter of debate precisely when Wagner heard the Ninth in Paris, and whether or not he only heard Habeneck rehearse the first three movements, or heard him conduct the whole symphony in concert).[14] While in Paris, Wagner also saw Berlioz conduct his *Roméo et Juliette* and *Symphonie funèbre*, both of which impressed him greatly.

The surprise acceptance of Wagner's opera *Rienzi* for performance by the Dresden Court Opera saved him and Minna from Parisian penury and took them back to Germany. Its world premiere on October 20, 1842 was a huge success, and Wagner was soon after allowed to stage his newest opera there, *Der fliegende Holländer*, whose premiere he conducted on January 2, 1843. One month later he was appointed a Royal Capellmeister for life (though he only spent the next six years in the job). Most of his conducting in Dresden was in the opera house, where he was again responsible for large chunks of the repertoire from Mozart to Donizetti. But Wagner occasionally also conducted in the concert hall, his most notable performances being those of Beethoven's Ninth Symphony in 1846, 1847, and 1849 (discussed in further detail below).

The Dresden Uprising of May 1849 came at a time when Wagner was yet again in debt. What's more, he had recently suffered the rejection of his plans for a reorganization of the Dresden Opera. So he joined the insurrection

---

12   Reproduced in Drüner (2016): 103 and Heinel (2006): 44.

13   Hiller: "Die Musik und das Publikum," in Hiller (1868): 220–63, here 231.

14   See, e.g., Voss (2015): 12.

against the old order, presumably thinking he had little to lose and much to gain. When it failed within a few days, however, he had to run. He fled first to Franz Liszt, who put him up, gave him some money, then sent him on his way to neutral Switzerland. Wagner used Zurich as a stopping-off point on his way to Paris, where he wanted to try his luck once again. When this proved as futile an endeavor as it had been ten years before, he settled back in Zurich. The city had already welcomed many exiles from the assorted European revolutions that had been raging since the previous year, and Wagner found there a wealthy, art-loving bourgeoisie ready to open their wallets and their wine cellars to the former Dresden capellmeister, now on the run.

Wagner never had a full-time conducting post again. At the suggestion of Liszt—who was growing weary of his friend's money-begging—Wagner began taking on occasional conducting jobs in Zurich to help pay the bills. The local concert orchestra, run by the Allgemeine Musikgesellschaft (General Music Society, hereafter AMG), was semi-professional, but its patrons were well-off and intrigued by the chance to work with the exotic exile in their midst. They even let Wagner dictate his terms of engagement. He declared himself willing to conduct, but only as a guest, only in works of his own choice (mostly Beethoven, occasionally Mozart and others), and at a fee that was vast for Zurich—he charged almost as much to conduct a single symphony as the orchestra's nominal music director, Franz Abt, was paid for two whole concerts. Abt was initially accommodating towards Wagner and even made a pilgrimage to Weimar to hear Liszt conduct the world premiere of *Lohengrin* in August 1850. But Wagner took a dislike to him—perhaps because Abt was popular in Zurich—and was soon successfully engaging in intrigues to get him out. Abt accordingly left to take up a post in Braunschweig in 1852.

In order to save time and energy in rehearsal, Wagner got the AMG's board to pay copyists (most notably one Adam Bauer) to enter his rehearsal letters and expression markings into the orchestral parts.[15] Wagner insisted on a strict rehearsal schedule in Zurich and introduced a zero-tolerance policy towards absenteeism, as we can see from a letter he sent to Hans Conrad Ott-Imhof of the AMG board on November 23, 1854:

> I hear that a large number of the musicians that you intend to place at my disposal will come from Winterthur and will not attend all rehearsals, but only the

---

15   For information on Wagner's Zurich copyists, see Walton (2007): 169–74.

last one. Once and for all I wish to explain that I am no longer able to rehearse if musicians are not present, and I must insist that all participants should attend the three rehearsals necessary for the concert.[16]

Wagner also conducted a few times in the city theater, where the players in the pit were more or less the same as those in the concert orchestra. In late 1850, Wagner evaded an attempt to appoint him music director of the Zurich theater by getting them to hire his new protégé instead: Hans von Bülow (1830–94) from Dresden, whom Wagner knew from his years as Royal Capellmeister there. Hans was visiting his father in his stately home in Canton Thurgau some forty miles north-east of Zurich in the summer of 1850 when he received the call from Wagner, and he accepted without hesitation. Wagner accordingly mentored von Bülow at the Zurich theater throughout the winter of 1850. Von Bülow did not last long—he had an argument with the main soprano and was on the losing end when their boss had to choose between them—but he must be regarded as Wagner's first, and arguably only, conducting student.

Zurich's music life also enjoyed several Wagnerian innovations that brought it more in line with the bigger centers. Thus he introduced concert program notes, though these were rarely printed separately for distribution on the night, but instead published in the local daily, the *Eidgenössische Zeitung*, edited by Wagner's new friend Bernhard Spyri. Wagner was also largely responsible for introducing the innovative concept of what we would call the "symphony concert," which replaced the earlier mish-mash of solos, songs, symphony movements and overtures with concert programs consisting (more or less) of an overture, a concerto, and then a symphony.

Wagner's biggest success in Zurich, however, was a three-concert festival of his own works that he organized and conducted around his 40th birthday in May 1853, with bleeding chunks from all his operas from *Rienzi* onwards. His genius for organization and publicity found its first full flowering here, and in all its aspects this Zurich festival can be regarded as an early trial run for the kind of measures Wagner later employed to organize his Bayreuth Festival, twenty-three years later. But just as in Dresden five years before, Wagner's enthusiasm got the better of him, and he began drawing up large-scale, expensive plans for the future music life of Zurich. He was turned down here too, and this was a factor that led him to withdraw from the local music scene in 1855. He did, however, accept an invitation to conduct

---

16   SB 6: 283.

a season of the Old Philharmonic in London in that year, where he had to cope with a huge repertoire ranging from Mendelssohn's *Italian* Symphony to arias by Spohr, Mozart, Meyerbeer, Cherubini, and others, along with several symphonies by Mozart and Beethoven (including the Ninth). Rehearsals were minimal, though Wagner was at least given a full two before conducting Beethoven's Choral Symphony.

Hector Berlioz had been the Old Philharmonic's first choice for the season, but had rejected their approach because he had already accepted an invitation to conduct its rival, the New Philharmonic, in June and July 1855.[17] Having both Wagner and Berlioz conduct at roughly the same time in the same city inevitably meant that they were compared in the press. Wagner came off decidedly worse. Matters were not helped by the partisan friendship Wagner inspired in one Ferdinand Praeger, a long-time German resident of London who briefly put up Wagner after his arrival in the city. Praeger began sending highly contentious articles to *The New York Musical Review and Gazette*, praising Wagner and fiercely attacking the London critics, especially the editor of *The Musical World*, James William Davison—who also happened to be the main music critic of *The Times*. Praeger's enthusiasm was such that he even let slip Wagner's authorship of the essay *Jewishness in Music* (something Wagner did not officially reveal until 1869), which was then openly mocked by Davison in *The Musical World*.[18] Given that Mendelssohn was still a kind of local hero to the English, the knowledge of Wagner's vicious anti-Semitic attack on him more or less scuppered any last hopes of a benevolent reception in London. On June 16, 1855, towards the end of the concert season, Henry Chorley—chief critic of the *Athenaeum* and a committed Mendelssohnian[19]—wrote that: "'The World' does well to stay away from execution so coarse and caricatured as Herr Wagner's treatment of Mozart's and Beethoven's symphonies." Two paragraphs later, by contrast, he wrote of the most recent concert of the New Philharmonic that "the appearance of M. Berlioz at the head of the band ensured as good a

---

17   James Davison: "Philharmonic concerts," *The Times* (March 14, 1855).

18   See the untitled editorial section on Wagner, his detractors, and supporters in *The Musical World* 33/19 (May 12, 1855), 299–300. For information on Praeger and the debate in and about the New York journal, see also Sessa (1979): 20–21.

19   For more information on Chorley, his Swiss teacher Jakob Zeugheer and their Mendelssohn connections, see Walton (2010).

performance of the music selected as was possible."[20] All in all, London was a flop for Wagner. Nor did the money he was paid stretch as far as he had anticipated. In *The Times*, James Davison summed up in devastating fashion the impression that Wagner had made: "Another such a set of eight concerts would go far to annihilate the [Philharmonic] society."[21] Wagner returned to the bosom of Zurich that summer, and did not visit London again for over twenty years.

The increasingly generous patronage of the silk merchant Otto Wesendonck and his wife Mathilde in Zurich meant that Wagner was able to realize his long-held desire for a proper home when he moved into his "Asyl" in mid-1857, a house on his patrons' estate (renovated, as it happens, by Leonhard Zeugheer, the brother of Henry Chorley's teacher).[22] Otto's money also meant that Wagner no longer needed to conduct in public to earn his living, and could devote himself to composition instead. Wagner's gratitude to Otto did not prevent him from trying to sleep with the man's wife; for her part, Mathilde enjoyed the attention of the famous composer, but kept him at arm's length. Wagner now embarked on the composition of *Tristan und Isolde*, which he saw as an allegory for his illicit passion, and also set five of Mathilde's own poems to music (the *Wesendonck Lieder*). He came out of his semi-retirement as conductor to direct a private performance of their song *Träume* in a version for violin and chamber orchestra on Mathilde's birthday, December 23, 1857, when Otto happened to be away in America. In an effort to restore some semblance of neighborly balance, Wagner took to the podium one more time in Zurich, this time for a private performance of assorted symphony movements by Beethoven for Otto's birthday the following March, also in the Wesendonck villa. Both these concerts involved members of the AMG Orchestra.

By spring 1858, however, Wagner's obsession with Mathilde had become public knowledge, and his continued presence in Zurich increasingly untenable. In mid-August 1858, he left behind his wife, his house, and almost all he owned, and embarked on a new series of wanderings: to Lucerne, Venice, Lucerne again, then to Paris, where he conducted three concerts of his own music in early 1860, then supervised—though did not conduct—a (disastrous) production of his *Tannhäuser* in early 1861. Then came Vienna, where

20   Henry Chorley: "Concerts of the Week," in *The Athenaeum* no. 1442 (June 16, 1855).

21   James Davison: "Philharmonic concerts" in *The Times* (June 26, 1855).

22   See Walton (2010).

he conducted several of his own works in concert in late 1862 and early 1863, then St. Petersburg in 1863, again to conduct excerpts from his works. According to Rimsky-Korsakov, Wagner was the first conductor in Russia to stand facing the orchestra, with his back to the audience, and set an example followed thereafter by all others.[23] Wagner then moved back to Vienna, all the while getting increasingly into debt (again) until the accession to the Bavarian throne of Ludwig II brought a temporary end to his worries in early 1864. Ludwig called Wagner to Munich, settled his debts, and installed him in comfort so he might proceed with composing. But Wagner's insatiable appetites, his political meddling, and his affair with Cosima von Bülow— wife of Hans and daughter of Liszt—made him so unpopular that Ludwig had to order him out of the country in late 1865. Wagner spent most of the next six years in Tribschen in Switzerland, where he set up home with Cosima. Living away from Munich naturally didn't stop Wagner from once again drawing up expensive plans (again unsuccessful) to reorganize the city's music life, most notably by proposing a festival theater for his works and a conservatory to train new generations of musicians in how to perform them. In 1872, the Wagners moved permanently to Bayreuth, which city had offered itself as the venue for his planned Festival Theater.

Wagner continued to conduct occasional guest concerts in these years, though his focus was on his own music. For example, he conducted his old *Faust Overture* in Berlin on April 30, 1871; then in Mannheim on December 20, 1871 he conducted a concert with the *Kaisermarsch* and odds and ends from *Lohengrin*, *Meistersinger*, and *Tristan* along with Mozart's *Magic Flute* Overture and Beethoven's Symphony no. 7 (he also tried out his *Siegfried Idyll* with full orchestra during the final rehearsal). A few months later, he conducted the *Eroica* and works of his own on May 12, 1872 in Vienna. Wagner celebrated the laying of the foundation stone of the Bayreuth Festival Theater on May 22, 1872 with a performance of Beethoven's Ninth in the Margravial Opera House in Bayreuth, for which he brought together instrumentalists and singers from across Germany (discussed in further detail below). Further occasional guest performances followed in Hamburg, Berlin, and elsewhere in order to raise money for the forthcoming Bayreuth Festival, and on March 2, 1876 Wagner conducted the whole of *Lohengrin* as a guest in Vienna. This was the first time in over a decade that he had conducted any of his operas complete, and it was the last time too. In 1877, Wagner undertook another concert tour to London, though he shared the conducting duties this time

---

23   See Rimsky-Korsakov (1909): 26.

with his protégé Hans Richter, and the repertoire was confined to works by Wagner, primarily excerpts from his operas. Wagner never in fact conducted the premiere of any of his own operas after *Tannhäuser* in Dresden in 1845. Liszt conducted *Lohengrin* in Weimar in 1850, when Wagner was already in exile; Hans von Bülow was entrusted with *Tristan und Isolde* in 1865 and *Die Meistersinger* in 1868, both in Munich; Hans Richter was assigned the *Ring* in Bayreuth in 1876 (though the first two operas, *Das Rheingold* and *Die Walküre*, had been performed under Franz Wüllner in Munich in 1869 and 1870 respectively, without Wagner's permission), and Hermann Levi conducted *Parsifal* in Bayreuth in 1882. Wagner famously took over the baton from Levi for the close of the final performance of *Parsifal* in Bayreuth in the summer of 1882, and his last performance as conductor was on Cosima's birthday, December 24, 1882, in the Teatro La Fenice in Venice, when he conducted his youthful Symphony in C major in her honor.

Wagner's conducting work up to his departure from Dresden was thus largely confined to the opera house with a permanent ensemble. From Zurich onwards, he worked mostly in the concert hall, always as a guest conductor, and in the last twenty years of his life he conducted very little altogether. Even when taking into consideration our lack of watertight statistics for his early years, we can with confidence state that Wagner conducted roughly the same number of concerts during his entire fifty-year career as did Wilhelm Furtwängler in his prime in a single season.[24] Reviews survive of Wagner's conducting engagements throughout his career, though regrettably for our purposes, by the time reviewing concerts had become a recognized profession across Europe in the mid-nineteenth century, Wagner had largely retired from the podium. There are several notable exceptions, however, that can offer us at least a sketchy idea of how Wagner actually conducted.

Wagner in Review

The collected reviews of Wagner's years in Dresden and Zurich have been published in book form,[25] though they offer little relevant information for our topic. Like most reviews of opera, those in Dresden were focused more on what happened on stage than on the technique or tempi of the conductor.

---

24   See the lists of Furtwängler's concerts in the 1930s in Trémine (1997): 33–47.
25   See Kirchmeyer (1967, 1968) for Wagner's Dresden years, and Zimmermann (1986 and 1988) for Zurich.

One exception is a review in the *Zeitung für die elegante Welt* of the performance of *Don Giovanni* given under Wagner's direction on April 26, 1843 in Dresden, which is notable because its anonymous author's criticism of Wagner's extreme tempi would be echoed by others over the years. In this case, however, the author believes he knows the reason for these tempi:

> In Paris, when German compositions are played, they consistently make the mistake of playing the slow tempi far too slowly, and the fast tempi far too quickly, and Mr. Wagner indulged in the same basic mistake yesterday from the start to the end of the opera. I confess that I find inappropriate tempi in Mozart incomprehensible in the case of a German musician. The French do not understand him; we can say without exaggeration that they haven't a clue about him ... yesterday's tempi were French. They are utterly reprehensible ... In some numbers, the capellmeister couldn't do things as he wished; he would set one tempo, but the singer began in another, to which [the conductor] had no choice but to yield.[26]

The author in question clearly knew that Wagner had just spent over two years in France. This seems to be the only instance in which Wagner was accused of conducting in a "French" manner, and it is fascinating because it casts new light on certain implicit contradictions we find a quarter of a century later in *Über das Dirigieren* and in his essay on Beethoven's Ninth Symphony. On the one hand, Wagner insists there on distinguishing his own, supposedly "German" style of conducting from that of everyone else, for which he often resorts to words of French origin to express his distaste at the un-Germanness of others (see his use of "elegant," "Tanz-Pas," etc., on pp. 29 and 74); but on the other hand, he also writes of how the French musicians under Habeneck in Paris had found the "right" tempi because they knew how to sing the music. Perhaps Wagner had learnt even more from Habeneck than he was willing to admit.

If there is little in the reviews of Wagner's Dresden period to help us "reconstruct" his art of conducting, there is even less from his Zurich years, where the local journalists were devoid of any specialist musical knowledge and compensated for their lack of an adequate vocabulary by resorting to florid adjectives. In any case, Wagner succeeded early on in dividing the press there, which meant that his artistic efforts tended to be assessed along party lines. Wagner's friend Bernhard Spyri was gushingly enthusiastic in the reviews he wrote for his own paper, the conservative *Eidgenössische Zeitung*,

---

26   Anon. (1843): 463–64.

which meant in turn that Zurich's rival daily paper, the liberal *Neue Zürcher Zeitung*, felt compelled to take a contradictory, skeptical position.[27] The closest Spyri gets to a description of Wagner's conducting approach is in a review of his *Tannhäuser* at the Zurich City Theater in 1855: "The rehearsals took place under the baton of the composer himself, and anyone who has ever attended a rehearsal of Wagner's will know what that means."[28] Sadly, we haven't, so we don't. The most detailed account we have is from Wagner's bosom friend at the time, the composer and choral conductor Wilhelm Baumgartner, though it too is in itself a sign of the paucity of sources, comprising but a single sentence: "He knew how to rule and inspire the orchestra like a military leader, full of life, spirit, clarity, and fire, with a clear conception of the work to be conducted."[29] (Making comparisons between Wagner the conductor and a military commander seems to have become second nature among those who approved of his methods.[30]) We do, however, have indirect proof that Wagner's conducting activities in Zurich inspired enthusiasm beyond the circle of his bedazzled local fans. The only other composer of note in German Switzerland at the time was Theodor Kirchner (1823–1903),[31] who (at Mendelssohn's own insistence) had been student no. 1 at the Leipzig Conservatory when it opened in 1843, and who was working as an organist and piano teacher in nearby Winterthur when Wagner arrived in Zurich. He was a brilliant pianist, so Wagner engaged him to accompany the first private performance of excerpts from *Die Walküre* in 1856, when the composer himself sang both Hunding and Siegmund. Kirchner's open admiration of Mendelssohn and Schumann meant he and Wagner were never going to be close, and Kirchner received only a disparaging mention in *Mein Leben* several years later. But he never lost his admiration for Wagner, and on at least one occasion said as much to Friedrich Nietzsche. On April 30, 1870, Nietzsche wrote to his friend Erwin Rohde to recommend Wagner's essay *Über das Dirigieren*, adding "Kirchner—one of Schumann's best pupils—told me the other day that he had never anywhere experienced performances as good as under Wagner."[32] Given that Kirchner's views on music were very

27   See also Walton (2007): 105–6.

28   Spyri in the *Eidgenössische Zeitung* (February 16, 1855).

29   Widmer (1868): 31.

30   See, for example, Tappert (1872): 392.

31   See Walton (2007): 122–29.

32   Nietzsche to Erwin Rohde, Basel, April 30, 1870, Nietzsche (2009–): www.nietzschesource.org/#eKGWB/BVN-1870,76 (accessed June 2019).

different from Wagner's, we have no reason to doubt the objectivity of his praise.

Despite the general antipathy of the London press towards Wagner in 1855, the critics there also offer us much more detail about his art of conducting than do their Zurich contemporaries. In *The Times*, James Davison noted Wagner's predilection for conducting without a score (though he did not approve).[33] After Wagner's concert of June 11, 1855, Davison also noted that Wagner preferred to play the symphonies of Beethoven and Mozart without repeats, except for the first movement of Mozart's *Jupiter*.[34] He praised Wagner for having a cello solo play throughout the Trio of the third movement of Beethoven's Symphony no. 8,[35] but, like the other London critics, he found much to criticize in Wagner's tempi and frequent *rubati*, and was astonished that Wagner tended to take the slow movements of Beethoven and Mozart much slower than was the custom there. He wrote of the opening movement of the *Jupiter* being

> tortured and spoiled by every species of affectation that could be expected from an ultra-sentimental boarding-school miss … '*Ritardando*' here, '*diminuendo*' there—false and unnatural accents without end—dragged back and tormented where its onward course should be impetus and unimpeded. The divine *andante*, played *adagio* (and '*senza*' instead of '*con sordini*') was so disfigured by unmeaning and unauthorized '*rallentandi*,' that its spirit evaporated and it sounded like a piece of maudlin insipidity. The *minuetto*, too, though marked '*allegretto*,' was somniferously dirge-like.[36]

The most often quoted report of that same concert was published in *The Sunday Times* by Henry Smart (nephew of Sir George, Carl Maria von Weber's host in London some three decades earlier). His criticism of Wagner's tempi is not so far removed from that of the Dresden critic of his *Don Giovanni* back in 1843, though he also takes aim at Wagner's tempo fluctuations:

> Firstly, he takes all quick movements faster than anybody else; secondly he takes all slow movements slower than anybody else; thirdly he prefaces the entry of an important point, or the return of a theme—especially in a slow movement—by

---

33   James Davison: "Philharmonic concerts," *The Times* (March 14, 1855).
34   James Davison: "Philharmonic concerts," *The Times* (June 12, 1855).
35   Ibid.
36   Ibid.

an exaggerated ritardando; and fourthly, he reduces the speed of an allegro—say in an overture or the first movement—fully one third on the entrance of its cantabile phrases.[37]

Given Henry Smart's obvious feelings of antipathy towards Wagner, we may assume that his report is somewhat exaggerated. But it does seem that Wagner indulged in far greater *rubato* than was the norm in London, for other critics raised similar concerns. Just a month earlier, Davison had written as follows in *The Times* about Wagner's performance of Mozart's Symphony no. 39, K. 543 (all italics are here original):

> A stranger performance of Mozart's symphony was never heard. The *allegro* was throughout too slow, but the first theme … was given in a manner that set not only tradition, but musical sentiment at defiance. There is no indication in Mozart's score for so abrupt a contrast between the opening *motive* and the rest. The *andante*—of all slow movements the most beautiful … was robbed of its character altogether by the tedious prolixity of the *tempo* Herr Wagner thought proper to indicate. The *minuetto* and *trio* were equally at variance with the reading consecrated by more than half a century; while the *finale*—singular to relate, after so much provoking slowness in the first three movements—was taken quicker than we ever heard it, so quick, indeed, that the stringed instruments at times could scarcely master the passages allotted them … According to Herr Wagner, the first movement should be *moderato*, the second *adagio*, the third *andante*, and the fourth *prestissimo!*[38]

Henry Chorley was more extreme in his comments, writing of the "caricatured slowness" of the *Andante*—and the *Finale* had been a "confused romp" played at "excessive" speed.[39] Wagner did not forget these reproaches. A memory of the hurt they must have caused seems to hover behind his brief discussion of the slow movement of K. 543 in his *Report to His Majesty King Ludwig II on Setting up a German Music School in Munich*[40] of 1865, and he mentioned his London critics (albeit not by name) four years later in

---

37 Henry Smart, *The Sunday Times* (June 17, 1855). By "cantabile phrases" Smart is presumably referring in particular to the second subject of a sonata-form movement, though he might also mean any such song-like phrase in the course of a movement.

38 James Davison: "Philharmonic concerts," *The Times* (May 16, 1855).

39 Henry Chorley writing in *The Athenaeum*, no. 1438 (May 19, 1855).

40 *Bericht an Seine Majestät den König Ludwig II. von Bayern über eine in München zu errichtende deutsche Musikschule.* Munich: Christian Kaiser, 1865.

Über das Dirigieren, turning things on their head in order to emphasize the rightness of his own approach to this movement; Wagner also discussed the tempo of this *Andante* in a letter of 1868 to Hans von Bülow (see footnotes 21, 38 and 95 in the translation of *Über das Dirigieren* above).

These London reviews are significant because much of what they mention remains relevant in later years. The tempo modifications they complain about are also strikingly similar to those discussed by Wagner in *Über das Dirigieren*. As for Wagner's stick technique, Davison complained that

> Herr Wagner's method of using the *baton* (like that of some other German musicians) must be very perplexing, at first, to those unacquainted with it. The confusion between the 'up' and 'down' beat, which he appears to employ indiscriminately—so unlike the clear and decided measure of his predecessor [Michael Costa]—requires a long time to get accustomed to.[41]

Amy Fay made a similar observation to this when she saw Wagner conduct in Berlin in 1871, writing that: "He didn't beat the time simply, as most conductors do, but he had all sorts of little ways to indicate what he wished. It was very difficult for them to follow him." However, she did not regard this as anything negative. On the contrary: "He is so great as a conductor, for the orchestra catches his frenzy, and each man plays under a sudden inspiration. He really seems to be improvising on his orchestra."[42] Her impressions are echoed by Richard Pohl in his review of Wagner's Mannheim concert in late 1871: he "has a wonderfully magnetic effect on his orchestra ... He knows how to inspire and enthuse every individual [in it] ... He 'plays' on the orchestra as if on a giant instrument."[43]

Arthur Nikisch played under Wagner in the *Eroica* in Vienna on May 12, 1872 and then in the Ninth Symphony two weeks afterwards in Bayreuth, and later wrote of how these two occasions were "decisive for my whole understanding of Beethoven, indeed for my art of interpretation with an orchestra in general."[44] While he, too, says almost nothing about *why* it was decisive, he unwittingly joins Davison and Fay by stating that Wagner "was certainly not what you'd call a 'routine capellmeister'; but his 'gestures' alone were music"[45] (see Gustav Gaul's

---

41   James Davison: "Philharmonic concerts," *The Times* (March 14, 1855).
42   Fay (1883): 119 and 120.
43   Pohl (1872): 15.
44   Nikisch (1920): 72.
45   Ibid.

sketches below, made at one of Wagner's rehearsals for his Viennese concert of May 12, 1872). If a late remark in Cosima's diary is accurate, Wagner made these gestures primarily through the wrist. On July 4, 1882, during the final rehearsals for *Parsifal*, she wrote that "we spend the evening with Jouk[ovsky], Stein and Levi. R[ichard] wants to show [Levi] how you govern [with?] the baton, because he finds he conducts far too much with his arm, whereas everything should be done with the wrist!"[46]

We do, however, have a long review of Wagner's *Eroica* in Vienna from the pen of Eduard Hanslick.[47] He spends his first four columns engaged in a polemic against Wagner and the supposed gullibility of his supporters, emphasizing Wagner's contempt for his contemporaries as expressed in essays such as his *Report to His Majesty* and *Über das Dirigieren*. But Hanslick then proceeds to discuss Wagner's interpretation of Beethoven in a detailed, objective manner. He acknowledges that Wagner is generally recognized as a "brilliant conductor," and admits that "his energetic, finely and unusually nuanced performance of the 'Eroica' was overall truly enjoyable," though he immediately states that this detracts not a whit from earlier, "excellent" performances of the work by the same orchestra under Johann von Herbeck and Felix Otto Dessoff—the latter being one of the conductors Wagner mocked in *Über das Dirigieren*, as Hanslick well knew (see p. 72). Hanslick goes on to say that

> What is new in Wagner's interpretation of the "Eroica," in brief, is a frequent "modification of the tempo" of it. This slogan, along with a second one, too— the "correct understanding of the melos," which is supposed to provide the key for the right tempo—are how Wagner himself describes the reform that he insists upon, and endeavors to practice, in performing Beethoven's symphonies.

Hanslick found these tempo shifts attractive in the last movement of the *Eroica*, as he felt that playing such a variation movement at the same tempo throughout could result in "vacuous formalism." He found the scherzo daringly quick, thought the slow movement "wunderschön," but also wrote that

> In other passages, Wagner seems to us to go too far with his "modifications," such as when he begins the first movement very quickly but promptly takes the second motive noticeably slower (dolce, 45th measure). This confuses the listener who has only just become accustomed to the basic mood, and shifts the "heroic" character of the symphony into the sentimental.

---

46 CWT 2: 975 (July 4, 1882).
47 The following quotes are all taken from Hanslick (1872).

What is notable here is how Hanslick relates Wagner's actual conducting to his essay *Über das Dirigieren*. This in itself raises a question that must be asked, even though it cannot be answered. If Wagner's critics were now judging him in the light of how he said one ought to conduct, did he in turn feel compelled to make the ideas expressed in his essay especially audible to his public? If his audiences, when given one of the increasingly rare opportunities to hear him, went in expectation of hearing the tempo modifications he had written about, did Wagner in turn feel compelled to intensify these modifications to ensure that people really noticed them? And was his retreat from the podium in these years perhaps in part because he did not want his own conducting to be compared too closely with the ideal of perfection in performance that his essay had more or less asserted to be his preserve alone? We can never know the answers, but these are pertinent issues to bear in mind.

Overall, Hanslick judged Wagner's concert in May 1872 to have been a great success, but he worried about how Wagner the conductor, like Wagner the composer, was wont to construct supposedly universal values from what were in fact mere personal preferences. "Hardly anyone doubts that these 'modifications' derive more from Wagner than from Beethoven," he wrote.

Just under two weeks after this concert in Vienna, Wagner conducted Beethoven's Ninth Symphony in Bayreuth at the commemoration for laying the foundation stone of the Festival Theater. This event and its aftermath are reported on in greater detail below, but the most interesting review—from our point of view at least—is worth quoting here at length because it offers an international perspective that complements Hanslick's comments from just a fortnight before. The author was Francis Hueffer, a German-born English resident who wrote music reviews for *The Times* for many years, and who reported back to its readers on the festivities in Bayreuth. While German reviewers such as Otto Lessmann and others glossed over the impact of the weather, focusing instead on the solemnity and gravity of the occasion, Hueffer wrote bluntly that "the ceremony proved a failure" because it was completely rained out, nor did he hold back about the culinary "horrors" of the banquet. His general bluntness means that his observations of Wagner on the podium are all the more worthy of consideration, and they touch on matters of personal magnetism that we would tend to disregard if emanating from the pen of one of the more hagiographical German commentators:

> although I have heard the Ninth Symphony at least three score and ten times, I never quite understood its wonderfully grand and harmonious structure till to-

day. Wagner indeed seems the born interpreter of this monumental work of musical genius. ... It is indeed one of the most interesting sights, to see the immediate *rapport* established between Wagner and his orchestra as soon as he raises his baton. Each individual member, from the first violinist to the last drummer, is equally under the influence of a personal fascination, which seems to have much in common with the effects of animal magnetism. Every eye is turned towards the master; and it appears as if the musicians derived the notes they play not from the books on their desks, but from Wagner's glances and movements. ... several artists in Wagner's orchestra and chorus assured me that they felt the fascinating spell of the conductor's eye, looking at them during the whole performance. Wagner in common life is of a rather reserved and extremely gentlemanly deportment; but as soon as he faces his band a kind of demon seems to take possession of him. He storms, hisses, stamps his foot on the ground and performs the most wonderful gyratory movements with his arms ... At other times, when the musical waves run smoothly, Wagner ceases almost entirely to beat the time, and a most winning smile is the doubly appreciated reward of his musicians, for a particularly well-executed passage. In brief, Wagner is as great a virtuoso on the orchestra as Liszt on the pianoforte, or Joachim on the violin.[48]

The inspirational aspect of Wagner's conducting also comes to the fore in a more gushing review four years later in early 1876, when he conducted his *Lohengrin* in Vienna as a guest. The critic of the *Wiener Abendpost* wrote—like Amy Fay—of how he seemed to conjure up the music "out of the moment." While admittedly unable to resist resorting to meteorological and sexual simile, this critic also confirmed how Wagner's gestures were not simply those of beating time, but determined by the content of the work he was conducting:

a glance, a slight lifting of the hand—the baton brandished now less, now more energetically—at a *diminuendo* his left hand makes a gently calming motion while the right continues beating the time—now come dotted notes and the graceful wave-like motion of the beats becomes sharply accentuated—a fiery effervescence and the baton jerks upwards like an ascending bolt of lightning— there is a brief chord in the whole orchestra, and his arm halts for a moment as if turned to stone.[49]

Informative reviews of Wagner's conducting methods are thus at a premium; the most interesting tend to be by those less well-disposed to him

---

48   Hueffer (1874): 294–96.
49   A. [*sic*]: "(Hofoperntheater)," in *Wiener Abendpost* no. 51 (March 3, 1876).

(negative criticism is often varied and fascinating; positive comments, like happy families, tend to be all alike). It is our misfortune that by the time the profession of music criticism had become established enough to offer more discriminating reports of Wagner's interpretive art, he had so divided musical opinion in his native land, and had so dreadfully insulted so many people, that few were able to remain objective (even Hanslick, the finest of them all, resorted to cheap shots when given the chance, as detailed below). But as we shall see, reliable sources of any kind are extremely scarce.

Wagner in the Picture

Wagner took a keen interest in science and technology. He mingled with scientists from at least the 1850s onwards, delighted in the possibilities of portrait photography, and kept abreast of new developments in stage technology from electric sunrises to moving panoramas to steam machines.[50] Since Thomas Edison invented his phonograph in 1877 and Eadweard Muybridge his stop-motion photography at almost exactly the same time, it would at least in theory have been possible to make some form of audio and visual documentation of Wagner as a conductor in the very last years of his life. But there is none. The earliest orchestral recordings of any kind were in any case only made several years after Wagner's death, and it took even longer before conductors were filmed in action (boxing kangaroos were better guarantors of success for early film-makers).[51] As it happens, one of the first-ever filmic depictions of a conductor was in Carl Fröhlich's silent centenary biopic *The Life and Works of Richard Wagner* of 1913. But despite having an actual conductor in the role of Wagner—one Giuseppe Becce, a former student of Arthur Nikisch no less— the scenes of him conducting are stilted and obviously staged for visual effect (in another odd instance of synchronicity, it was in that same "Wagner year" that Arthur Nikisch made his first orchestral recording—Beethoven's Fifth Symphony—in which we hear the kind of *rubato* of which Wagner writes in the essays translated in the present volume).

While it is not surprising that we have no film of Wagner conducting, nor do we have any photograph of him on the podium either.[52] And even if such a photograph were to surface today, it would be of limited value. A

50   See Walton (2007): 90–93.
51   See Goldsmith et al. (2016): xvii.
52   See Braam (2015).

single, staged moment would tell us less about Wagner's conducting than about what he might have wanted us to think. Several artistic depictions of Wagner as conductor do exist, however. The silhouettes of Wagner on the podium by Otto Böhler (1847–1913) are well known, and were apparently made after observing him conduct in Vienna in 1875 (Böhler became a keen Wagnerian, and attended the first Bayreuth Festival a year later). But a comparison with Böhler's other silhouettes of conductors—from Grieg to von Bülow, Mahler and others—shows that he must have regarded their conducting gestures as pretty much interchangeable.

The Viennese artist Gustav Gaul (1836–88) sketched Wagner as conductor on three separate occasions. Gaul was well connected in Vienna. His father, Franz Gaul, was an artist and engraver whose double-eagle design graced the reverse of all Austrian coins in the second half of the 19th century; Gustav's brother Franz (1837–1906) was also an artist, who like Gustav dabbled in caricature, but achieved fame as a costume designer and was in charge of costumes at the Viennese Court Theaters from 1868 onwards. He thus designed costumes for Wagner's operas in Vienna, and stayed in his job long enough to work with Mahler. Gustav Gaul made a name for himself as a portraitist of royalty and the aristocracy in Vienna and also specialized in painting well-known singers and actors (his brother's theatrical contacts no doubt helped). It seems that Gustav first got to know Wagner in October 1861, when he drew him in his rooms in the Hotel Kaiserin Elisabeth. His first drawing of Wagner the conductor was made in Vienna in January 1863, and according to the artist himself it depicts Wagner conducting his "Ride of the Valkyries" at a concert that featured excerpts from his operas at the Theater an der Wien (Wagner gave three of these, featuring a largely identical program each time, on December 26, 1862, and on January 1 and 11, 1863).[53] It has a strong element of caricature about it, but is all the more alive for it.

This was followed nine years later by three "action" sketches dated May 10, 1872, that were presumably made at a rehearsal for Wagner's concert on May

---

53   I here reproduce Gaul's engraving; the drawing on which it is based is marked "I Concert Theater a. d. Wien 1863"; since Wagner's first concert at the theater was actually on December 26, 1862, Gaul probably means the first concert of the year, on January 1, 1863. The "Ride of the Valkyries" was given at all three concerts, and was a big success. See, for example, the review of the concert of January 1 by "z." in *Blätter für Musik, Theater und Kunst* 9/2: 5–6, which mentions that the "Ride" was one of the pieces that the audience demanded be repeated. Gaul's original drawing is in the Österreichische Nationalbibliothek, shelfmark Autogr. 194/3(1–22).

Figure 5.1. The interchangeable conductor. Otto Böhler's silhouettes (clockwise from top left) of Wagner (Austrian National Library, ÖNB Wien, Pf 692:D(7)), Hans von Bülow (public domain), Edvard Grieg (public domain), and Gustav Mahler (ÖNB Wien, Pk 2770,10). Grieg's silhouette is here given as a mirror image for purposes of comparison.

Figure 5.2. "The Ride of the Valkyries" conducted by Wagner in Vienna in January 1863, engraving by Gustav Gaul. ÖNB Wien, PORT_00002880_01.

12, 1872 in Vienna, when he conducted Beethoven's *Eroica* Symphony and excerpts from his own operas. These are perhaps the most expressive sketches that we have of Wagner on the podium, and while they too tend to caricature, they convey a similar theatricality to what we can observe in sketches by Henry Holiday and "Spy" at Wagner's London concerts five years later (see below). As already mentioned, Arthur Nikisch played in the orchestra for Wagner's concert of May 12, 1872, and later wrote how "his 'gestures' alone were music."[54] Gaul's final sketch of Wagner in the act of conducting was made on February 27, 1875, again in Vienna, at a rehearsal for another batch of concerts featuring

---

54   Nikisch (1920): 72.

excerpts from his operas. The expressive use of the baton-less left hand is something we find again in the picture by "Spy" in London in 1877.

Two years later, the English Pre-Raphaelite artist Henry Holiday (1839–1927) sketched Wagner during rehearsals for his London concerts of 1877, and then made more detailed drawings during the actual concerts, when he made sure to sit behind and above the orchestra in order to have a clear view of the conductor. His rehearsal sketches have not survived, but four drawings from the concerts have come down to us.[55] Holiday was a friend of the London Wagnerian Edward Dannreuther, and had only recently published illustrations commissioned by Lewis Carroll for the first edition of *The Hunting of the Snark* (in the second of the two images given below, it's tempting to think the Master might be about to attack a frumious Bandersnatch). Wagner seems to be using a baton roughly half a meter in length, which happens to be the length recommended by Berlioz back in the mid-1850s in his *Le chef d'orchestre*.[56] The other images of Wagner on the podium, whether by Gaul or "Spy," suggest that he generally preferred a slightly shorter baton.

In two of Holiday's four sketches, Wagner has his left hand in his pocket (just as Richard Strauss recommended in the rules for young conductors that he drew up in the 1920s). His assistant director for the first Bayreuth Festival, Richard Fricke, also wrote of Wagner keeping his left hand in his pocket while conducting his American Centennial March in Bayreuth in 1876, adding that "he only lifts [his left hand] when he wants a *piano*, but for *forte* he conducts with all fours."[57]

The Wagner Museum in Bayreuth holds the baton that Wagner used to conduct his *Siegfried Idyll* in Tribschen in 1870: it is 0.7 cm. square and 34.4 cm. in length. But since Wagner only needed a dozen musicians in Tribschen, perhaps he used a longer baton when conducting a much larger ensemble (as was the case in London in 1877, when Holiday drew him).

This Tribschen baton is made of natural wood, with no alteration having been made to its color. Wagner wrote of having used a wooden baton wrapped in white paper when he conducted in Dresden,[58] and it seems that he continued to use such batons for several years afterwards (one survives in a private collection that dates from the early 1860s).[59] The fact that Wagner

---

55   For a description of these drawings and their history, see Föttinger (2011).
56   Berlioz (1856a): 300.
57   Fricke (1906): 115.
58   See his reminiscences of Spontini in this volume.
59   See www.opera-online.com/en/articles/lohengrin-wagners-baton (accessed April 2020).

Figure 5.3. Wagner conducting in Vienna on May 10, 1872, drawn by Gustav Gaul. By kind permission of the Austrian National Library. ÖNB Wien: Autogr. 194/3–4.

Figure 5.4. Wagner conducting in Vienna on February 27, 1875, drawn by Gustav Gaul. ÖNB Wien: Autogr. 194/3–7.

Figure 5.5. Henry Holiday, Sketches of Wagner conducting in London in May 1877. Städtische Galerie Dresden—Kunstsammlung. Museen der Stadt Dresden, Inv.-Nr. 1981/k 1928, 1929, 1930; bottom right: Nationalarchiv der Richard-Wagner-Stiftung, Bayreuth (the inscription is: "Richard Wagner conducting the Huldigungsmarsch").

Figure 5.6. Wagner's wooden baton for conducting the *Siegfried Idyll* in Tribschen in 1870 (34.4 cm long, with a diameter of 0.7 cm), with a US 5-cent coin for scale. Photograph by John Keller. Owned today by the Nationalarchiv der Richard-Wagner-Stiftung Bayreuth.

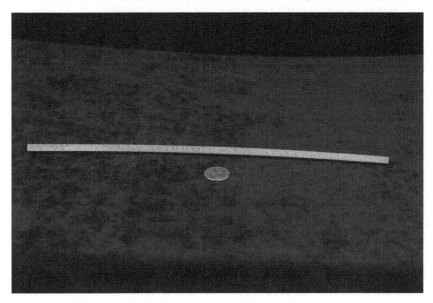

was conducting so few musicians in Tribschen might have meant the extra visibility provided by a white baton was simply unnecessary (in fact, some of the musicians were situated out of Wagner's sight anyway).[60] Berlioz recommended using a white baton,[61] though Mendelssohn seems to have varied between black and white. Two of his batons are held today by the Bodleian Library in Oxford, one of which is made of whalebone wrapped in white leather, while the other is made of ebony and has a silver tip.[62]

On at least three occasions, Wagner was presented with elaborately designed batons as a gift. The first was made of ivory to a design by Gottfried Semper, was commissioned by Mathilde Wesendonck, and was presented to Wagner at a Beethoven concert in the Wesendonck villa in March 1858; the second was made of ebony and inlaid with silver and precious stones, and was a gift from King Ludwig on the occasion of the world premiere of

---

60   See Walton (2012).

61   Berlioz (1856a): 300.

62   See https://wayback.archive-it.org/all/20190828095848/https://genius.bodleian.
      ox.ac.uk/exhibits/browse/conducting-batons-belonging-to-felix-mendelssohn/
      (accessed April 2020).

Die Meistersinger in 1868; and the third is a similarly elaborate item, though made of ivory inset with jewels. Only Semper's sketches survive of the first of these,[63] the second is held today in a private collection in Bavaria, and the third by the Reuter-Wagner-Museum in Thuringia.[64] However, it is clear that all three would have been far too unwieldy and heavy for practical use; and in any case, a physical object such as a baton can only offer limited information on how it might have been used.

Most pictures of Wagner in the act of conducting are caricatures. Some of them are fascinating because they can heighten traits or aspects of their subject that are less discernible in traditional portraiture, and the boundary between caricature and real-life portraiture is in some cases fluid (as we can observe in the drawings of Gustav Gaul, for example). But many caricatures are of little to no use at all as documents of the activity of conducting. We cannot even be sure if some of the artists in question had ever seen Wagner on the podium, for he seems equipped with a conductor's baton merely to signify him as a musician with supposed delusions of power—such as in his portrayal as a duck-drawn Lohengrin/Don Quixote in the Russian satirical journal *Iskra* in 1868, at the time when *Lohengrin* was first performed in St. Petersburg; here, the baton seems intended as a substitute for Quixote's lance in his battle against the windmills.

In a caricature by "Cham" for the French journal *Le Charivari* in 1860, Wagner is depicted conducting his "musicians of the future"—an orchestra of toddlers. In the wake of the Franco-Prussian War of 1870, French magazines began depicting Wagner as an archetypal militaristic German, often wearing a Prussian helmet. In Jules Renard's caricature for *L'Eclipse* of August 7, 1870, published before the routing of the French forces, Wagner is shown as a military drummer, his conducting baton doubling as a drumstick while he holds the reins of his horse in his other hand. And on the title page of *Le Sifflet* on August 27, 1876, Henri Meyer depicts him both wearing a Prussian helmet and standing on one (the first Bayreuth Festival of that summer seems to have inspired caricaturists everywhere). In this case, the helmet on Wagner's head is largely obscured by a laurel wreath, while the helmet on

---

63   Held today by ETH Zurich; see https://www.deutsche-digitale-bibliothek.de/item/PV2KFVQCZNQW4C7SZAVYV7BRC7CHQY63.

64   The "Ludwig" baton was exhibited at the "Mineralientage" in Munich in October 2019; see https://muenzenwoche.de/munich-show-zeigt-preziosen-europaeischer-monarchen/ ; for the baton in Thuringia, see www.eisenach.de/kultur/museen/thueringer-museum-eisenach (both accessed September 2020).

Figure 5.7. "Лознгринъ" = "Lohengrin": Wagner as Lohengrin/Don Quixote, drawn by a duck, not a swan, and with a baton instead of a lance for his battle against windmills. An anonymous cartoon, published in *Iskra* in St. Petersburg in 1868. Source: Kreowski (1907): 49.

which he stands is apparently inserted into his nether regions (hence, presumably, the pursed facial expression).[65]

In some caricatures, the baton is clearly used to signify Wagner the musician, just as mid-20th-century caricaturists would naturally include a cigar in a cartoon of Churchill. In these cases, the baton tells us no more about Wagner the conductor than Churchill's cartoon cigar might inform us about insipient anarcho-syndicalism in Cuban tobacco factories. Apart from Gustav Gaul's above drawings, the caricature of Wagner-as-conductor that is perhaps the most expressive was made in London in 1877 by Leslie Ward (known as "Spy")—thus at roughly the same time that Henry Holiday was sketching the composer. Wagner is standing in Gaul, seated in Spy, but in each picture he seems animated, caught in mid-gesture, with the same foot raised—here,

---

65   For further examples of Wagner caricatures, both with and without baton, see Kreowski and Fuchs (1907).

Figure 5.8. Wagner conducting "the musicians of the future"—an orchestra of toddlers—as depicted by Charles Amédée de Noé (*aka* Cham) in *Le Charivari* on February 27, 1860. Musée Carnavalet, Histoire de Paris, inv. no. G.21963(7) (public domain).

Figure 5.9. Jules Renard, "Wagner, generalissimo of the German forces. — They're counting on his music to put the French to flight." Published in *L'Eclipse: journal hebdomadaire politique, satirique et illustré* no. 133 (August 7, 1870), p. 4, as one vignette on a full page of assorted cartoons with the overarching title "Prussian Fantasies." This issue presumably went to print before news arrived of the Battle of Wörth of August 6, which was the first major defeat of the French in the Franco-Prussian War of 1870.

Figure 5.10. Wagner, "the musician of the future," by Henri Meyer, published in *Le Sifflet* on August 27, 1876. Bibliothèque nationale de France. The inscription on the Prussian spiked helmet refers to the Charenton lunatic asylum, whose inmates were in the early 19th century allowed to express themselves through art; the Marquis de Sade died there in 1814.

one thinks of the above remarks by Hueffer in 1872, that Wagner would occasionally stamp his foot when conducting, and by Fricke in 1876, of him conducting "with all fours." In his review of Beethoven's Ninth in Bayreuth 1872, Wilhelm Tappert also wrote of Wagner conducting "with hand, foot, mouth and eye."[66]

There are, however, two significant things that all these pictures can tell us about Wagner. First, it seems he sometimes conducted with a score before him, sometimes not. We cannot be sure about this, because an artist might consider a music stand a mere visual prop, to be included or omitted at his own discretion (thus Spy drew him in 1877 sitting down, without a music stand, though clearly in concert dress, whereas Holiday drew him standing, with a music stand).[67] Secondly, he seems to have conducted (or at least rehearsed) wearing glasses or pince-nez. We know that Wagner had been wearing glasses since at least the late 1840s, because it is stated in the description of him on the "wanted" notice issued by the police after he fled the Dresden Uprising in 1849.[68] Wagner never wore glasses for any of his official photo shoots, but Gaul, Holiday, and Spy all depict him thus, and these are in fact just about the only extant pictures of Wagner in which we see him wearing glasses at all. This fact alone confirms that Gaul, Holiday, and Spy must have drawn him from life. The glasses are in themselves of interest, because in his reminiscences of Spontini, Wagner wrote specifically about how the man conducted *without* glasses despite his very poor eyesight. According to Spontini, this helped him keep a better grip on the orchestra (see p. 13). Recent research has suggested that Wagner suffered from a squint in his left eye and myopic astigmatism.[69] Since the short-sighted do not generally wear glasses to be able to read close up, this could mean that he wore them to be able to see his musicians, which in turn suggests that this was his primary concern, and that it was less important for him to follow the score. This, again, would tie in with reports that he often rehearsed and conducted

---

66   Tappert (1872): 392.

67   There is another such example in Brown (2012): 16. He prints an amateur caricature of Wagner, sketched by one Joseph Kühn at or after his concert in Mannheim on December 20, 1871 that shows him conducting in front of an (admittedly empty) music stand; the review of that concert by Pohl (1872): 15 states, however, that Wagner conducted from memory, implying that he did not have a music stand before him.

68   Reproduced in many books, e.g., Strecker (1951): 29.

69   See Trimble et al. (2019).

Figure 5.11. Wagner in 1877, drawn by "Spy" (*aka* Leslie Ward). © The Trustees of the British Museum.

from memory. Just because a conductor has a score in front of him does not mean he needs to read it. Conversely, if Wagner's eyesight made it difficult for him to follow a score while focusing on his musicians, then memorizing the music might have been a countering strategy. A conductor who peers short-sightedly at the music, as if unable to find his place, can rapidly become a figure of fun. Orchestral players often have a near-feral sensitivity to weakness in their conductors.[70]

Numerous contemporaries of Wagner spoke of his magnetic impact before an orchestra. In Hueffer's account of the Ninth in Bayreuth, for example, quoted at length above, he specifically mentions how the players in the orchestra felt that "the conductor's eye [was] looking at them during the whole performance."[71] Quite besides any personal magnetism on Wagner's part, this might actually have been a serendipitous side-effect of his wandering left eye. If it looked constantly elsewhere than the right, this could have left his musicians unsure as to the precise object of his gaze, resulting in each of them assuming it was *him*. All we can safely say is that wearing glasses does not seem to have detracted from Wagner's ability to inspire his musicians on the podium or in the pit.

The few images we have of Wagner as conductor thus provide very few answers. If anything, they pose even more questions about his conducting technique, his health and his rehearsal practices. We are on somewhat firmer ground when it comes to the physical documentation of his conducting activities in the form of scores and parts—though here, too, sources are not as copious as we might hope.

---

70   As confirmed by numerous orchestral players among the present writer's friends and colleagues; I also spent three years managing a symphony orchestra.

71   The ability to convince a large number of people that you are looking straight at each of them individually is something that today seems to be cultivated especially by politicians. The present writer experienced something along these lines at a university function in Pretoria attended by Nelson Mandela—already well into his eighties—who was able to walk past a long line of people (including me) while conveying the impression that he was making eye contact with each of us individually.

Annotated Scores and Parts

Wagner did not travel with a stock of his own orchestral parts and scores when he went on tour as a conductor (in this he differed from Berlioz, who took his scores and parts with him when he went out and about). Such luxuries were probably beyond Wagner's financial means, and his disorderly, peripatetic existence would in any case have made such long-term planning impossible. Circumstances several times compelled him to leave his place of residence in something of a hurry, whether fleeing his creditors in Riga in 1839, fleeing the failed Dresden Uprising in May 1849, fleeing domestic entanglements with the Wesendoncks in Zurich in 1858, or fleeing yet more creditors in Vienna in 1864. Such precipitous moves made it impossible for him to maintain a large, traveling library. In any hunt for traces of Wagner's conducting exploits, we are thus mostly dependent on the archives of institutions for which he conducted.

Orchestral parts for several of Wagner's own operas have indeed survived that were used under his direction, the earliest thus far discovered being those for *Der fliegende Holländer* used at the world premiere in Dresden in 1843.[72] But as already mentioned above, Wagner did not conduct the world premieres of his own operas after *Tannhäuser*, and in fact rarely conducted them at all after that, except occasionally as a guest. The frequent fires that consumed opera houses in the 19th century were hardly conducive to the preservation of combustible matter such as scores and parts, which makes it rather surprising that anything from that time has survived at all (the Zurich Theater burnt down on New Year's Eve 1889, destroying the building, its stage sets, parts, and scores; the Dresden Opera House had suffered a similar fate already in 1869). What's more, theater directors in the mid-19th century, at least in the smaller houses, were as expendable as soccer managers today, with short-term failure resulting in a rapid turnover of personnel at the top.[73] And when a director moved on—if he hadn't gone bankrupt first—he would sometimes pack up the parts and scores used by his musicians and singers, and take them to his next place of work (this was the fate of the parts for Wagner's supposed "arrangement" of Mozart's *Don Giovanni*

---

72   See the corresponding documentation for a project of the Bern University of the Arts HKB at www.hkb-interpretation.ch/index.php?id=93 (accessed October 2019).

73   For an account of the trials and tribulations of running the Zurich Theater in its early years, see Walton (2007): 26.

made for Zurich in 1850, which were taken away by the then theater director Philipp Kramer when he left the city not long afterwards).[74] As for Wagner's erstwhile places of employment in Magdeburg, Riga, Königsberg, and elsewhere, much of whatever managed to survive theatrical fires and pilfering personnel was probably destroyed in the Second World War anyway. It is highly unlikely that we shall ever discover parts or scores used there under Wagner's baton.

The orchestral parts used under Wagner's direction were never treated as relics, but kept in circulation and scribbled upon by later generations of musicians, generally making it impossible to tell what was annotated when, by whom, and at whose behest. In most places where he conducted as a guest, Wagner did not have the time or the authority to ensure that all parts were marked as he wanted (as noted above, his mammoth concert programs in London, for example, were almost all done on a single rehearsal). Some orchestral parts have survived in Zurich, however, that can be proven to include Wagner's desired markings. His main copyist, Adam Bauer, had a recognizable hand, and his invoices—paid by the concert society, not Wagner—specifically mention expression markings added on Wagner's instructions. Even these parts, however, are mostly incomplete.[75] There are parts for excerpts from Wagner's own *Rienzi*, but the most informative are annotated string parts for Mozart's *Jupiter* Symphony;[76] then there are a few parts for Beethoven's Fifth Symphony with meager expression markings in the *Adagio*, a viola part for Haydn's Symphony no. 104, and a seemingly full set of annotated parts for his arrangement of Gluck's overture to *Iphigenie in Aulis*, whose expression markings—devised by Wagner specifically for his performances in March 1854—largely match those given in his essay on the work in the *Neue Zeitschrift für Musik* on July 1, 1854, with the difference that the sudden dynamic shifts occur on the beat in the copied parts, but on the upbeat in the later article (see the illustrations below).[77]

---

74 See Walton (2007): 168–69; the "arrangement" probably existed more in marketing hype than in actual fact.

75 See the discussion of Wagner's conducting activities in Zurich and a list of his concerts in Walton (2007): 162–82. The extant performing materials are listed on the website of the Zentralbibliothek Zürich, at www.amg-zürich.ch/rubrik-dokumentationen/dirigenten/wagnerdirigent.pdf (accessed February 2019).

76 See Walton (2007): 171–72 and Moor (2019): 62–87.

77 See SSD 5: 111–22.

Figure 5.12. All traces of Wagner expunged: the Zurich Theater after the fire of New Year's Eve 1889; thanks to quick-thinking staff, the public was led out without any outbreak of panic, and no one died (the ETH Zurich, the Federal Institute of Technology, built by Wagner's friend Gottfried Semper, can be seen on the hill in the background to the right). Photo by Robert Breitinger, 1890. Zentralbibliothek Zürich, Breitinger, Cabinet III, Altstadt, C, Theaterbrand, 964, 965, 966/55/1890, http://doi.org/10.7891/e-manuscripta-34686 / Public Domain.

Wagner must have annotated scores of the works that he conducted, otherwise Adam Bauer and his other copyists would have had nothing to copy from. But no conducting score of Wagner's from the Classical or Romantic repertoire has survived with any autograph annotations. He had something of a bibliophile sensibility and was apparently loathe to make pencil markings in the books that he owned (his Bayreuth library is in general almost devoid of pencil annotations),[78] so it is also possible that he did not like marking up his scores except when copyists such as Bauer needed them. What's more, his own somewhat vagabond existence up to the time of his "rescue" by King Ludwig II meant that whatever conducting scores he might have owned could well have been left behind with the rest of his library

---

78   See Friedrich (1999): 13.

Figure 5.13. Gluck, Overture to *Iphigenie in Aulis*, mm. 51–82, first violin part copied by Adam Bauer for Wagner's performances in Zurich on March 7 and 21, 1854, with expression markings as stipulated by Wagner. Zentralbibliothek Zürich, AMG I 314: 4, http://doi.org/10.7891/e-manuscripta-16 / Public Domain.

Figure 5.14. Gluck, Overture to *Iphigenie in Aulis*, mm. 62–74. Music example from Wagner's article in the *Neue Zeitschrift für Musik* of July 1, 1854, explaining his interpretation of the work. Assuming that Bauer copied Wagner's expression markings accurately for the performances in the previous March, Wagner has by now moved his sudden dynamic changes to the eighth-note upbeat each time, where before they were placed on the first beat of the measure.

whenever he was compelled to move on. We can assume that he will have left behind any conducting scores when he and Minna fled from their creditors in Riga in 1839; when he fled from Dresden in 1849, he had to leave behind his library, only for it to be confiscated to pay off his debts.[79] When he fled Zurich (and Minna) nine years later, his abandoned wife got her revenge by publicly selling off their household goods, and presumably dispersed much of his library, too, though we have no details of that.[80]

We must also consider the possibility that Wagner did not need to conduct with annotated scores because he stored them in his head. We know that Wagner was able to conduct from memory, though we have few details of how often he did so, nor of how often he also rehearsed without a score. His friend Gustav Kietz wrote that Wagner rehearsed and conducted Beethoven's Ninth in Dresden from memory in 1846 (see p. 18 above), so he presumably conducted that symphony from memory again at his subsequent performances of it in Dresden. There are no reports of his having conducted from memory in Zurich—but likewise, there are none of his having expressly conducted with a score either. We know that he conducted from memory at his guest concerts in London in 1855, because this was mentioned twenty years later in the *Musical Standard*,[81] though again we have no details about whether this applied to just the standard classical repertoire or to all his concerts (probably the former, since Wagner had to conduct a large repertoire with very little rehearsal, including works by local composers that he had never conducted before, and never would again). By early 1872, in a review of Wagner's recent concert in Mannheim that featured works of his own, Beethoven's Seventh Symphony, and the Overture to Mozart's *Magic Flute*, Richard Pohl was able to remark that "Wagner always conducts from memory";[82] and Adolf Wallnöfer's report of Beethoven's Ninth under Wagner in Bayreuth on May 22, 1872 states clearly that he rehearsed and conducted the work without a score. From the 1860s onwards, however, Wagner's concerts mostly comprised extracts from his own works and a small number of standard repertoire works by Mozart, Beethoven, & Co. that he had already conducted several times over the years. Conducting a Classical symphony from memory is not so difficult if the orchestra is well trained,

---

79   See von Westernhagen (1966): 75–76.

80   See Walton (2007): 77.

81   Anon.; short news notice without title, in *The Musical Standard* 9/581 (September 18, 1875), 193. See also p. 158 above.

82   Pohl (1872): 15.

because it can usually run on autopilot if the conductor loses his way for a moment. But rehearsing from memory, as Wagner clearly did on occasion, is a very different matter. One has to be able to stop, start, repeat passages, and give instructions to individual musicians. To rehearse Beethoven's Ninth without a score, as Wagner clearly did on more than one occasion, was by any measure a major feat of memory and concentration (not least because he conducted it so rarely). It was surely also intended as a theatrical gesture to strike his musicians with awe, and ensure that they gave him their full attention.

Two scores have nevertheless survived that bear annotations based on Wagner's interpretation. His friend Heinrich Sczadrowsky (1828–78), music director in St. Gallen in the mid-1850s, copied out Wagner's anno-tated score of the Overture to *Iphigenie* in spring 1856—a fact confirmed by Sczadrowsky himself in a note on the inside cover ("Aus Wagners Partitur kopirt [*sic*] StGallen, Frühling 1856"). The original is lost, but Sczadrowsky's copy recently surfaced and has been donated to the Zentralbibliothek Zürich;[83] its annotations (see below) largely match those in the parts in the Zentralbibliothek Zürich already discussed above. And as is discussed in greater detail below, Adolf Wallnöfer, who was a member of the chorus for the 1872 Bayreuth performance of Beethoven's Ninth, took the trouble to annotate his own copy of the orchestral score with Wagner's copious instruc-tions and expression markings as communicated in rehearsal. Wallnöfer later donated it to the Bayreuth archives.

As outlined above, the last time that Wagner was able to rehearse and per-form his preferred concert repertoire on a regular basis was in Zurich from 1850 to 1855; the last time he conducted such a broad repertoire at all was in London in the latter year (albeit with next to no rehearsal time). So when one considers how the impact of Wagner's interpretation of certain works can still be heard in recordings from the mid-20th century, it is astonishing to consider how rarely he himself conducted them. To give just one exam-ple: he conducted Weber's Overture to *Der Freischütz* only five times, the last of these being in Vienna in late 1863, as he himself recalls in *Über das Dirigieren* (see p. 64). And yet conductors such as Felix Weingartner—born in the same year as Wagner's Viennese performance—were over seventy years later still performing this work as Wagner had stipulated in the aforemen-tioned essay (see footnote 84 in chapter 3).

---

83   Shelfmark Ms Q 861.

Figure 5.15. Gluck, Overture to *Iphigenie in Aulis*, mm. 63–69, Heinrich Sczadrowsky's copy of March 1856, presumably made from Wagner's personal score (since lost). The dynamic changes occur here on the upbeat each time, as in Wagner's article in the *Neue Zeitschrift* (see Figure 5.14). Zentralbibliothek Zürich, Ms Q 861, http://doi.org/10.7891/e-manuscripta-16406 / Public Domain.

Conductors, commentators, and critics alike are unanimous in maintaining that Richard Wagner overall had a more significant impact on the history of conducting than any other musician of the 19th century. He successfully initiated a tradition of performance practice that spread across the western world, and to which all manner of musicians pledged allegiance even long after his death, from Gustav Mahler and Richard Strauss to Wilhelm Furtwängler, and which echoes on in the work of conductors today such as Christian Thielemann. As we shall see below, Wagner's actual performances seem to have had less of an impact on performance practice than did his writings on interpretation—primarily the texts given in translation in the present volume.

Writing on Conducting—Mania, Helmsmen, and Theory

A number of music treatises of the 18th and early 19th centuries offer a brief discussion of the ways and means of beating time and directing an ensemble,[84] but it was only after the emergence of conducting as an independent art in the second quarter of the 19th century that a discourse truly began to form around it. One of the first to write an essay specifically on conducting was Robert Schumann, in a front-page article in his *Neue Zeitschrift für Musik* on April 15, 1836 (the author is actually named as "mr," but Schumann's contemporaries seem to have assumed that he was the author, and current scholarship believes the same).[85] However, this "Vom Dirigiren und insbesondere von der Manie des Dirigirens" (About Conducting, especially about the Conducting Mania) was primarily polemical, and hardly appreciative of the new genre of musician: "A good orchestra … only needs to be conducted in symphonies, overtures etc. at the start of a movement and when the tempo changes. Apart from that, the conductor can stand calmly at his music stand, read the score and listen for when his commands are necessary again."[86] Eyewitnesses admittedly testify to having occasionally seen both Weber and Mendelssohn cease beating time during a performance, so Schumann's stance was perhaps just an extreme version of what seems to have been a dwindling tradition. But by all accounts, Weber and Mendelssohn rehearsed meticulously enough to ensure a fine ensemble with or without their constant intervention. Given that neither rehearsing, nor man-management, nor time-beating, were strongpoints of Schumann himself, it is small wonder that his own later attempt at a conducting career was disastrous.[87]

Just eight years after Schumann's article, conducting had become established enough for it to warrant a whole treatise of its own. In 1844, the Austrian composer and violinist Ferdinand Simon Gassner (1798–1851) published his *Dirigent und Ripienist für angehende Musikdirigenten,*

---

84 See, for example, chapter 5 ("Taktschlagen und Doppeldirektion im 18. Jahrhundert") in Schünemann (1913): 116–253, and Christensen (2001).

85 Did "mr" perhaps mean "Meister Raro"? Raro was one of the many pseudonyms Schumann used in his journal; see Vosteen (2001): 1, xxv. Richard Pohl (*aka* "Hoplit") wrote in the *Neue Zeitschrift für Musik* on January 1, 1854 that Schumann was presumably the author of the article in question; since he knew Schumann, and since Schumann read the journal and seems to have made no attempt to correct this claim (his breakdown still lay several weeks in the future), we may assume that Pohl was correct. See [Pohl] (1854): 6 and Stollberg et al. (2015): 79, 93, 144.

86 [Schumann] (1836): 129.

87 See the summary of Schumann's conducting by a local critic in Anon. (1853); it is admittedly something of a hatchet-job, but other contemporary reports suggest that it is not too far from the truth.

Musiker und Musikfreunde (Conductor and Ripienist, for Aspiring Music Conductors, Musicians and Music-Lovers), comprising 160 pages of solid advice and information, much of which has lost none of its validity—such as how a conductor must check for mistakes in his score, and ensure that the score and all the parts have the same markings and the same rehearsal numbers. He explains about tuning up, the importance of sectional rehearsals, how the tempo must vary depending on the acoustic of the hall, and how to beat different meters. Gassner also includes an appendix with orchestral seating plans for different institutions, from Berlin to Dresden, Munich, Vienna, and elsewhere.

Wagner only began to engage with the topic of conducting in his writings in the early 1850s, after having completed various big theoretical works and an autobiography in his Swiss exile (*Art and Revolution, The Artwork of the Future, Opera and Drama* etc., then his memoir *A Communication to my Friends*, all written from 1849 to 1851). There is a certain logic to this; after having described his aesthetic ideas and the story of his life thus far, the next natural step was to put into prose how conductors and directors should translate his ideas into practice on stage and in the pit. *Tannhäuser* was enjoying a surge of popularity in 1852, but the continuing validity of the arrest warrant on Wagner in the German states meant that he was stuck in Switzerland, unable to cross the border to oversee or conduct any of the productions being organized. The only way he could hope to ensure "correct" performances was by sending out instructions in writing. Many of Wagner's extant letters from 1852 are devoted to ensuring that theaters and conductors had the right materials and knew what he wanted. But by the second half of the year, he had decided that issuing a general set of guidelines for staging *Tannhäuser* was the most sensible way forward. The result was a small, standalone volume of just over forty pages published by Schulthess of Zurich in the fall of 1852.[88] It is entitled *Über die Aufführung des Tannhäuser. Eine Mitteilung an die Dirigenten und Darsteller dieser Oper vom Dichter und Tonsetzer derselben* (On the Performance of Tannhäuser. A Communication to the Conductors and Performers of this Opera by the Poet and Composer of the Same; it seems Wagner assumed people would already know his name, which is otherwise absent here).

Despite the title of this little book, Wagner's prime concern is not how to conduct his work, let alone to offer any theoretical considerations about the

---

88   Wagner mentions writing this book in a letter of August 14, 1852 to Theodor Uhlig. See SB 4: 443–45, here 444.

art of conducting in general, but how the scenic representation and the music of *Tannhäuser* can best function together. "The musical conductors in our theaters have become almost completely accustomed to ignoring the stage setting … while our stage directors … completely ignore the orchestra,"[89] he complains, and his recommendations to conductors here are couched largely in terms of establishing a rapport between stage and pit. He wants all the singers to be brought together at the start for a dramatic reading of their roles, with the chorus director present to read the chorus part, and the stage director and the conductor similarly at hand to oversee it all. What's more, this rehearsal should be repeated as often as necessary until everyone has internalized their parts, he says. Only then may the sung rehearsals begin.[90] The vocal line (with text) should be included in every orchestral part so that the musicians in the pit know exactly what is happening on the stage at any time (as far as we are aware, Wagner never managed to achieve this whenever the orchestral parts to his operas were copied or published). Wagner then explains at great length how he had been compelled to cut assorted passages in *Tannhäuser* in Dresden, and why these cuts have to be reversed in future. From p. 23 in the original edition, he finally provides three pages of detail about how the Overture to the opera should be performed. But while he does ask here or there for an *accelerando* or a *decelerando*, he is mostly concerned with making minor corrections to the printed score—deleting an accent in the first violin part, changing a *fortepiano* to just *piano*[91]—or reminding the conductor to get the balance right when the strings are divided, to make sure the clarinet isn't obscured by the violins, and suchlike.[92] The reason for this sudden specificity lies in Wagner having copied much of this passage from a letter of March 18, 1852 to his friend the conductor Gustav Schmidt in Frankfurt, who had written to ask his advice in advance of a planned performance of the Overture.[93] Wagner had only recently conducted the Overture in Zurich himself, so he knew exactly where he wanted changes made to the score of it. Many of his extant letters of early 1852 are to string players whom he needed to bolster his numbers in the Zurich orchestra, and this experience is reflected in his booklet later that year, where he insists that the string section has to be "especially large" for the Overture, though his

89   SSD 5: 124.
90   Ibid.: 126–27.
91   Ibid.: 142–43.
92   Ibid.: 143.
93   SB 4: 315–18.

insistence on at least "four good violists" suggests that he knew he had to be economical with his ambitions for provincial German orchestras.[94] By contrast, Berlioz's orchestration treatise in both its first and second editions, of 1843 and 1855 respectively, recommended six violas for the opéra-comique, eight for grand opéra and eighteen for a concert orchestra.[95]

Occasionally, Wagner touches on an issue that he revisited at much greater length in the essays published in the present volume—such as when he insists on the wind playing the melody of the Pilgrims' Chorus as if they were singing it, all breathing at the same time (though he adds that when the trombones later play this theme *forte*, they should breathe as often as they need to ensure strength of tone).[96] "Singing" by the orchestra is a major concern of Wagner's in *Über das Dirigieren*, nearly two decades later (see the section on "melos" below). However, Wagner here still recommends the use of his metronome markings—albeit with the caveat that the tempi are not to be regarded as fixed, but are to be adapted according to the musical and dramatic situation.[97] In *Über das Dirigieren*, Wagner would reject the use of the metronome altogether.

This essay on performing *Tannhäuser* was followed by a shorter text on performing *Der fliegende Holländer*, in which Wagner is once again concerned more with the unity of music and action than with the mechanics of conducting (his very first sentence insists on how conductor and stage director must work together). The closest Wagner gets to discussing interpretive details for conductors is in his brief essay of 1854 on performing Gluck's Overture to his *Iphigenie in Aulis*, already mentioned above, in which he offers a few details of his desired dynamics (see Figures 5.13 and 5.14) and insists on a constant tempo throughout, instead of a shift to a swifter tempo after the introduction, as had been customary until then. All these essays intimate a growing desire to communicate his ideas about performing music, though his prime concern remains how to perform *his* music. And in those instances where he discusses the works of other men—as in his concert essays on Beethoven's *Eroica* Symphony or the *Coriolanus* Overture,[98] also from 1852—he still subscribes to the kind of programmatic description such as he had devised for Beethoven's Ninth Symphony in Dresden in 1846, when he

---

94   SSD 5: 145.
95   See Berlioz (1843): 285 and (1855): 294.
96   SSD 5: 142.
97   Ibid.: 144.
98   SSD 5: 169–72 and 173–76.

came up with a "program" for that work based on Goethe's *Faust*. Since the topic of the present book is Wagner's art of conducting, I have not included these essays in translation here.

The first member of the "New German School" to write about conducting *per se* (though that school was not yet designated thus) was Franz Liszt, who published a letter in the *Neue Zeitschrift für Musik* on December 16, 1853 in response to criticism of his own conducting at a recent music festival in Karlsruhe. It is just three columns long, but occupies an important place in the history of the art because Liszt here touches on issues that Wagner and others would later expand upon. He insists that music from late Beethoven onwards (thus including works by Wagner and Berlioz) requires a new, progressive approach to all parameters of interpretation, from rhythm to phrasing. He insists that simply beating time would be a death sentence to this music. He uses the word "Taktschläger" (time-beater) pejoratively, as would Wagner several years later (see pp. 80 and 102), and towards the close he sums up the function of a conductor in words that were often quoted thereafter: "Wir sind Steuermänner und keine Ruderknechte" (We are helmsmen, not oarsmen).[99] Shortly afterwards, over the space of four issues in the same journal, Richard Pohl published an article entitled "The Conducting Mania," in which he referred back specifically to Schumann's article of 1836 in order to bolster Liszt's arguments against "time-beating"—Pohl clearly shared Schumann's belief that a good conductor ought to do very little on the podium indeed. He nevertheless endeavored to square his chosen circle by offering extensive praise of Hector Berlioz as conductor, despite the fact that he "beat every measure clearly."[100] Pohl's sympathies were generally with the progressives of his day (his wife was a harpist in Liszt's Weimar orchestra), but he also had high praise for Mendelssohn's conducting. He mentions Wagner, however, only with regard to his instructions on conducting his *Tannhäuser*, not in his capacity as a conductor himself.

Just eighteen months later, in the summer of 1855, Berlioz wrote the first-ever comprehensive guide to conducting: *Le chef d'orchestre. Théorie de son art* (The Conductor: [The] Theory of his Art). It had been commissioned by Alfred Novello of the English publishing company that bore his name, though it was first published in the original French, in Paris, in late 1855 as a supplement to a revised edition of Berlioz's treatise on orchestration.[101]

---

99   See Liszt (1853).
100 See [Pohl] (1854): 37 (on Mendelssohn), 38–39 (on Berlioz).
101 Berlioz (1855): 299–312.

Translations into German and into English (the latter by Novello's sister, Mary Cowden Clarke) appeared the following year.[102] This essay on conducting was also serialized in the *Revue et gazette musicale* in Paris in early 1856, published separately by Schonenberger that same year,[103] and serialized in English by the *Musical Times* (Novello's house journal) in the summer of 1856.[104] Berlioz's international reputation as a conductor no doubt helped to popularize the ideas he expounded in his essay. He offers primarily practical advice, with diagrams of beating patterns, a discussion of how and where the conductor should stand, and so forth. Richard Wagner waited until after Berlioz's death, fourteen years later, before finally making his own contribution to the discourse on conducting.

Berlioz the Catalyst?

It is clear from the documentary sources that Wagner spent at least one and a half decades planning his own essay on conducting before finally putting pen to paper in late 1869. It is possible that his original idea had been for someone else to write it. After settling in Zurich in 1849, Wagner engaged in a detailed correspondence with his friend Theodor Uhlig (1822–53), a sometime violinist in the Dresden orchestra and now a noted critic. Uhlig had done much to shift the *Neue Zeitschrift für Musik* away from a Schumannian aesthetic under its new editor Franz Brendel, making it instead a mouthpiece for Wagner's ideas. Uhlig was clearly Wagner's closest confidant at the time— he was even allowed to read *Opera and Drama* before its publication—and had been much impressed by Wagner's interpretations of Beethoven back in Dresden. In the same letter of late February 1852 in which Wagner first mentions meeting the Wesendoncks, he suggests that Uhlig should write an article entitled either "On the Direction of Beethoven's Instrumental Works" or "R.W. as Conductor of B.['s] Instrumental Works."[105] Wagner offers concrete suggestions as to what Uhlig should write; his prime concern is here neither tempo nor melody nor transitions of any kind—all major

---

102 Berlioz (1856c and 1856b).

103 Berlioz (1856a).

104 For details of the genesis and early publication history of Berlioz's essay on conducting, see Macdonald (2002): xxiii–xxv. I am also grateful to Julian Rushton for providing information on Berlioz.

105 SB 4: 297–302, here 299.

topics in *Über das Dirigieren* nearly two decades later—but to emphasize how only he, Wagner, has thus far understood Beethoven, because only he has discerned the "poetic content of [Beethoven's] musical works."[106] He also suggests that Uhlig could reprint the program to the Ninth Symphony that Wagner had written and disseminated for his first Palm Sunday performance of the work back in Dresden in 1846—and he goes on to criticize Mendelssohn for having misunderstood Beethoven and for supposedly getting his tempi wrong (this, by contrast, is indeed a topic that crops up again in *Über das Dirigieren*).

Uhlig did publish a series of articles about Beethoven later that same year, though they were entitled "Über den dichterischen Gehalt Beethoven'scher Tonwerke" (On the Poetic Content of Beethoven's Compositions), and their topic was the extra-musical content of Beethoven's music, not any nitty-gritty about how one might perform them. Wagner's poetic program for the Ninth was (re-)printed as the second installment of Uhlig's essay,[107] his program for the *Eroica* Symphony in his third installment,[108] that for *Coriolanus* in the fourth.[109] Uhlig was everywhere at pains to explain how identifying the "program" behind a work was necessary for its performance; he even quotes Wagner's Zurich musicians as having demanded to know the program behind his *Tannhäuser* Overture, because "then they would play it better."[110] Uhlig was one of the few writers whom Wagner ever truly trusted to put the composer's ideas into the writer's own words. But we shall never know if Wagner had intended his friend to write more about his conducting aesthetic, because Uhlig died (presumably of tuberculosis) on January 3, 1853, just a few weeks after the publication of his last installment on Wagner and Beethoven.

As Egon Voss has remarked, an essay entitled *Über das Dirigieren* is first mentioned by Wagner in a list of articles he made at around the turn of the year 1856–57, possibly earlier[111]—though it is clear that this was something he was merely planning at the time, not a finished product. A careful reading of the first page of Wagner's essay of 1869 suggests that we should

106 Ibid.
107 Uhlig (1852): II.
108 Uhlig (1852): III.
109 Uhlig (1852): IV.
110 Uhlig (1852): III, 166.
111 Voss (2015): 91.

indeed date the gestation of *Über das Dirigieren* to the mid-1850s. Wagner writes:

> My assessment of things is not addressed to conductors themselves, but to musicians and singers, for they alone can sense properly whether they are being conducted either well or badly … I do not intend to construct any system here.[112]

When Wagner insists that he is "not" going to do something, it is often reasonable to assume an inferred criticism of someone else who has done just that. This last sentence could thus be interpreted as a riposte to some unnamed party who had indeed endeavored to construct a "system" of conducting. We have a prime candidate for this: Hector Berlioz, whose *Le chef d'orchestre* was published at the very time that Wagner seems to have begun planning his own article. Wagner must have known that Berlioz had been the Old Philharmonic's first choice of conductor in London back in 1855, for it was openly mentioned in the press (we know that Wagner read the London critics, because he was still complaining about them in *Über das Dirigieren* fourteen years later). Alfred Novello secured the English rights for Berlioz's treatise on orchestration and commissioned his essay on conducting towards the end of June 1855.[113] This was when Wagner was about to leave London, though he too had mingled with the Novellos—the soprano Clara Novello, sister to both Alfred and Mary, Berlioz's soon-to-be translator, sang solo arias in two of Wagner's London concerts. Wagner was probably aware of Berlioz having been offered a contract to commit his conducting precepts to paper—and if he didn't yet know it, he soon would, given the essay's rapid dissemination in journals and in book form in the months thereafter, in English, German, and French. It will have been bad enough for Wagner's ego that Berlioz got better concert reviews in London, but for him to be given the opportunity to publicize his conducting "theory" too will have rankled all the more.

Wagner and Berlioz had known each other since the former's first sojourn in Paris from 1839 to 1842. Berlioz was ten years older than Wagner and already famous at that time, whereas Wagner was a penniless would-be artist whose ambitions were far greater than his achievements and clearly starry-eyed and -eared at what he heard by Berlioz in Paris. His *Roméo et Juliette* Symphony impressed Wagner most of all. Berlioz helped Wagner to publish

112 SSD 8: 261 and above, p. 23.
113 Berlioz's letter of acceptance is dated June 30, 1855 (the same day that Wagner arrived back in Zurich). See Berlioz ed. Citron (1989): 122.

articles in the French musical press, and Wagner repaid the compliment by heaping praise on him in his "report from Paris" of May 5, 1841 for the *Abend-Zeitung* in Dresden (as a composer, he is "brilliant," his *Symphonie fantastique* a "miracle," and "among Berlioz's most superb characteristics, we have to mention his ability as a conductor").[114] Wagner is not wholly uncritical, but his reservations really only serve to underline his praise. Two years later, when Wagner was capellmeister to the Court Opera in Dresden, Berlioz visited as a guest and the two renewed their acquaintance. They met again on Wagner's visits to Paris in the years immediately after the failed Dresden Uprising of May 1849. Wagner's early *Faust Overture* had been partly inspired by *Roméo et Juliette*, and Berlioz's technique of thematic transformation bore obvious similarities to the leitmotif technique that Wagner developed in the early 1850s. Their relationship remained superficially cordial, though the varying fortunes of the two men over the years inevitably meant that mutual admiration was tempered by a certain degree of rivalry.

Liszt had known Berlioz for far longer. His piano transcription of the *Symphonie fantastique* had played a major role in its wider propagation back in the 1830s, and the early 1850s saw Liszt utilize his position as music director in Weimar to invest increasing energies in promoting Berlioz's music. This worried Wagner, who had several times depended on Liszt's help since fleeing Dresden in 1849, and who tended to assume that others shared his own opinion of his uniqueness. Wagner's shifting opinion of Berlioz found expression in *Opera and Drama* in 1850–51. Back in his report from Paris of May 5, 1841, he had stated unequivocally that Berlioz had understood Beethoven's symphonies;[115] now he made it clear that Berlioz had not.[116] He even mocked him as a false "Messiah" of the musical world,[117] much as he would Johannes Brahms nearly two decades later in *Über das Dirigieren*. When Liszt staged Berlioz's opera *Benvenuto Cellini* in Weimar as part of a Berlioz week in March 1852, Wagner even wrote to Hans von Bülow to complain that Liszt's insistence on conducting works by Berlioz and Meyerbeer could "completely destroy everything that he has done for me up to now," and he expressed astonishment that his ideas in *Opera and Drama*

---

114 *Pariser Berichte für die Dresdener Abendzeitung no. III*, as printed in SSD 12: 87–95, here 90.

115 SSD 12: 88.

116 See the passages about Berlioz in *Opera and Drama*, SSD 3: 282–86, especially 286 here.

117 SSD 3: 283.

had clearly not been properly understood (Wagner apparently assumed that Liszt would have read his sprawling tract from cover to cover and agreed with everything).[118]

Liszt's own correspondence with Wagner leaves no doubt that he knew of the latter's envy of Berlioz, though he remained unconcerned. The following November, he organized further performances of *Benvenuto Cellini* as part of a festival to which the composer himself was invited as a guest conductor. Hans von Bülow was involved in the preparations, and now became an enthusiastic convert to the Berliozian cause himself. (It was perhaps not by chance that Wagner decided to organize a "Wagner festival" of his own, half a year later in Zurich, in May 1853—though in the absence of any infrastructure akin to Weimar's, he had to do almost all the organizing himself.) Wagner's envy of Berlioz—and of the attention Liszt was giving him—found strange expression in a letter from Wagner to Liszt of September 8, 1852, in which he complained how Berlioz did not understand drama because he didn't have the right librettist.

> He needs a poet who fulfils him through and through, who *compels* him with rapture [Entzücken], and who is to him what man is to woman ... Can I help him? You don't want [my own libretto for] Wiland [i.e. *Wieland der Schmied*] ... Do you want to offer it to Berlioz?[119]

The word "Entzücken" signified many different degrees of delight in Wagner's time (as also in our own), up to and including sexual climax (as in the "vollste[s] Entzücken" or "fullest rapture" that Tannhäuser enjoys "in Venus's arms," as Wagner would write in his 1854 essay on performing *Tannhäuser*).[120] Wagner had already introduced the gendered metaphor of the male poetic seed fertilizing music-as-woman in his recent *Opera and Drama*. But the imagery of a barren Berlioz in need of forceful penetration and fertilization by Wagner's seed is quite extraordinary (whether the "rapture" involved is to be experienced by the penetrator, the penetrated, or both, remains unclear). Metaphors of rape are otherwise uncommon in Wagner's writings (though an oblique one does occur in *Über das Dirigieren*; see p. 69).

---

118 Wagner to von Bülow, undated, but clearly February–March 1852, SB 4: 250–53, here 251.

119 Wagner to Liszt, September 8, 1852, SB 4: 457–61, here 459.

120 See SSD 5: 123–59, here 152.

In April 1854, Berlioz even seems to have come close to being appointed *de facto* to Wagner's old job in Dresden. In a letter of that month, Hans von Bülow wrote a glowing report to Liszt about Berlioz's recent concerts in the city, and mentioned that August von Lüttichau, the intendant of the Dresden theaters, was hoping to appoint the man as capellmeister.[121] No such post materialized, but we may assume that Wagner got wind of it, given his many existing contacts back in Dresden. By the time he and Berlioz conducted their rival orchestras in London in mid-1855, Wagner thus had reason enough to see Berlioz as a serious competitor who was encroaching more and more on "his" territory, and perfectly capable of swaying the affections of the men he had hitherto imagined he could count on the most.[122]

Wagner had been in London for several weeks by the time Berlioz arrived in the early summer of 1855. They met on cordial terms; Berlioz wrote to Liszt on June 25, 1855 after Wagner's last concert to assure him that they had become the best of friends,[123] and Wagner made sure to say the same to Liszt two weeks later, in a letter of July 5.[124] But matters between them were far from straightforward, and Berlioz was not above a spot of *Schadenfreude* himself. Feeling assured of his own superior popularity, he wrote to August Morel on June 2, 1855 that Wagner was "succumbing to attacks from all the English press. But they say that he is remaining calm, being assured that he will be the master of the music world *in fifty years.*"[125] The London journal *The Musical World* had begun serializing Wagner's *Opera and Drama* in translation the previous spring (discussed in detail below), and on June 30, 1855, just days after Wagner left London, it took the opportunity to publish a long passage from that book in which Wagner criticized Berlioz as a "lamentable" composer, a "tragic victim" who had aspired but failed to understand and emulate Beethoven.[126] Publishing this now was probably the editor's way of making Wagner seem petty towards his more popular rival, and a letter

121 Hans von Bülow to Liszt, letter of April 30, 1854, in [Lipsius] (1898): 75–81, here 77.
122 For an in-depth discussion of the relationship between Wagner and Berlioz, see Kolb (2009).
123 Berlioz to Liszt, June 24–25, 1855, in Berlioz ed. Citron (1989): 115–18.
124 Wagner to Liszt, July 5, 1855, SB 7: 238–41, here 240.
125 Berlioz ed. Citron (1989): 95–96, here 96. Emphasis in original.
126 Wagner: "Opera and Drama. Part I. Opera and the constitution of music. Chapter V," *The Musical World* 33/26 (June 30, 1855), 407–9, here especially 408–9.

of July 3, 1855 from Berlioz to his friend Théodore Ritter makes it evident that he was indeed riled, and now doubted the sincerity of Wagner's recent protestations of affection. As for Wagner's conducting style, Berlioz wrote to Ritter merely that "he conducts in the free style like [Karl] Klindworth plays the piano."[127]

Whether or not Wagner sensed Berlioz's apparent feelings of superiority, he got his own back in *Mein Leben* anyway, where he accorded him that strange, condescending form of praise that was his specialty.[128] Poor, exhausted Berlioz had gone to London because he needed the money, says Wagner, whereas *he* had gone there merely to provide himself with a welcome distraction (Wagner was in fact as desperate as anyone to get his hands on English pounds). Wagner's praise of Berlioz's "superb" conducting back in 1841 was now forgotten; he might be a "formidably talented" man, wrote Wagner in *Mein Leben*, but he was really only a "vulgar time-beater." What's more, Berlioz had supposedly been envious of the "enthusiasm" that Wagner now claimed to have inspired in London—though this was a shameless, complete reversal of the facts.[129] Wagner rarely forgot or forgave being upstaged.

Berlioz is never mentioned by name in *Über das Dirigieren*, but it seems likely that he had in fact been the principal catalyst for it. His own essay on conducting is indeed "systematic," with his subtitle itself declaring his intention to explain the "theory" of the conductor's art (*Théorie de son art*). Unlike Berlioz, Wagner offers no practical advice about beating patterns or the like, and when he does write about beating time, he focuses on *rubato*—essentially beating "out" of time. Wagner also rejects the use of metronome markings, and does so with such insistence that this, too, might be an implicit rejection of Berlioz, who highly recommends their use in his own treatise (see p. 39 above). The fact that Berlioz died on March 8, 1869 might even have emboldened Wagner to commit his essay to paper at last—after all, there was now no danger that Berlioz would ever pen a reply to it in turn. Wagner was repeatedly drawn to write about music in reaction to the activities of men towards whom he was ambivalent (especially when he deemed them successful enough to pose some kind of threat). So just because Berlioz remains unmentioned in *Über das Dirigieren* does not mean that he was not its real point of origin. As Peter Bloom has observed, and as Cosima's diaries prove,

127 Berlioz to Théodore Ritter, July 3, 1855, in Berlioz ed. Citron (1989):123–26, here 125.
128 For a discussion of Wagner's ambivalence towards the talented, see below.
129 ML: 533–34.

Berlioz was very much on Wagner's mind at this time.[130] Wagner began an article about him after hearing the news of his death, though it remained only a fragment,[131] and he complained to Cosima on April 7, 1869 that the man's passing meant he could now write only good things about him[132]— which gives us a pertinent reason why Berlioz's name is absent from *Über das Dirigieren*. He remained an intermittent topic of conversation between Wagner and Cosima into the summer of 1869, and returned again when they began reading his *Mémoires* in the spring of 1870, just a few weeks after Wagner published the final installment of his conducting essay.[133] On July 5, 1870, Wagner criticized him for having been unable to construct his themes "so that the main melody always sounds through," naming the appearance of the "love theme" (the *idée fixe*) in the ball scene of the *Symphonie fantastique* as such an instance ("it sounds like the bass line," he said).[134] This seems distinctly evocative of the insistence Wagner had placed on the primacy of the melodic content in *Über das Dirigieren* just a few months earlier. It is also significant that Wagner wrote *Über das Dirigieren* at roughly the same time that he was dictating to Cosima his reminiscences of his conducting activities in Zurich and London, which naturally meant recalling his conducting rivalry with Berlioz in the latter city.[135] Berlioz thus seems to have been haunting Wagner throughout much of 1869 and 1870.

Über das Dirigieren—Early Impact

Wagner published his first installment of *Über das Dirigieren*—About Conducting—in the *Neue Zeitschrift für Musik* on November 26, 1869. Further installments appeared over the next eight numbers, up to and including the fourth issue of the next year's journal, published on January 21, 1870. Wagner's contributions were in each case featured on the front page, except for issue 1 on January 1, 1870, which began with an article

---

130 Bloom (2000): 246.
131 "Fragment eines Aufsatzes über Hector Berlioz," in SSD 12: 312.
132 CWT 1: 82.
133 See CWT 1: 223.
134 CWT 1: 254.
135 We cannot date these passages precisely, but Wagner added the footnote "written in the year 1869" to his reminiscences of autumn 1853. See ML: 514. His reminiscences of London begin not long after; see ML: 527.

by Ludwig Nohl about the forthcoming Beethoven centenary.[136] The complete essay was issued in book form in spring 1870 by Kahnt of Leipzig, and was included in the eighth volume of Wagner's collected writings, published by Fritzsch in Leipzig in 1873.

Über das Dirigieren did not have the immediate transnational impact that Berlioz's essay had enjoyed back in the mid-1850s, though it did appear in spring 1870 in installments in the German-language journal *New Yorker Musik-Zeitung* and attracted some attention in the Francophone and Anglophone worlds. On April 21, 1870, *Le guide musical* of Brussels and Paris included an anonymous, brief notice that Wagner had just published a book entitled "sur l'art de conduire l'orchestre" (On the Art of Directing the Orchestra), adding merely that "the title is more inoffensive than the content of this opuscule."[137] Excerpts from the essay itself were published in English from June to August 1870 in *Dwight's Journal of Music* in Boston and then reprinted in part later that summer by the London journal *The Orchestra*, which referred to Wagner's "celebrated pamphlet 'Ueber das Dirigieren'"[138] (see the section "Wagner in Translation" below for further details).

When we consider the early reception history of this essay, however, "celebrated" seems a considerable exaggeration. To be sure, the Wagnerites were delighted with it. It was one of Wagner's essays about which Nietzsche remained long enthusiastic; in a letter to Carl von Gersdorff of March 11, 1870, he compared it favorably to Schopenhauer's essay "Über die Universitäts-Philosophie,"[139] and he praised it again in *Richard Wagner in Bayreuth* in 1876.[140] But the immediate response to *Über das Dirigieren* was actually rather muted—so much so that in his review of the book for the *Neue Freie Presse* in Vienna of June 25, 1870, Eduard Hanslick remarked that it "has received strikingly few reviews in the journals."[141] Some critics

---

136 See Nohl (1870).

137 Listed in the column "Allemagne," *Le guide musical*, 16/16 (April 21, 1870), no page numbers.

138 Anon.: "Wagner on conducting," *The Orchestra*, 14/365 (September 23, 1870): 417.

139 Schopenhauer (1877): 51-212. See Nietzsche to Carl von Gersdorff, Basel, March 11, 1870. Nietzsche (2009–): www.nietzschesource.org/#eKGWB/BVN-1870,65 (accessed June 2019).

140 Nietzsche (1992): 283.

141 Hanslick (1870).

were less than impressed—Ferdinand Hiller wrote at length in the *Kölnische Zeitung* on April 15, 1870 of how it was "brimming with falsities and injustices"—but this was hardly surprising, since he himself is mocked in its pages, and he was in any case already engaged in a longstanding battle against Wagner and the "New German School."[142] Hanslick was scathing about the essay, though, as was his wont, he offered concrete reasons for his criticism. He rightly called *Über das Dirigieren* a pendant to *Jewishness in Music*, and expressed astonishment at Wagner's continuing obsession with the supposedly malign influence of Mendelssohn. It was, thus Hanslick, "without precedent that a creative artist should judge his colleagues in so disdainful, arrogant a manner." Wagner is only interested in himself, says Hanslick: he is "the greatest living egoist."[143] The review by Heinrich Dorn in the *Neue Berliner Musikzeitung* was only slightly less unfavorable. He made fun of Wagner's supposedly deep insights, finding them at times blindingly obvious—such as his insistence on how the tempo and the melodic content are mutually dependent on each other. Dorn did praise certain things, such as Wagner's emphasis on the cantabile element in Beethoven, but he found the criticism of colleagues repellent, and a reflection of Wagner's "boundless vanity." At the close, Dorn offers an alphabetical list of all the musicians whom Wagner criticizes in his essay, from Eduard Bernsdorf to Dionys Weber: twenty-five names in total.[144] But we should also note that little trust existed between Dorn and Wagner, with the latter having accused the former of stealing his job in Riga back in the 1830s when Wagner had happened to be incapacitated by illness.[145] Dorn could also have added his own name to Wagner's blacklist of twenty-five, for as a former conductor of the Berlin Court Orchestra, he was presumably one of those whom Wagner intended to insult in his blanket criticism of that orchestra's music directors (see p. 27).

A few German-language essays and booklets on conducting appeared in the years immediately before and after the publication of Wagner's essay, though the latter group did not engage with it much. The music scholar Franz Ludwig Schubert (1804–68; no relation to the famous composer) had published a little booklet on conducting in 1864 in which he deals primarily with everyday matters of concern to conductors of amateur ensembles in the provinces. These include how to beat time, and what the different

---

142 See Schubert (2014).
143 Hanslick (1870).
144 Dorn (1870): 58.
145 See Wagner's letter to Theodor Apel of September 20, 1840. SB 1: 407.

instruments can do; he has clearly been influenced by Berlioz. The last quarter of the roughly eighty pages of Schubert's book is taken up with repertoire lists.[146] Hermann Zopff's *Der angehende Dirigent* (The Budding Conductor) of 1881 and Carl Schroeder's *Handbuch des Dirigierens und des Taktierens* (Handbook of Conducting and Beating Time), first published in 1889 and thereafter in several editions over the ensuing decades, are not much longer than Schubert's book, and similar to it in intent. They too describe the orchestral instruments and offer instruction in time-beating (though Schroeder includes far more music examples than Zopff). They both also offer advice to inexperienced conductors grappling with the basic repertoire in the concert hall and the theater (two institutions that were a feature of even tiny German towns at the time).[147] Wagner remains largely ignored. Zopff does feature Wagner's *Über das Dirigieren* in his recommended reading list, however, and insists—like Wagner—that a sympathetic musician must add the necessary expressive "nuances" to Mozart's "cantilenas" (two of Wagner's favorite words) and may not rely solely on what is given in the score.[148] For his part, Schroeder's second chapter begins with what seems an obvious paraphrase of Wagner's insistence on the importance of getting the tempo right in performance.[149] However, by the time one Josef Pembaur published the first edition of his own little guide to conducting in 1892, just three years after Schroeder (entitled, rather daringly, *Über das Dirigieren*), Wagner looms large and is even plagiarized shamelessly.[150]

The initial response to Wagner's essay was thus sluggish and devolved largely along party lines. But within a few years it became one of his most widely read and often quoted tracts. We can state without hyperbole that by the end of the 19th century it was the most influential text by far on the art of conducting, and it has lost little of its significance since—witness the praise accorded to it by the assorted conductors quoted at the opening of this essay (its sister article on performing Beethoven's Ninth Symphony, published three years after *Über das Dirigieren*, had a more specific impact, but was similarly significant). The first translations into French of the essay on the Ninth and of *Über das Dirigieren* were both published in 1874, by Maurice Kufferath in Belgium and by Guy de Charnacé in France respectively; within

---

146 See Schubert (1864).
147 See Schroeder (1921).
148 Zopff (1881): 100.
149 See Schroeder (1921): 33.
150 See Pembaur (1892): 32.

twenty years of their publication, these and other theoretical writings by Wagner had also found their way into English (see the section on "Wagner in Translation" below).

The two most important books on conducting to be published in French in the late 19th century—by Édouard-Marie-Ernest Deldevez and Maurice Kufferath in 1878 and 1890 respectively—also quote liberally from Wagner's own essay on conducting.[151] The only other French-language conducting tract of note, Édouard Blitz's *Quelques considérations sur l'art du chef d'orchestre* (Some Considerations on the Art of the Conductor), published in Leipzig and Brussels in 1887,[152] is much shorter—under a hundred pages—and with its beating patterns and seating plans is closer to Berlioz or the German-language booklets of Schubert, Schroeder and Zopff. When Wagner's former assistant Anton Seidl edited a coffee-table book *The Music of the Modern World* in New York in 1895, he included two essays of his own, entitled "On Conducting" and "About Conducting," the second of which drew heavily on Wagner's ideas on tempi in Beethoven and elsewhere.[153] Seidl closed it by considering in turn the three conductors he regarded as the finest of the age—Berlioz, Liszt, and Wagner—stating unequivocally that "Wagner is not only the mightiest of all musical geniuses, but also the greatest conductor that ever lived."[154] The international impact of Wagner's essays on conducting was initially sluggish, but by the late 19th century, they had become the gold standard across much of the western world.

Über das Dirigieren—Structure, Context, and Meta-Text

Wagner's stated avoidance of any "system" in his essay was probably intended to excuse in advance its haphazard organization. It was obviously conceived without much of a pre-planned structure, its individual installments written presumably just in time for submission to each new issue of the *Neue Zeitschrift*. But the word "system" also had a deeper significance for Wagner, as we find it throughout his writings, mostly (though not always) with negative connotations, signifying something dry and abstract (such as

---

151 Deldevez (1878) and Kufferath (1890).

152 See Blitz (1887); reprinted, along with Deldevez's bigger book, in Navarre (2005).

153 Seidl (1895a and 1895b).

154 Seidl (1895b): 214.

"an abstract, scientific system" and "an arbitrarily contrived system," both from *Opera and Drama*,[155] or "the whole sorry system of performance on the part of our opera singers today" from *Letter to an Actor about the State of Acting*.[156] It also tends to merge with his anti-Semitism (Wagner's essay *On Jewishness in Music*, for example, includes a mention of a supposed "new Jewish system" in music derived from Mendelssohn).[157] There is also a striking correlation here with the Third Reich's later use of the word to describe the Weimar Republic—again with anti-Semitic connotations.[158] However, in this instance we must take care not to assume any causal relationship when we have no precise proof, and the word had in fact also been used to castigate Wagner's own music. It is thus possible that the word "system" in Wagner's *Über das Dirigieren* was also a reference to Eduard Hanslick's pejorative use of it in the third edition of his *Vom Musikalisch-Schönen* of 1865, where Hanslick accused Wagner's "endless melody" of being "formlessness raised to a principle, a systematized non-music."[159] Suggesting such a connection might seem a little far-fetched, but Wagner was in fact given to reading and remembering the negative things that others wrote about him, and could quote from them years later. For example, in a letter to Johannes Brahms of June 26, 1875, Wagner quoted (without specific reference) the wording of a review published by Hanslick back in 1862.[160] We know that Wagner possessed a phenomenal memory, not least because of his habit of rehearsing and conducting classical symphonies without the aid of a score, as detailed elsewhere here.

Wagner wrote essays throughout his life, though the bulk of his literary output—aside from his own librettos—can be grouped into three distinct periods: his early essays written in around 1840–43, mostly in Paris or just after, including his first, brief autobiography of 1843; his Zurich writings, when his work as a composer more or less came to a halt for five years and he began codifying his aesthetic instead in works such as *The Artwork of the Future* (1849) and *Opera and Drama* (1851), and including another

---

155 See SSD 3: 99 and SSD 4: 205 respectively.

156 SSD 9: 271.

157 See *Das Judentum in der Musik*, SSD 5: 86. On Wagner's anti-Semitism, see, e.g., Millington (2012): 183–91.

158 For Victor Klemperer's discussion of the Nazis' use of the word "System," see Klemperer (1996): 127–28.

159 Hanslick (1865): x.

160 Kloss (1909): 570.

autobiography, *A Communication to my Friends* (1851); and then the series of writings that he embarked upon in 1864 after he was "saved" by Ludwig of Bavaria, culminating in his biggest autobiography, *Mein Leben* (which he began dictating to Cosima in 1865) and essays on all kinds of topics ranging from politics to animal rights, the arts and music education (it is important to note that Wagner did not dictate all his prose to Cosima; he also penned essays himself, as was the case with *Über das Dirigieren*).[161]

Several of Wagner's texts from around 1870 are obviously aimed at presenting himself as Beethoven's heir (most notably his essay *Beethoven* that was published during that composer's centenary year, just a few months after *Über das Dirigieren*). Taken as a whole, the writings of this late period seem to constitute a kind of meta-text, for it is as if they all existed as a single, vast text in Wagner's mind, from which he chose to publish different excerpts at different times. They are like the surface excretions of a vast subterranean fungus of ideas, all interlinked and interdependent.

Reading *Über das Dirigieren* without reference to Wagner's other writings of the time is almost like reading every other chapter in a novel, and Wagner himself occasionally makes this intertextuality explicit. For example, early on in the second published installment of this essay, he refers the reader to his *Report to His Majesty on Setting up a German Music School in Munich* of 1865, specifically to his discussion of Mozart and the slow movement of the Symphony in E flat no. 39; "those who seriously wish to follow my arguments [should] read the relevant passages there," he says. This passage must have been of particular importance to Wagner, because he paraphrases it in two other places in *Über das Dirigieren* (one of which, oddly, refers to a different slow movement by Mozart).[162] But this *Report* also foreshadows other topics that are dealt with at greater length in *Über das Dirigieren*, such as their author's antipathy towards the academic study of music,[163] and the importance of "singing" the melodic line in Beethoven's instrumental works.[164]

---

161 See the discussion of the autographs of *Über das Dirigieren* in Wagner's hand in Voss (2015): 89–90.

162 See SSD 8: 146 (*Report*) and fns 21, 38 and 95 in *Über das Dirigieren* above.

163 SSD 8: 140.

164 SSD 8: 168.

Then there are other places where Wagner's arguments seem to flow freely across different published texts. For example, there is a strange *non sequitur* in the following passage from *Über das Dirigieren*:

> I received the best guidance with regard to the tempo and the performance of Beethoven's music from the soulful, carefully accentuated singing of the great *Schröder-Devrient*; it has been impossible for me since then to let the inspiring oboe cadenza in the first movement of the C minor Symphony

Example 5.1. Beethoven, Symphony no. 5, 1st movement, m. 268

be so embarrassingly blown in that same manner in which I have otherwise always heard it.[165]

It remains unexplained why a general description of the art of Schröder-Devrient should lead directly to a specific discussion of how oboists play Beethoven's Fifth Symphony. This passage makes sense, however, if we read it in the context of a passage from *Mein Leben* that he dictated to Cosima at this time:

> In the [Zurich] orchestra I even discovered several truly talented musicians who were capable of being trained with rare success. Of these I wish to mention by name [Philipp] Fries the oboist ... In the Beethoven symphonies, he had to rehearse his highly important part privately with me as if it were a vocal line. When we performed the C minor Symphony for the first time, I managed to get this peculiar man ... to play the small "song" passage marked *Adagio* in the first movement in a marked and gripping way such as I have never heard equaled since.[166]

If we conflate these two passages, we arrive at what Wagner probably meant:

> In the Beethoven symphonies, Fries the oboist had to rehearse his highly important part privately with me like the soulful, carefully accentuated singing of the great Schröder-Devrient. When we performed the C minor Symphony for the

---

165 See p. 32 above.
166 ML: 470–71. See also Walton (2007): 165, and Walton (2002).

first time, I managed to get this peculiar man ... to play the small "song" passage marked *Adagio* in the first movement in a marked and gripping way such as I have never heard equaled since.[167]

It was natural for Wagner to mention Fries in his autobiography, but he presumably refrained from doing so in *Über das Dirigieren* because praising a provincial oboist in a semi-amateur orchestra might have drawn mockery in an essay that otherwise criticizes the major German professional orchestras from the Leipzig Gewandhaus to the Dresden Hofkapelle.

These cases where Wagner's prodigious mind strayed unencumbered from one text to another are probably also a result of publishing essays in installments while he was at the same time dictating *Mein Leben* to Cosima. Nietzsche was one of the first to appreciate how Wagner's practice of dictating his writings was a determining factor in their often haphazard structure and haranguing vocabulary. In his *Richard Wagner in Bayreuth*, he wrote of how this resulted in passages that were at times "artificial," "heavy" and "bloated,"[168] but at other times possessed of beauty:

> It seems to me as if Wagner often speaks as if addressing enemies—because all these writings are in the style of someone speaking them, not writing them, and you will find far more clarity in them if you hear them spoken well to an audience of enemies with whom [Wagner] can feel no sense of familiarity.[169]

While this overarching meta-text of his ideas must have made complete sense in his own mind, Wagner's often disjointed prose reads almost like a stream of consciousness, flitting from one half-uttered idea to another, and is at times oddly reminiscent of Tristan's delirious ramblings in the third act of his opera (it is noteworthy that Édouard Dujardin, one of the literary pioneers of the stream of consciousness technique, openly regarded Wagner as one of his prime influences).[170] *Über das Dirigieren* is one of the more extreme examples. Its vocabulary is occasionally repetitive (such as when Wagner describes how his *Meistersinger* can't be ruined by even a bad conductor, which is first an "oddly comforting realization," then a few lines later a "strangely comforting conclusion"). Nor can he help adding positive adverbs to enhance his successes. Thus, for example, the Leipzig audience at the first

---

167 This is discussed in Walton (2007): 165–66.
168 Nietzsche (1992): 283.
169 Ibid.
170 See Huebner (2013).

performance of his *Meistersinger* Prelude did not just demand an encore: they did so "animatedly" (see p. 102 above); there are many such examples. Wagner jumps blithely back and forth from one topic to another—see, for example, his recollection of conducting the *Freischütz* Overture in Vienna, which is suddenly interrupted by a discussion of the second subject of the Overture to Weber's *Oberon*, only for the tale of the *Freischütz* Overture to resume (pp. 66–67). Sometimes he'll tell us it's superfluous to explain things further—and then proceeds to explain them anyway. In both *Über das Dirigieren* and his later report on performing Beethoven's Ninth, Wagner appears to announce the conclusion of his essay, only to veer off again because something else has just occurred to him. The structure of these essays is at times reminiscent of a satirical novel such as William Beckford's *Azemia*, or perhaps prescient of a Monty Python sketch, for what is tangential can suddenly dominate, and an apparent peroration can be a new beginning.

Occasionally, we even see Wagner reacting as if in real time to something that has suddenly obsessed him. In the installment of *Über das Dirigieren* published on January 1, 1870, for example, Wagner includes two jibes at Eduard Bernsdorf, who on the preceding December 6 had published a review praising Johann Christian Lobe for his ironic treatment of Wagner's essay *On Jewishness in Music*. Wagner probably also hadn't forgotten that Bernsdorf had written a scathing review back in 1850 of the anonymous first publication of his anti-Semitic essay (while Bernsdorf presumably did not know the identity of its author at the time, that will have been immaterial to Wagner). In his conducting essay, Wagner now lumps Lobe and Bernsdorf together with another of his hate figures, capellmeister Reissiger, referring sarcastically to "Lobe/Bernsdorf's 'eternal laws' of the genuine and the true, which were presumably also guarded over by Reissiger back then."[171] The content here is as devoid of real sense as the choice of names seems arbitrary. Wagner is so determined to bundle all three men together in a single, pejorative sentence that he forgets to explain what they are actually guilty of. Like a dog that can't stop returning to dig up an old bone and gnaw on it, Wagner gravitates time and again back to these various *bêtes noires*, many of whom were fellow conductors whom he despised, ranging from Reissiger, as in this case, to Ferdinand Hiller and—of course—Felix Mendelssohn.

Besides his adjectives and adverbs of love and hate, there is much else in Wagner's vocabulary that reflects the circumstances under which he conceived and wrote *Über das Dirigieren*. It is full of superlatives that impart a

---

171 See p. 73 above.

degree of urgency on his part, even desperation, to convince his reader of the rightness of his opinions. Wagner had always been fond of superlatives, but a perusal of their use in his writings suggests that they reached a peak in the 1860s and early 1870s; there are nearly one hundred of them in his conducting essay alone.[172] It is worth noting that Wagner seems not to have infected Cosima with them, despite dictating much of his prose to her. Her diaries use them far more sparingly.

Wagner employs his superlatives to both positive and negative rhetorical effect. One of the most notable instances of pejorative intent in *Über das Dirigieren* occurs when discussing Mendelssohn, "dem es doch wahrlich nicht an den ungewöhnlichsten Kenntnissen und Begabungen fehlte."[173] Wagner had no compunction about criticizing Mendelssohn's background, his family or his wealth, but clearly hesitated to denigrate in print the actual abilities of a man so prodigiously gifted. Instead he praises him, but in a sub-clause with an implicit double negative combined with a negatively connoted verb placed at the end, presumably to enhance its negative impact on the otherwise positively connoted nouns that precede it. It is odd, but double negatives in Wagner rarely seem to signify their opposite; second and third negatives in a sentence tend to signify instead an intensification of the first.

Of "Elegance" and Anti-Semitism

Wagner's use of superlatives might well have been an instinctive act of which he was only vaguely aware himself, but his antipathy to Mendelssohn and his circle comes quite intentionally to the fore in his repeated criticism of the

---

172 For example: allerbestimmtesten, allereigensten, allereinfachsten, allerernstlichst, allergründlichst, allerkombiniertesten, allerkonfusesten, allermeisten, allernichtssagendsten, allerschnellsten, allerschwierigsten, allertiefsinnigsten, allervieldeutigste, allervorzüglichst, angesehensten, bestimmendsten, dürftigsten, energischesten, entgegengesetztesten, erkenntlichsten, gelindesten, gewissenhaftesten, lebhaftesten, naivsten, namhaftesten, niederschlagendsten, seltsamsten, steifesten, theilnehmendster, unverhülltesten, verständnisvollsten, vollendetsten, vorzüglichst, wundervollster, zartesten. This list was compiled by conducting a full-text search of all words in *Über das Dirigieren* ending in "sten," "isten," "lichsten" and so forth, taking care not to count words such as "Bratschisten," which is presumably considered a superlative only by violists.

173 "who truly did not lack the most unusual knowledge and talents." See also above, p. 30.

new conservatories of music and all those who study at them. He had already given voice to this criticism in his *Report to His Majesty* of 1865 (to which Hanslick referred in his *Eroica* review of 1872, quoted above). Wagner continued in the same vein in 1869–70 in *Über das Dirigieren*. He writes:

> there is a real call for "musical greats" to come and help out. The theaters have no such conductors; but the singing academies and concert organizations can apparently churn them out … These are the "music bankers" of our time, such as have emerged from Mendelssohn's school, or who have been recommended to the world as having been his protégés. They are a very different kind of person from the inept progeny of our old bewigged capellmeisters. They are musicians who haven't grown up in the orchestra or in the theater, but have received a respectable education in the newly founded conservatories, composing oratorios and psalms and attending the rehearsals of subscription concerts. They have also been given tuition in conducting, and have been educated elegantly such as had never before been the case among musicians.[174]

Apart from the crass jibe at Mendelssohn, whose father helped run the family bank in Berlin, Wagner's use of the word "elegant" here is noteworthy, for it occurs several times in this essay, acquiring a negative connotation in the process. The manner in which Wagner takes an otherwise innocuous or positive adjective in order to pervert its meaning until it signifies its own opposite is something he might have learnt from Shakespeare's *Julius Caesar*, a play he knew well: "So are they all, all honorable men."[175]

We first find the word "elegant" in Wagner's writings about Paris in the early 1840s (hardly surprising, given that the word is French in origin), but then barely at all until *Über das Dirigieren*. It then reappears again soon afterwards, in his ghastly pseudo-satire *Eine Kapitulation* about the Franco-Prussian War.[176] "Elegant" clearly became for Wagner a signifier of something either French or Jewish, but in any case something that in his eyes wasn't "German" (a category he clearly regarded as excluding the previous two). But the word also seems to have acquired for him an anti-intellectual connotation, for when he writes of "der elegante Kapellmeister neuesten Schlages" (the elegant capellmeister of the newest type: see p. 31), he means conductors

---

174 See pp. 28–29.

175 See Mark Antony's funeral oration in *Julius Caesar*, Act 2, Scene 2. In *Mein Leben*, Wagner recalled Eduard Devrient reciting Mark Antony's speeches to him and his friends when visiting Zurich in 1858 (ML: 564–65).

176 SSD 9: 3–41.

with an academic or conservatory training. Wagner's antipathy towards the new institutions of musical learning was in part a result of his feelings towards Mendelssohn, who had founded and run the Leipzig Conservatory, in part a consequence of his envy towards those who had enjoyed a better education than he, and in part a resentment caused by his own recent failure to set up a conservatory in Munich to promote his own ideas and aesthetic. We should also note the possibility that the word "elegant" encompassed for Wagner a more visceral, even sexual form of envy, for it generally signifies fine manners, tastes, and external appearance—just the kind of attributes he must have recognized in the dashing figure of the upper-class Mendelssohn, and to which the diminutive, gnarly-faced, chronically flatulent Wagner[177] clearly aspired with his yearnings for perfumes, frilly silks, and velvets. It is also noteworthy that Wagner cannot help referring to Mendelssohn as a "master" (see, for example, p. 94). While there is presumably some irony intrinsic to its use here, it is a word that for Wagner had generally positive connotations (Beethoven, for example, is for him often "der Meister"), and reveals a greater degree of admiration for his older contemporary than he was willing to admit openly.

In *Über das Dirigieren*, it seems at times as if all roads lead back to Mendelssohn. The chronological proximity of this essay to the revised, expanded version of *Jewishness in Music* (published just a few months before), along with the textual overlaps among Wagner's diverse essays referred to above, means that we are here confronted with some of the author's crassest instances of anti-Semitism. From his snide references to "music bankers" to his binary constructs of what is "German" and supposedly "other" (French/ Jewish/Italian/whatever), there are numerous instances in *Über das Dirigieren* that are explicitly offensive and that lie as monstrous, steaming *non sequiturs* in Wagner's prose. The most recent translator to grapple with this essay, Robert L. Jacobs, decided to omit Wagner's anti-Semitic tirades from his edition, as he openly states in his introduction.[178] During my work on the present translation, I found myself sympathizing with Jacobs more and more, and at times I began to worry that by translating the essay entire I might in some way be facilitating the dissemination of its author's more odious beliefs. But at a time when anti-Semitism is once again daily news in the west, jettisoning the most offensive passages here would be tantamount to pretending

---

177 See Walton (2007): 95–102 for details of Wagner's digestive complaints.
178 Wagner, trans. Jacobs (1979): ix–x.

that they do not exist. It is far better, I believe, to lay everything open than to sanitize Wagner.

Publishing Wagner's text entire is also vital if we are to give him the benefit of the doubt, which is our scholarly duty. We must not follow his example, neither by letting our own antipathies determine our actions, nor by constructing our own binary oppositions—such as between what we find offensive, and what we do not, then excising the one to "cleanse" the whole. Jens Malte Fischer rightly observes in his study of *Jewishness in Music* that anti-Semitism was one of the "central obsessions of [Wagner's] life,"[179] though it is also often impossible to determine what in Wagner's arguments is cause and effect. We must consider the possibility that his aesthetic stance also provided him with valid artistic grounds for criticizing the art of interpretation as practiced by Mendelssohn and his successors. Since this criticism was inevitably filtered through Wagner's personal obsessions (including his anti-Semitism), we also risk obscuring his artistic purpose if we excise what he says because how he says it is deeply offensive. Few commentators managed to rise above the vitriol of the day, but on May 13, 1870 the *Musikalisches Wochenblatt* published a noteworthy article by the composer Ludwig Hartmann—a student of both Liszt and the Leipzig Conservatory, and thus well placed to bridge the increasing aesthetic gap between them. Hartmann here condemns *Jewishness in Music* in the harshest possible terms, but also writes that one should not judge Wagner by his "arbitrary invective" alone, and concedes that his essay on conducting, despite its occasional hyperbole, contains "an exceptional number of true, accurate remarks."[180] And in spring 1873, the same journal published an article by the Swiss violinist Carl Courvoisier, who had played in the Gewandhaus Orchestra in the late 1860s. He defends Joseph Joachim against Wagner's criticism in *Über das Dirigieren*, asserting that Wagner would have a better opinion of the man it he took the trouble to hear him play (though Wagner is nicer to Joachim the musician than Courvoisier seems to think). All the same, Courvoisier then goes on to confirm Wagner's assertion (see p. 40) that the Gewandhaus Orchestra occasionally did play works very quickly in order to hide its lack of precision in performance.[181]

Throughout *Über das Dirigieren* Wagner is unable to refrain from denigrating those musicians of his time whose practices he regards as opposed to

---

179 Fischer (2015): 13.
180 Hartmann (1870): 312.
181 Carl Courvoisier (1846–1908). See Courvoisier (1873a): 307.

his own. Some of them happened to be Jewish, others were not (as already mentioned above, Heinrich Dorn's review of the essay listed no less than twenty-five men whom Wagner excoriates).[182] Wagner's antipathies extended far beyond anti-Semitism and are important signifiers of his insecurities. It is in moments when his negative emotions get the better of him that he lets his guard down, inadvertently letting us perceive his frailties beneath the bluster. The more he criticizes certain contemporaries, the more we can be sure how much he actually respected them (or feared them, or even desired to emulate them). *Mein Leben*, for example, is full of examples of Wagner's inability to praise talented colleagues (regardless of their nationality, faith or family background) without qualifying that praise by means of a subsequent negative comment.[183]

We must bear in mind, too, that Wagner was just one of several musicians at the time who used the press to publicize their opinions as forcibly as possible, regardless of the consequences. Ferdinand Hiller comes off badly in *Über das Dirigieren*, but Wagner was himself responding to Hiller's own recent book *Aus dem Tonleben unserer Zeit* (vol. 2 of 1868), which reprints Hiller's review from 1857 about a music festival in Aachen. Hiller here explained at length why Liszt was a really bad conductor who failed to practice what he preached, and he specifically complained about the "extreme monotony" evoked when Liszt conducted Wagner's *Tannhäuser* Overture.[184] Wagner had already published a vitriolic reply to Hiller at the time,[185] but the criticism clearly still rankled,[186] and Wagner understandably seems to have regarded Hiller's republication of the article a decade later as a renewed declaration of hostilities.

Wagner's opponents certainly did not hold back. His relations with King Ludwig II were a matter of open scorn by mid-1870 at the latest, when the *Allgemeine musikalische Zeitung* (edited by Brahms's friend Friedrich Chrysander) wrote of Wagner's "fawning [*kriechend*], unmasculine manner" towards the king in what was presumably a veiled reference to the latter's

---

182   See, for example, Wagner's criticism of the conductors Felix Otto Dessoff, Ferdinand Hiller, Franz Lachner, Carl Reissiger, and others.

183   For Wagner's opinion of Emilie Heim and Theodor Kirchner, for example, see ML: 545 and 553, and my discussion of this in Walton (2007): 117–18.

184   From Hiller's report on the 1857 music festival in Aachen, as reprinted by him in book form. See Hiller (1868): 140 and 183.

185   See Wagner's "Ferdinand Hiller" in SSD 8: 213–20.

186   See Schubert (2014).

homosexuality[187] (Wagner avenged himself by publicly assailing Chrysander in turn six months later).[188] And in 1877, Chrysander's line of attack was taken to extreme lengths when the *Neue Freie Presse* (Hanslick's paper) outed Wagner as a transvestite. In a vicious front-page article, the *Presse* printed embarrassing excerpts from Wagner's correspondence with the seamstress who had made his frilly satin underwear back in the 1860s.[189] The accompanying commentary by the journalist Daniel Spitzer employed highly sexualized vocabulary to emphasize Wagner's supposedly abnormal desires. Just as Wagner strings together *non sequiturs* as a means of vilifying his enemies in his prose, so does Spitzer casually drop in random references to Italian castrati, quotes from Wagner's own writings about "music as woman," and lines from his dedications to King Ludwig II. The cumulative effect is to portray the composer as effeminate, emasculated, and potentially homosexual. And while Wagner by all accounts was not gay, such an accusation, if only implicit, could nevertheless have had serious, legal consequences; paragraph 175 of the recently established German penal code had made homosexuality punishable by either prison sentence or the loss of one's civil rights.[190] It was assumed at the time that Spitzer would not have been able to publish his article without the encouragement or acquiescence of Hanslick himself.[191] Just because one party resorts to vitriol—be it homophobic, anti-Semitic or anything else—it does not excuse another from doing the same. But we must acknowledge that Wagner's prose writings, including *Über das Dirigieren*, were situated in the context of a wider, angry, aesthetic and political debate in which there were absolutely no holds barred to the vocabulary, tone or content of the arguments expounded on all sides.

---

187 Anon. [Friedrich Chrysander?] (1870).

188 See Wagner's "Offener Brief an Dr. phil. Friedrich Stade" of December 31, 1870, in which he quotes Chrysander's use of the word "kriechend." See SSD 16: 103–8, here 105.

189 Spitzer (1877).

190 See Schwarze (1876): 142.

191 See Wilhelm Tappert's comments in the *Musikalisches Wochenblatt*. Tappert (1877).

Wagner and the Academy

Wagner's mistrust of the new institutions of musical learning, as expressed at length in *Über das Dirigieren*, extended to the emerging field of musicology. The 1860s had seen the establishment of Beethoven scholarship, with Gustav Nottebohm, Otto Jahn, and others publishing his sketches, letters, and the like, and insisting on philological scrupulousness as the key to understanding his oeuvre.[192] We know that Wagner was aware of their work, and we can be sure that he did not like them either. Nottebohm was a former student of Mendelssohn and Schumann and was friendly with Brahms, while Jahn had already publicly criticized Wagner's own music.[193] We should also note that Eduard Hanslick was given a chair of music history and aesthetics in Vienna in 1861 and was made a full professor there in 1870.

The first scholarly, complete edition of Beethoven's works had begun publication in 1862, and had declared its claims to primacy on its title page: "Vollständige kritisch durchgesehene überall berechtigte Ausgabe. Mit Genehmigung aller Originalverleger" (Complete, critically reviewed, thoroughly authorized edition. With the permission of all the original publishers). The editors included Jahn, Nottebohm and assorted practical musicians connected to Mendelssohn and his circle, none of whom was likely to gain Wagner's favor (the piano works, for example, were edited under the auspices of Carl Reinecke, a composer and conductor whom Wagner nastily singled out in *Über das Dirigieren*; see p. 102). Judging from his comments on their activities, Wagner seems to have feared that the work of this new generation of music scholars would in future determine the reception of Beethoven's music that he felt was his preserve alone. Competition was also coming from France. Berlioz included several essays on Beethoven in his book *À travers chants*, published in 1862, including a 45-page study of the nine symphonies; Liszt's acolyte Richard Pohl published the book in German translation just two years later.[194]

---

192 See Nottebohm (1865) and Jahn: "Beethoven und die Ausgaben seiner Werke" in Jahn (1866): 271–337. Cosima wrote in her diary on Saturday, May 15, 1875 that she and Wagner had been studying Nottebohm's edition of the sketches for Beethoven's Ninth (CWT 1: 917). This volume is not in Wagner's Wahnfried library today, however.

193 See Jahn: "Tannhäuser, Oper von Richard Wagner," in Jahn (1866): 64–86; see also Walton (2014): 16.

194 Berlioz (1862) and Berlioz, trans. Pohl (1864).

Wagner's writings from the late 1860s onwards place a particular emphasis on interpreting and understanding Beethoven, which was probably in part a response to what he seems to have felt was a real, new threat to the sovereignty of his own interpretation of Beethoven's music. Wagner's reaction to this increasing academicization of the music world in general, and of Beethoven reception in particular, is significant because he now embarked on a strange balancing act that had a long-lasting impact on how others played music and thought about it. In *Über das Dirigieren* and its sister essay on Beethoven's Ninth, Wagner insists on maintaining complete fidelity to the text, performing Beethoven "wie der Meister es sich dachte"—as the Master had himself intended (see p. 37). This was surely an acknowledgement of the recent trend towards textual rigor as evinced by the aforementioned title page to the Beethoven *Gesamtausgabe*. But at the same time, Wagner insists no less on an organic approach to performance and interpretation in which the ideal conductor (clearly meaning him, Wagner) could and should adjust the tempo in order to maintain unity in diversity within a work, and could and should adapt the musical text itself in order to fulfil what he, Wagner, regarded as having been the composer's true intentions.

Wagner and Beethoven's Ninth

The reception of Beethoven's Ninth Symphony was long dominated by Wagner. Much of the literature refers to his performance of the work on Palm Sunday in Dresden in 1846 as having been a major turning point in the work's history. In his early biography of Wagner, Carl Glasenapp wrote that

> Undoubtedly, Beethoven's mighty last symphony only truly came to life for the first-ever time thanks to its Dresden performance [under Wagner on April 5, 1846]; it was on this date that our deeper understanding of this work began, which until then had had such a negative reputation.[195]

In his Wagner chronology, published after the Second World War, Otto Strobel called his Palm Sunday performance in Dresden the "grandiose revival of this work!"[196] And this still seems to be the general opinion today. Even the chapter on "Performance and Tradition" in Nicholas Cook's *Cambridge*

---

195 Glasenapp (1923): 2, 402.
196 Strobel (1952): 30.

Handbook on the Ninth plunges almost straightaway into a discussion of Wagner's interpretation of the work and his 1846 performance.[197]

This impact is remarkable when we consider that Wagner only ever conducted the work five times—five and a half, to be precise, for he conducted a private performance of the middle movements for Otto Wesendonck in early 1858 as a kind of unspoken apology for trying to sleep with the man's wife.[198] The dates of Wagner's performances were April 5, 1846, March 28, 1847, and April 1, 1849 (all in Dresden with the Court Orchestra of which he was capellmeister), March 26, 1855 in London with the Old Philharmonic, March 31, 1858 in Zurich (only the scherzo and *Adagio*), and May 22, 1872 in the Margravial Opera House in Bayreuth, to commemorate laying the foundation stone of the Festspielhaus.

It is true that Beethoven's Ninth Symphony was regarded as a strange, unwieldy work by many in the mid-19th century. But Wagner was not alone in recognizing its significance. As already mentioned above, Wagner himself praised Habeneck's Paris performance of 1840, though his report is admittedly phrased as if Habeneck had been an outlier, with the symphony really waiting to be properly rediscovered back in its German homeland. But even in this, Wagner was pipped to the post, because Otto Nicolai conducted the Vienna Philharmonic Orchestra in a highly successful performance of the Ninth on March 19, 1843 in Vienna. Nicolai had founded this orchestra just a year earlier, and was already making Beethoven's symphonies a permanent fixture in his programs. Judging by the reviews, Nicolai's performance of the Ninth in 1843 was considered a real turning point for the work at the time. Carl Kunt, writing in the *Wiener Zeitschrift für Kunst, Literatur, Theater und Mode*, was wildly enthusiastic:

> [This concert] was a journey of the Argonauts to win the Golden Fleece that
> is Beethoven's Ninth Symphony. And how did this daring endeavor succeed in
> becoming such a brilliant event under the guiding hand of its masterly leader? A
> thousand delighted people can tell you. Enthusiastic, passionate, and yet calm,
> we saw the multitude defy the raging seas of music; no sea-surge held them back,
> no cliffs deterred them, no struggle against the agitated elements of sound dampened their majestic progress ... no one could manage what this performance
> achieved, with the orchestra of the Court Opera under the profound, energetic,
> poetic direction of Capellmeister Nicolai.[199]

---

197 Cook (1993): 48–64.
198 See Walton (2007): 76–77.
199 Kunt (1843): 475–76.

The reviewer concluded by mentioning Habeneck's performance of the work in Paris two years before, but only to assure his readers that "the greatest perfection of performance" had now also been achieved in Vienna.[200] Charles Gounod was among those who heard Nicolai conduct the Ninth, and years later listed this Viennese performance alongside Habeneck's in Paris as the two that had impressed him the most.[201] Berlioz experienced Nicolai when he visited Vienna for concerts of his own in the winter of 1845–46 (though he heard him conduct Beethoven's Fourth, not the Ninth). He was mightily impressed, later writing in his Memoirs that Nicolai was "one of the most excellent orchestral conductors I have ever met."[202]

Nicolai's performance of the Ninth in 1843 was noticed far beyond his own city. The *Zeitung für die elegante Welt* in Leipzig—the same magazine that had published Wagner's first autobiography a few weeks earlier—brought a glowing review of this Viennese performance in its issue of April 12, 1843, stressing how Nicolai had achieved the "greatest perfection" thanks to his "tireless diligence" and his many rehearsals, and how he had managed to turn this misunderstood work, supposedly composed against the very rules of music, into such a huge public success that people demanded he give a repeat performance the following week. Since Wagner had connections to the magazine and its editor Heinrich Laube, we can assume that he will have read this review. It won't have pleased him much.

It is possible that Wagner's efforts to make a success of his Ninth in 1846 were in part prompted by a desire to outdo Nicolai's Viennese success of three years before. As Nicholas Vazsonyi has shown,[203] Wagner conducted an extensive marketing campaign before his concert, publishing anonymous articles in the local press to get the public interested, and he also wrote a program for the symphony based on Goethe's *Faust* that was reprinted numerous times thereafter. The press response was very positive, if largely confined to Dresden; the only dissenting voice was that of Julius Schladebach, the critic of the *Abend-Zeitung* in Dresden and an implacable opponent of Wagner's, whom Vazsonyi has suggested might have been one of the models for

---

200 Ibid.: 478.
201 Gounod actually gives the year 1842 for Nicolai's performance, though he presumably means 1843; he was writing thirty-one years later, so the confusion is perhaps understandable. See Gounod (1874): 189–90.
202 Berlioz (1870): 353.
203 Vazsonyi (2010): 66–77.

Beckmesser in *Die Meistersinger von Nürnberg*.[204] The Ninth Symphony later figured large in Wagner's theoretical writings in Zurich, where it is presented as the final step on the road to Wagnerian music drama. But Wagner writes there in abstract terms, without reference to his own performances. Nor did he consider his Dresden performances of it significant enough to mention in his autobiography *A Communication to my Friends* of 1851. Theodor Uhlig does mention the Dresden Ninth in his abovementioned series of articles on Beethoven and Wagner of late 1852, but he too was focused on Wagner's invented program for it, not on his actual interpretation of the work or how he rehearsed and conducted it.[205]

Wagner dictated his reminiscences of his Palm Sunday concert of 1846 to Cosima in the late 1860s as part of his autobiography *Mein Leben*,[206] but he then published this section separately under the title *Report on the Performance of Beethoven's Ninth Symphony in Dresden in 1846* in the second volume of his collected writings in 1871,[207] alongside the program he had written back in 1846 and other texts from the 1840s. This situated his report "chronologically" at the time of the performance it was describing. Despite Wagner stating clearly that it is an extract from his memoirs, most commentators have accepted Wagner's description of his performance (and its purportedly resounding success) as if it were an accurate, objective contemporary report (even the *New Grove* and *MGG Online* list this essay as dating from 1846 in their chronological lists of Wagner's writings).[208] But this essay was essentially a retrospective marketing campaign for his view of the work that was, if anything, even more successful than the campaign he had carried out at the time. The many commentators since who either explicitly or implicitly situate Wagner's 1846 performance of the Ninth at the heart of the work's 19th-century reception[209] are actually following Wagner's own example. One could even argue that another performance of the Ninth, just six weeks after Wagner's, was at least of equal significance in the history of

204 Ibid.: 73–75.

205 Uhlig (1852): II, 133.

206 ML: 341–46.

207 Wagner: *Gesammelte Schriften und Dichtungen*. Vol. 2. Leipzig: E. W. Fritzsch, 1871. The *Bericht über die Aufführung der neunten Symphonie von Beethoven im Jahre 1846 in Dresden* was printed there on 65–74, the program on 75–84.

208 Deathridge and Dahlhaus (1984): 189; the current online *New Grove* keeps the date given there. See also Döge (2016).

209 See, for example, Cook (1993): 49; Eichhorn (1993): 72, and many more.

the work—namely its first performance in North America, given by the New York Philharmonic Society on May 20, 1846.[210] To be sure, Wagner's performance of Beethoven's Ninth in Dresden in 1846 was hardly insignificant. As Raymond Holden has remarked, his physical arrangement of the orchestra and chorus, with the latter placed in semi-circular tiers behind the former, later became the norm everywhere.[211] And the members of the audience included the teenage Hans von Bülow, who would later play such a major role in the performance history of the work. All the same, it is undeniable that the discourse around Wagner's 1846 performance did not really begin until twenty-five years afterwards, when he published his own report of it to tell the world just how crucial it had been. By that time, no one could remember it well enough to argue against him. Wagner's glowing account was thus little more than "fake news"; but when everyone else started repeating it, it assumed the status of actual truth.

The Bayreuth Performance of Beethoven's Ninth in 1872

Wagner's retrospective report of 1871 on conducting the Ninth in Dresden in 1846 also helped to prepare the way for his performance of it in Bayreuth, just a few months later in 1872. In fact, his report might well have been intended primarily as part of a new marketing campaign for that forthcoming event. He had actually been asked by the Gesellschaft der Musikfreunde to conduct the Ninth Symphony in Vienna in 1870 at that city's Beethoven centenary celebrations, but he had refused because Hanslick was on the committee responsible (Hanslick even mentioned this rejection in his review of *Über das Dirigieren*). Wagner told Cosima: "When I'm home at last, I'll perform the symphony, but I want nothing to do with that rabble."[212]

Wagner's dislike of Hanslick had only intensified in recent months. It is notable that Hanslick had published his large-scale history of Vienna's concert life just a few months before the Viennese invitation to Wagner. In it, he spent several pages praising Otto Nicolai's Philharmonic concerts from 1842 to 1847, singling out his performances of the Ninth Symphony as his

---

210 The program for the evening can be viewed online in the New York Philharmonic Archives, at https://archives.nyphil.org/index.php/artifact/079d4d73-e2e7-4c8b-9ab6-294cab67d9de-0.1/fullview#page/1/mode/2up (accessed May 2019).

211 Holden (2011a): 5.

212 CWT 1: 230 (May 13, 1870).

crowning achievement. Hanslick also lists the conductor's concert repertoire of the 1840s, which was remarkably similar to that of Wagner in Zurich in the 1850s—Beethoven's symphonies, the last symphonies of Mozart and Haydn, Gluck's Overture to *Iphigenie in Aulis*, Weber overtures and so forth, even down to Beethoven's complete *Egmont* music with linking declamations.[213] We have no proof that Wagner read Hanslick's book (nor it is held in his Wahnfried library), but it is likely that he had at least heard of it. Perhaps publishing his own report of his Dresden performance of 1846 was in part a response to Hanslick's Nicolai; following this up with his Bayreuth performance of 1872 and his subsequent report on *that* in turn was perhaps a final attempt to wrest the history of Beethoven reception back to his own person. If so, it was highly successful—no one bothered to talk about Nicolai's Beethoven any more after that.

One might imagine that Wagner would have wanted to organize a concert solely of his own works to commemorate the laying of the foundation stone in Bayreuth on May 22, 1872. Instead, he chose Beethoven's Ninth as the main item on the program, and had a clear ulterior motive for doing so. The Ninth was already regarded in the mid-19th century as a kind of "monument" in sound;[214] Wagner now aimed to elevate it into a monumental precursor to his *Ring*. Every great undertaking needs its own genealogy, and to this end, Wagner had already begun reinventing Beethoven in his own image. He did so on three fronts: by emphasizing the Ninth's aesthetic significance as a symphonic construction that found its ultimate fulfilment in combining words and music (thus foreshadowing Wagnerian music drama); by performing it to commemorate laying the foundation stone for the Festival Theater in Bayreuth, which essentially meant staging the symphony itself as a metaphorical "foundation stone" for the *Ring*; and by organizing that same performance as a quasi-national event of social and political significance, uniting musicians from all over Germany under his own direction. Not for nothing did Wagner choose a date of dual import for his performance. It was both his own birthday and the first Wednesday after the feast of Pentecost, when the Church celebrates the descent of the Holy Spirit onto the Apostles (this did not go unnoticed either; Otto Lessmann's report on the event in the *Neue Berliner Musikzeitung* was actually entitled "Pentecost in Bayreuth").[215]

---

213 Hanslick (1869b): 314–17. The praise of the Ninth is given on p. 317.
214 See Eichhorn (1993): 300–301.
215 See Lessmann (1872).

Figure 5.16. Louis Sauter, Wagner conducts Beethoven's Ninth in the Margravial Opera House in Bayreuth on May 22, 1872. Note that he is conducting from memory, without a music stand. The male semi-chorus for "Seid umschlungen Millionen" is placed in the boxes to the left and right of the stage. Nationalarchiv der Richard-Wagner-Stiftung, Bayreuth.

Wagner's performance of the Ninth in Bayreuth was widely reported in the assorted music journals of the day, from Lessmann's abovementioned review to Francis Hueffer's report for *The Times* (already quoted above) and Wilhelm Tappert's essay in the *Musikalisches Wochenblatt* (this journal also included a list of all the orchestral players, as did the anonymous report in the *Neue Zeitschrift für Musik*).[216] To make sure the world read of the event in the way he wanted, Wagner also appointed his acolyte Heinrich Porges (1837–1900) to write up a detailed report, which was first published in installments in the *Neue Zeitschrift für Musik* over several weeks, beginning on June 21, 1872, and then in booklet form that same year.[217] And just a few months after that, Wagner followed it up with a report of his own—*On Performing Beethoven's Ninth Symphony*, included in the present volume—in

---

216 See Tappert (1872) and Anon. (1872): 232.
217 Porges (1872).

which he took his performance of the Ninth as the starting point for a general discussion about how the work ought to be performed. Wagner initially published this essay in installments in the *Musikalisches Wochenblatt*, no doubt because it was the house journal of the same publisher, Fritzsch of Leipzig, who was now responsible for bringing out his collected writings. Wagner's standing was now such that Fritzsch announced the imminent publication of the essay on the front page of his journal on March 21, 1873; the essay itself was published over two issues (each time beginning on the front page), on April 4 and 11, 1873.[218] The essay was then included in the ninth volume of Wagner's collected writings, published by Fritzsch later that same year.

Wagner here lists numerous adjustments that he had made to the text of the symphony, such as filling in gaps in the trumpet parts where Beethoven had simply omitted notes unplayable on natural trumpets (see p. 122), and smoothing out the melody in the first flute where Beethoven had written ungainly leaps to avoid high notes that were similarly unplayable on contemporary instruments. Wagner also altered passages where he felt that Beethoven's loss of hearing had made him incapable of judging how best to bring out the principal melodic line (see pp. 127f.), and furthermore specified certain changes to the orchestration that he would make in future, were he ever to perform the symphony again (which he did not). The most significant of these was intended to attain the correct balance at measure 93ff. in the scherzo by adding more wind instruments to the main theme (see p. 120). Some disagreed with his suggestions, though occasionally they seem to have done so on principle, like Charles Gounod. In late spring 1874, he read a brief report about Wagner's essay in the English journal *The Orchestra*, and promptly published a long letter explaining that no one should dare to tinker with the works of a master like Beethoven; he didn't need Wagner's Beethoven, because Beethoven's Beethoven was enough for him (it seems that he never heard Wagner conduct the Ninth, nor did he read the actual essay he was criticizing).[219] Heinrich Schenker was another who later castigated Wagner's amendments, finding it impossible to believe that Beethoven's scores were as full of miscalculations as Wagner insisted.[220] But there are instances where Beethoven's autographs prove that, in his flute parts at least, he had indeed originally envisioned precisely the kind of

---

218 Wagner: "Zum Vortrag der neunten Symphonie Beethoven's," *Musikalisches Wochenblatt* 4/14 and 15, 209–13 and 225–31 respectively.

219 Gounod (1874): 189.

220 See Schenker (1901): 268.

solutions that Wagner proposed in his essay of 1873, but had then changed the musical text before publication because he had meanwhile realized that what he had written was actually unplayable on the instruments of the day (we find such instances in both the Eighth and Ninth symphonies; for details, see the footnote on p. 124).

Such dissenting voices seem to have been rare, however, and many conductors adopted several of Wagner's proposals over the next eighty years. These included not just Mahler and Strauss (who were keen to preserve the Wagnerian inheritance) but even men such as Toscanini, who adopted most of Wagner's octave changes to the *espressivo* wind passage at measure 138 in the first movement and at the parallel passage in the recapitulation at measure 407; he also added horns and trumpets to the scherzo to solve the balance problem at measures 93ff., and adopted Wagner's recommendations for extra notes in the trumpets at the opening of the last movement[221]—proof surely (if it were still needed) that the popular image of Toscanini as everfaithful to the letter of the text, and thus an antithesis to the Germanic *espressivo* of Wilhelm Furtwängler & Co., is a gross simplification.[222]

If post-Wagnerian conductors felt they had to justify amendments to Beethoven's text, they were able to do so by specific reference to Wagner's elastic notions of textual fidelity. When Mahler was attacked for "retouching" Beethoven's Ninth in Vienna in 1900, he had a handbill printed and distributed to explain that he was being utterly faithful to Beethoven's intentions, merely after the manner of Richard Wagner.[223] It is noteworthy that Wagner's own proposed adjustments to this symphony also seem to have prompted a debate about whether other works by Beethoven might profit from similar treatment: in the *Neue Berliner Musikzeitung* on January 7, 1875, the Berlin pianist and pedagogue Alexis Hollaender used Wagner's arguments to suggest similar minor changes to certain piano works by Beethoven.[224]

It is ironic that Mahler and others felt they were being faithful to Wagner by following the ideas expressed in his 1873 essay, because Wagner never put all those ideas into practice himself. The only reliable musical source we have for Wagner's Bayreuth performance of the Ninth only resurfaced in the new millennium—the score that the Viennese baritone Adolf Wallnöfer took

221 Toscanini's annotated score is held by the New York Public Library: Shelf locator: JPB 90-1, folder A42.

222 See, for example, Fairtile (2003).

223 See the facsimile of the handbill in Martner (2010): 124.

224 See Hollaender (1875).

with him to rehearsal when he sang in the chorus. Wallnöfer was just 18 at the time, and had been one of the many young admirers thronging around Wagner when he conducted Beethoven's *Eroica* and several of his own works in Vienna on May 12, 1872 (the same concert reviewed so extensively by Hanslick; see above). Wagner urged them all to come to hear the Ninth in Bayreuth ten days later, and Wallnöfer took him at his word.[225] Since he already knew Carl Riedel, one of the men in charge of organizing the chorus, Wallnöfer was allowed to join in. When he wasn't actually singing, he faithfully noted down everything Wagner said and did in the score he'd brought with him. The many correlations between his annotations and the contemporary accounts of Wagner's rehearsals and performance by Porges and Tappert leave little doubt that Wallnöfer was an accurate witness (in some cases, a close comparison of Porges, Tappert, and Wallnöfer suggests that Wallnöfer was in fact the most attentive and most accurate of them all).[226] Apart from occasional changes to the notes—such as filling in the trumpet "gaps" in the melody already mentioned above—Wallnöfer's score is particularly notable for its many *crescendi, decrescendi, stringendi* and suchlike that reflect Wagner's Romantic approach to the Ninth, his delight in tempo modification and his preference for the gradual instead of the abrupt. The last movement is the one with the fewest annotations—hardly surprising, since this was the movement in which Wallnöfer had to sing—but the exception here is one of the most fascinating passages, for he meticulously notated how Wagner wanted the basses to perform their "recitative," including *ritardandi* and a *stringendo*, and an altered upbeat to measure 81 that is mentioned in no other source. It would seem that Wagner's approach to this passage had altered over the years, because when he conducted it in London in March 1855, George Hogarth, the music critic of the *Daily News*, had written that the "recitative … was rendered excessively difficult by being taken in strict time, without the relaxation hitherto allowed."[227] Incidentally, the "mystico" Wallnöfer mentions here at the "joy" theme coincides with the vocabulary of

---

225 See Wallnöfer (n.d.): 16–17.

226 See Walton (2019a).

227 As quoted in Ashton Ellis (1900–1908: 5, 203–4). George Hogarth (1783–1870) was himself a cellist, and secretary of the Philharmonic Society at the time of Wagner's visit. He was also the father-in-law of Charles Dickens, who had founded the *Daily News*.

Figure 5.17. Double bass part from Adolf Wallnöfer's score of Beethoven's Ninth Symphony, annotated during Wagner's rehearsals at Bayreuth in 1872, fourth movement, mm. 63–101. Nationalarchiv der Richard-Wagner-Stiftung, Bayreuth.

Heinrich Porges, who was present at the same rehearsal, and later wrote of the "mystic unison"[228] of this passage.

Two years later, Wallnöfer auditioned for the part of Donner at the first Bayreuth Festival, but was turned down on account of being relatively small in stature (though he was in fact taller than Wagner). As I explain in greater detail below, he nevertheless stayed in Bayreuth to help out, first with copying, then later with rehearsing the singers for the first festival. He even helped Felix Mottl and others to manipulate the machinery that made the Rhinemaidens "swim" in 1876. Wallnöfer later changed *fach* to become a heldentenor, and went on to sing all the major Wagner roles in opera houses

---

228 Porges (1872): 29.

from New York to St. Petersburg, working under conductors from Mahler to Seidl—though he was never invited to sing in Bayreuth.[229]

Finding a Vocabulary for Conducting

Wagner's journalism and forays into fiction of the early 1840s are generally couched in a lively, readable style. This changed, however, when he embarked on his career as a music theorist in exile in 1849. His new home, Zurich, had overnight become a leading intellectual center of the west because so many of the continent's intelligentsia had flocked to neutral, democratic Switzerland after the failed Europe-wide revolutions of the past year. In Dresden, Wagner had rubbed shoulders with all manner of musicians who could recognize his genius even if they disliked his person. But in Zurich, he found himself mixing with high-powered academics instead: scientists, historians, philologists, and linguists. His prose now turned dense and convoluted, perhaps on account of a desire to assert himself among these men whose prime mode of communication was not music, but words. Wagner had left full-time education at the age of just 18, and must at times have felt out of his depth at Zurich's après-concert gatherings (it is noteworthy that in his apparent "competition" with Otto Wesendonck for the favor of the latter's wife Mathilde, Wagner should have made repeated reference to Otto's cultural ignorance and lack of a proper education. He probably realized that one of the best ways to hide one's faults is to project them openly onto others).[230] By the time Wagner came to write *Über das Dirigieren*, his prose had become so opaque that it is sometimes difficult to determine what he is saying at all. His fondness for multiple negatives, coupled with his heavy-handed irony, even comes close to obscuring whether he is actually in favor of something or against it.[231] This was remarked upon at the time; his brother-in-law and early translator, Guy de Charnacé, wrote:

229 See Walton (2019b).

230 See, for example, Wagner's letters to Mathilde Wesendonck of May 2, 1860 and December 21, 1861, in SB 12: 137 and SB 13: 339 respectively, and Walton (2007): 193.

231 The present writer is a native English speaker—albeit a Swiss national and a resident of the German-speaking world for more than two decades—but the same exasperation with Wagner's prose is shared (so they assure me) by my Wagnerian colleagues whose mother tongue is German.

"What preoccupies M. Wagner least of all is making himself understood to musicians ... clarity is the quality that [he] lacks the most ... [but] he reaps only what he sows."[232] Wagner must on some level have been aware of the obscurity of his essays, in both their manner of presentation and their prose style, otherwise he would hardly have insisted time and again on the necessity for "clarity" in all its forms. This word, in its adjectival form "deutlich" and noun form "Deutlichkeit," appears no less than twenty-seven times in his essay on the Ninth Symphony, which is surely protesting too much; Heinrich Schenker even wrote of Wagner's "Deutlichkeitsmanie" (clarity mania) in his criticism of Wagner's essay on the Ninth.[233] "Deutlichkeit" was also Wagner's final exhortation to his performers on August 13, 1876, before the world premiere of the *Ring*.[234]

In order to give a greater scholarly veneer to his arguments, Wagner also drew on the work of famous writers. In his essay *Beethoven*, for example, he openly appropriates Schopenhauer's highfalutin vocabulary for discussing different types of dreams, even using the philosopher's obscure adjective "fatidik" (derived from the Latin), to mean "prophetic" dreams.[235] This word even perplexed Thomas Mann, who underlined it in his copy of Wagner's collected writings and added a question mark in the margin.[236] And in *Über das Dirigieren*, Wagner adopts Friedrich Schiller's terminology for "naïve" and "sentimental" literature, applying it instead to what we describe today as Classical and Romantic music (Wagner's terms do not coincide exactly with ours; he clearly regarded Beethoven's first two symphonies as naïve, whereas Mozart's and Haydn's last symphonies were to him already sentimental). Wagner also developed an interest in etymology—encouraged, no doubt, by his friendship in Zurich with the philologist Ludwig Ettmüller, who was an expert in old Germanic languages, and who helped him with the sources for his *Ring des Nibelungen*. This developed into a lifelong fascination for the derivations of words in general. In *Beethoven* in 1870, for example, Wagner expounded on how "Schönheit" (beauty) was supposedly descended from "Schein" (appearance) and

232 Charnacé (1874): 228–29.

233 Schenker (1912): 71

234 SSD 16: 160. A facsimile of the original is given in Heinel (2006): 268.

235 See Walton (2014): 19.

236 Shelfmark Thomas Mann 601: 9–10, 69, in the Thomas-Mann-Archiv of ETH Zurich. Mann used the same sixth edition of Wagner's writings, abbreviated elsewhere here as SSD.

"Schauen" (looking)— another instance that prompted Thomas Mann to a marginal line and a question mark in his copy of the essay.[237] These issues no doubt had less to do with any philological rigor than with Wagner's general interest in organic transformation, but they are important not least because they fed into Wagner's creative work. In the second act of *Parsifal*, for example, Kundry begins her seduction of the title hero with an etymological explanation of his name, deconstructing it as the cod-Persian "fal parsi," supposedly meaning a fool who is pure ("tör'ger Reiner").

These varying linguistic interests on Wagner's part also coalesced in a long-lasting endeavor to create his own (pseudo-)scholarly vocabulary about music. He made tentative steps in this direction already in the theoretical writings of his Zurich period, though it became more pronounced in *Über das Dirigieren*, and he in fact only explained his practices in 1872 in the preface to the third volume of his collected writings, where he says:

> At the time [i.e. in around 1850] I was vividly inspired by reading several texts by Ludwig Feuerbach, prompting me to appropriate different designations for concepts that I then applied to artistic ideas, though they were not always able to correspond to them clearly.[238]

Wagner made a similar point about German writers in general in his essay *Public and Popularity* of 1878, where he complained that the French, Italians, and Greeks all had a vocabulary adequate to their needs, whereas "each of our great poets and wise men first had to create his language."[239] So at some point in around 1850, when he first discovered Feuerbach's writings, Wagner seems to have begun trawling through scholarly literature in order to create his own aesthetic vocabulary, and clearly continued doing so for many years thereafter. In all this, one word in particular became of central importance to him: *melos*.

Melos and the Body

Wagner's sprawling essay on conducting focuses on two related concepts: recognizing the melodic content of a work, and playing it at the right tempo, with each dependent on the other. The key factor, says Wagner, is to perform

237 Shelfmark Thomas Mann 601: 9–10, 71.
238 SSD 3: Preface.
239 SSD 10: 66.

a work as if you were singing it. Thus he writes as follows about his epiphany upon hearing Habeneck conduct Beethoven in Paris: his "marvelous orchestra *sang* this symphony." Wagner's emphasis on uniting the symphonic with the sung was naturally an integral aspect of his own music dramas.[240] From our perspective, it hardly seems worthy of an epiphany to draw parallels between the instrumental lines of a Classical or Romantic symphony and the natural act of inhaling and exhaling that is the fundamental characteristic of performing music with and through the body. But many great post-Wagner conductors have referred specifically to these passages in *Über das Dirigieren*, which suggests that making a link between instrumental music and vocality is not always obvious. Even Hermann Scherchen found it necessary to discuss this in his own textbook on conducting, duly referring back to Wagner as he did so:

> Singing is not just a prerequisite for shaping a melody properly, but also gives you the tempo in which it is to be performed (we here refer to Richard Wagner's essay "Über das Dirigieren," which explains the basics of a musical theory of tempo in a general fashion). The Italian and the French instrumentalist plays his music by singing, the German primarily with his instrument. In other words, instead of subordinating his technique to song, he burdens the latter with the habits of his technique.[241]

And when Scherchen wrote an admiring letter to Willem Mengelberg in 1933, he reserved his main praise for the way he got his orchestra to "sing"— just as Nikisch had done before him, he claimed.[242]

"Singing" an orchestral phrase could naturally entail a conductor resorting to physical demonstration. In his *Report to His Majesty* of 1865, Wagner claimed that Mozart himself had sung to his orchestral musicians in rehearsal to explain the phrasing of his music,[243] and there are reports of Wagner having done the same.[244] Singing to an orchestra was not infrequent among

---

240 For a detailed discussion of Wagner's approach to melody, his forebears, his aesthetic, and his debt to Italian music, see Trippett (2013).
241 Scherchen (1929): 39.
242 Zwart (2019): 2, 1165.
243 SSD 8: 145.
244 See Praeger (1892): 241 and 242. Praeger is proven to have been something of a fantasist, but since he was intimate with Wagner during the latter's stay in London in 1855, his report of Wagner singing to the orchestra is probably accurate.

Wagner's successors from von Bülow down to von Karajan, though the significance it is accorded in the extant oral and written sources suggests again that it was not as common as we might assume. When several of Mahler's former musicians from the New York Philharmonic recorded interviews about him for his centenary in 1960, two of them recalled specifically how Mahler would explain things by singing to his orchestra, and how he made them play so as to "breathe" physically between phrases.[245]

We should here bear in mind that Wagner's own musical frame of reference was primarily vocal. He had never learnt to play the piano well (nor any other instrument), but he will have grown up hearing his elder brother Albert sing, and Richard by all accounts also developed a fine singing voice (he took pleasure in singing his own roles to piano accompaniment, both in private and in semi-public performances). And right from the start of his career as chorus master in Würzburg, Wagner's daily tasks involved working with singers and learning to accompany them in the opera—which means "breathing" with them and accommodating their physical needs and eccentricities of the moment (for one singer will breathe differently from the next, and this affects all aspects of phrasing, tempo and *rubato*). If one listens to recordings today by conductors who from the start of their career have been focused on the concert hall, rarely or never working in the theater, then one can arguably discern a different attitude to phrasing than among those conductors more accustomed to "breathing" with singers in the opera house.[246]

When Wagner came to describe the melodic content of Beethoven's music, he decided to use a word borrowed from the Greek: "melos." He probably came across it first in one of the several books about ancient Greek music and literature which were published in the early 19th century, or perhaps he perused Gottfried Schilling's well-known music encyclopedia and found it there.[247] Its fourth volume, published in 1841, gives a three-line entry for "Melos," stating cursorily that it is Greek for "Gesang, Lied, auch Gesangspoesie" (singing, song, and also sung poetry), and that the adjective derived from it, "melisch," is used in German to mean "melodic."

Wagner's writings appear to contain only two instances where he used the word "melos" before *Über das Dirigieren*. In *The Artwork of the Future* of 1849,

245 Malloch (1960).

246 This was affirmed by several participants in the discussions at the conference on conducting held at the Royal Academy of Music in London in April 2019 in collaboration with the Bern University of the Arts.

247 See, for example, Drieberg (1835): 103, or Schilling (1841): 653.

he used it specifically to describe the emergence from folksong of Haydn's melodic style in the slow movements of his symphonies;[248] two years later, in the third book of *Opera and Drama,* he again used it to describe how instrumental music came forth from folksong.[249] Then, in *Über das Dirigieren* in 1869, Wagner uses "melos" to mean the melody or melodic content in Beethoven's orchestral works, as in "das neue Beethovensche Melos" (the new Beethovenian melos) or: "Nur die richtige Erfassung des Melos, giebt aber auch das richtige Zeitmaaß an" (Only by properly recognizing the melos can one achieve the correct tempo).

Wagner had a smattering of ancient Greek, and later claimed to have translated the first twelve books of the *Odyssey* into German in his early teens.[250] A couple of letters exist in which Wagner includes a quotation from the Greek of just a few words each time,[251] but it seems he never mastered the language properly, and as an adult he read the great tragedies in German translation. So he presumably used the word "melos" primarily because it seems more scholarly than "melody." A foreign word often sounds clever, especially when it's taken from a language hardly anyone speaks. "Melos" was not the only foreign flourish in Wagner's essays on conducting; we find splashes of French and English, and even the odd phrase from the Latin, such as "ultima ratio" and "monstrum per excessum," the latter almost certainly quoted from Schopenhauer; I have already mentioned his adoption of "fatidik" from Schopenhauer above. These instances were presumably intended to make Wagner appear erudite, though they often serve merely to confirm the perfunctory state of his erudition (see, for example, his corruption of the English phrase "time is money" into "time is music," on p. 58, where his apparent desire to find a clever, anti-Semitic jibe to use against Mendelssohn leads him into linguistic nonsense). But regardless of the extent to which all these foreign words might have been an intellectual sham, Wagner succeeded brilliantly in his purpose in the case of "melos." While some found it pompous at the time—Heinrich Dorn's review of *Über das Dirigieren* mocked Wagner's use of the word "melos" on account of its lack of clarity[252]—such

248 SSD 3: 91.
249 SSD 4: 187.
250 SSD 1: 5. Wilhelm Tappert (1883): 12 claims it was only the first three books, but there is no proof either way.
251 For example his letter of December 19, 1855 to Prosper Sainton (SB 7: 319–21, here 320), or that of January 7, 1862 to Hans von Bülow (SB 14: 38).
252 Dorn (1870): 49.

criticism was soon forgotten. "Melos" had a huge impact, entering into general use whenever people wrote about melodic content in the context of conducting orchestral music. Being a Greek word, it also sounds just as clever in French and English. Most of the early Wagner translators kept it—Émile Guillaume in French,[253] Julio Gómez in Spanish,[254] Ferruccio Amoroso in Italian,[255] and Walter Lawson, Edward Dannreuther, and William Ashton Ellis in English. Only Guy de Charnacé in 1874 stuck to basics, translating "melos" simply as "mélodie" in his abridged French version.[256]

"Melos" has proven just as popular with later conductors and commentators, regardless of their native tongue, from Bruno Walter[257] to Felix Weingartner,[258] Wilhelm Furtwängler,[259] Vittorio Gui,[260] and John Barbirolli.[261] It seems that everyone finds it more attractive to say that a conductor has to draw out the melos, rather than just saying he lets us hear the tune. Apart from sounding cleverer, it also seems to imply a more general category of melodic content beyond what is clearly on the surface—though this latter fact is arguably a later accretion that has become its own justification for using the word. Thus Charnacé, as stated above, assumed it meant only "melody," though when Dannreuther came to it several years later, he felt compelled to add a footnote to his translation to explain that "melos" means "melody in all its aspects."[262] By the time Amoroso came to translate the essay some fifty years after that, he went even further, asserting that "'melos' … is a word that can't be reduced to any logical or technical definition."[263] Over time, everyone seems to have begun to assume that the word must surely mean more than it says, whereas Wagner presumably just

---

253 Wagner, trans. Émile Guillaume (1888): 153.
254 Wagner, trans. Gómez (1925).
255 Amoroso (1940): 18.
256 See Charnacé (1874): 286.
257 Walter (1957): 162.
258 Weingartner (1923): 24.
259 Furtwängler: "Vom Handwerkszeug des Dirigenten," in Furtwängler (1956): 97–106, here 102.
260 Gui (1940): 197.
261 Holden (2007): 136.
262 Wagner, trans. Edward Dannreuther (1897): 15; Wagner, trans. Ellis (1895): 303.
263 Amoroso (1940): 376.

wanted to seem erudite, and might just as easily have chosen any suitably foreign-sounding word for the purpose.

This use of "melos" in a Wagnerian context had already become widespread in the general musical discourse before the First World War. In 1911, the prominent German writer Paul Stefan praised Mahler as the embodiment of Wagner's ideals in realizing the "melos," which Stefan regarded (obviously paraphrasing Wagner) as the true "task of the conductor … All written notation is but signs: only in the melos and in its sounds does it acquire life."[264] One year later, Heinrich Schenker published his monograph on Beethoven's Ninth Symphony, in which he writes extensively about the "melos," using the word over thirty times; as Nicholas Cook once observed, this is a book "haunted by Wagner."[265] Just one year later, the critic Richard Aldrich of the *New York Times* could write of Arturo Toscanini's performance of the Ninth Symphony in New York in April 1913 that he

> met in an unusual degree Wagner's criterion of the *melos*, of keeping unbroken the essentially melodic line that underlies it. The orchestra sang throughout; and in all the nuances of his performance the melodic line was not interrupted; nor, in all the plastic shaping of phrase was the symmetry of the larger proportions of the organic unity of the whole lost sight of.[266]

Aldrich had studied in Germany in the 1890s, which perhaps also explains his emphasis on the "organic" unity of Beethoven's symphony and his use of the word "nuance," which was another of Wagner's favorite words of foreign origin ("nüancieren," meaning expressive modifications; we also find this word used in a similar context by Wagner's friend Bernhard Spyri, the newspaper editor in Zurich, when he wrote of Wagner's performances in the 1850s).[267]

One of the first commentators to dispute Wagner's approach to Beethoven and to offer concrete reasons for his opposition was Heinrich Schenker. Wagner was convinced that Beethoven had intended his "melos"—the principal thematic line—to be clearly audible throughout, and assumed that when this was not the case, then it had to be a miscalculation resulting either from Beethoven's deafness, or from the technical inadequacies of the instruments at his disposal. In such cases, said Wagner, adjustments to the part-writing or

---

264 Stefan (1911): 42.
265 See Schenker (1912) and Cook (1995): 94.
266 Aldrich (1941): 396.
267 Zimmermann (1986): 20.

the orchestration were desirable. Schenker's criticism of Wagner, as expressed extensively in his abovementioned monograph on the Ninth Symphony, was founded on his belief that Beethoven had not in fact intended one thematic line to dominate, but had at times wanted it to be more veiled (*verhüllt*). Reducing Beethoven's textures to a kind of melody-plus-accompaniment, wrote Schenker, brought with it the risk of monotony. Given Wagner's antipathy to much that was Italianate in music,[268] it is deliciously ironic that Schenker now accused Wagner of misunderstanding Beethoven and of treating him as might a "superficial" Italian opera conductor devoted to tunes above all else.[269] But, as Nicholas Cook has observed, when Wagner postulates the existence of a background melodic structure in a Beethoven symphony (what Aldrich called the underlying melodic line), he in fact seems from our perspective to be pointing towards Heinrich Schenker's notion of the *Urlinie*, however much Schenker might have abhorred Wagner's approach to what he, too, still called Beethoven's *melos*.[270] Schenker only later coined his own term for the underlying melody in a Beethoven movement (that *Urlinie*), but we are here faced with the peculiar fact that Wagner's vocabulary, presumably chosen just to impress others, seems to have led indirectly to a new generation of musicological terminology in Schenker that has itself had a profound impact on scholarship.

Schenker was actually not alone in associating Wagner with Italian operatic practices. His ideas find an unexpected correlation in remarks made by Richard Strauss to his sometime assistant Hans Swarowsky, who in later life recalled how Strauss had envied Verdi for taking the vocal line as his starting point when composing. Instead he, Strauss, "always started out with the orchestral textures when writing his operas, only afterwards 'inserting' the vocal parts, which he regarded as one of his own unalterable mistakes."[271] Strauss regarded this as a natural result of having begun his mature composing career with symphonic poems. When Wagner's stepdaughter Daniela once showed Strauss a musical sketch for the dispute of the Masters in the first act of *Die Meistersinger*, Strauss "was astonished to find that 'the Master'

---

268 See, for example, Hans Sachs's famous disparagement of "welscher Tand"—Latinate frippery—in the closing scene of *Die Meistersinger*. "Welsch" in German signifies things either French or Italian.

269 Schenker (1912): 49.

270 Cook (1995): 101.

271 Swarowsky (1979): 252.

had set about things no differently from Verdi,"[272] namely that Wagner, too, had composed from the vocal line outwards.

Wagner's insistence on identifying the primary melodic line in a symphonic work and on bringing it to the fore had numerous consequences for the performance of instrumental music over the ensuing decades. It was quite possibly one of the points of origin of the Second Viennese School's predilection for specifying the "Hauptstimme" (the main voice) in their non-tonal music, and *Melos* was even chosen as the title of a new music journal set up by Hermann Scherchen in 1920.[273] This did not necessarily mean that conducting adherents of Wagnerian "melos" naturally felt an affinity for the new music of their own time. Furtwängler insisted on the necessity of making the "melos" sing in a symphonic work in whichever instrumental part it was to be found,[274] but when confronted with Schoenberg's *Variations for Orchestra*, op. 31, it seems he was unable to find that "melos" anywhere but in the uppermost line, a fact that displeased the composer. Walter Goehr recalled hearing a telephone conversation between Schoenberg and Furtwängler after the work's premiere, in which the former complained: "Herr Furtwängler, you are an experienced enough musician to know that the melody is not always in the first violin part."[275]

Regardless of how it might have been interpreted by the Schoenbergians, the prime impact of Wagner's "melos" was clearly felt in how post-Wagnerian conductors performed the Classical repertoire. We have already noted how many still followed Wagner's example, many decades after his death, by strengthening the brass in the scherzo of Beethoven's Ninth Symphony in order to bring out the melody. Others undertook similar measures in other works. Otto Klemperer, for example, added the horns to the melody in the bass at the recapitulation in the first movement of Beethoven's Eighth Symphony (measure 190), and was proud that the horns themselves were barely audible, the result being merely a strengthening of the melody

272 Ibid.: 253.

273 *Melos. Halbmonatsschrift für Musik*, edited initially by Hermann Scherchen, ran from 1920 to 1934, and it afterwards continued in different guises until it was merged with the *Neue Zeitschrift für Musik* in 1975. The first issue in 1920 included articles on Busoni and Schoenberg.

274 Furtwängler: "Vom Handwerkszeug des Dirigenten," in Furtwängler (1956): 97–106, here 102

275 Quoted in Goehr (2004): x.

without any noticeable alteration to the sound colors.[276] And numerous conductors applied the same principles to the works of other composers, including Mozart. Christoph Moor has observed how several of them adjusted the dynamics, the orchestration, or both in the famous passage of five-part invertible counterpoint at the close of Mozart's *Jupiter* Symphony in order to make the movement's main four-note motif better audible when it appears in the bass at measures 388–91; the fanfares in the brass at this point mean that the motif in question recedes into the background, and conductors in the Austro-German tradition in particular seem to have assumed that this must have been a miscalculation. Bruno Walter had the horns play it, Hermann Scherchen doubled the bassoons, and Fritz Reiner even had the timpani play the four-note motif, *forte*.[277] But unlike the case of Beethoven in his Ninth, no one could argue that Mozart had made a mistake because of deafness, or that the instruments available to him were inadequate for his intentions. When he wrote this symphony in 1788, Mozart was at the height of his powers, presumably able to achieve whatever effect he desired with the forces at hand. So we may assume that Mozart indeed intended to shift our attention away from his motif during these measures. The conviction among numerous conductors that one *has* to make the motif more prominent here, regardless of how drastic the means might be to achieve it, is surely a direct result of Wagner's insistence on keeping the "melos" prominent at all times.

It is worth noting that Wagner's affinity for the corporeal aspect of music seems to have encompassed more than vocality. His description of Beethoven's Seventh Symphony as the "apotheosis of the dance" in his *Artwork of the Future* is often quoted,[278] but it is less well known that on at least one occasion he also put these words into practice. In his autobiography, Siegfried Wagner recalled how Franz Liszt played Beethoven's Seventh Symphony for Cosima, Princess Hatzfeld and other friends during his visit to the Wagners in the Palazzo Vendramin in Venice in late 1882: "We children listened in the adjoining room. Suddenly, at the Scherzo, we saw our father enter and start to perform the most adroit, graceful dance, unnoticed by Liszt and his audience. You would have thought you were watching a twenty-year-old youth in front of you."[279] A similar tale was told by Richard Fricke, the ballet master who served as Wagner's assistant director at the first

---

276 Related to the present writer by Klemperer's daughter Lotte in 1999.
277 See Moor (2019): 293.
278 SSD 3: 94.
279 Siegfried Wagner (1923): 20.

Bayreuth Festival in 1876. In his diary of that year, he wrote on May 10 of how Wagner asked his house pianist Joseph Rubinstein to play "my favorite Sonata by Beethoven, op. 54, minuet tempo," i.e., the first movement, marked "In Tempo d'un Menuetto." Rubinstein began, but then Wagner interrupted him:

> Wagner immediately corrected the tempo: "Ask our ballet master how it should be done." I indicated the tempo. "That's right!" And now he moved through the room in accordance with the rhythm, in solemn steps, in the funniest manner, gesticulating, and beating the time with his legs and arms.[280]

Beethoven's minuets were of particular interest to Wagner; he devotes a long passage of *Über das Dirigieren* to the "Tempo di menuetto" movement of the Symphony no. 8, insisting that it be performed thus, not at the quicker tempo of a scherzo (see p. 45 above). And two years later, he offered an instance in which dance and melody both determine the tempo, when he sang the D major *Andante* section of the slow movement of Beethoven's Ninth to Cosima, adding: "It's really a dance, a minuet theme."[281]

Tempo Modification

Tempo is the second fundamental concept that occupies Wagner in *Über das Dirigieren*, alongside melody. As Egon Voss has remarked,[282] Wagner seems to have regarded tempo as existing in a kind of continuum from the "sustained tones" of *Adagio* at one extreme to the swift figurations of *Allegro* at the other, though both are derived from song, with the *Allegro* arising when a cantilena is refracted by means of quicker figurations. The true *Adagio* cannot be played slow enough, writes Wagner, nor the true *Allegro* quick enough, and when we reach the one extreme, it makes us yearn for the other. But having specified these extremes, Wagner goes on to discuss in greater detail how to effect gradual modifications of tempo along that continuum, to which end one has to recognize the inherent vocality of a work's melodic lines. As we have seen in the reviews quoted above, it was Wagner's tempo modifications that seem to have struck critics everywhere, from London to Vienna. *Rubato* in all its forms was nothing new—the word itself was in

---

280 Fricke (1906): 46.
281 CWT 2: 112 (June 8, 1878).
282 See Voss (2015): 101.

common currency among German musicians in the 18th and 19th centuries. *Pace* Wagner, Mendelssohn too was adept at altering his tempi within a work, albeit apparently within tighter parameters than was Wagner's custom; the violinist Wilhelm Wasiliewski (1822–96), Schumann's concert master in Düsseldorf, observed Mendelssohn closely in the Leipzig Gewandhaus in the 1840s and wrote in his memoirs of how, "if he allowed himself small divergences in tempo in performance with improvised ritardandos or accelerandos, these were achieved in such a manner that you would have thought he had rehearsed them."[283]

Numerous aspects of *rubato* practices are already described in the literature in the first half of the 19th century. The 1827 piano tutor by Mozart's pupil Johann Nepomuk Hummel, for example, mentions the practice of slowing down for the lyrical passages in an *Allegro* movement, though Hummel expressly states that good taste is expected to prevail, lest a performance become "too rhapsodic."[284] As we know from many critics from Smart to Davison to Hanslick, slowing down for the second subject of a sonata movement was something practiced by Wagner, and he also specifically recommends it in *Über das Dirigieren* (see, for example, his discussion of Weber's *Freischütz* Overture on p. 68 above). This practice was later continued by conductors such as Strauss, Mengelberg, and Furtwängler, as can be heard in their recordings of the symphonic repertoire: in later life, Strauss even stipulated in writing that "the cantabile second subject should in general be taken rather more calmly" in Mozart's symphonies.[285] Wagner's tendency to slow down for the recapitulation of a first subject—mentioned above by Smart in 1855—is something that we also find mentioned in Czerny's piano tutor of 1839.[286]

There was thus nothing new in modifying the tempo in a work, nor should we suppose that Wagner was alone in his era with his tempo modifications. As in so many areas, Wagner is keen here to erect binary oppositions in order to emphasize the rightness of his own practice, and the wrongness of others. Since we naturally have no recordings from the time, it is almost impossible to tell when Wagner is exaggerating for effect, and when not. But there is at least one sound document that might serve as a cautionary example. When

---

283 Wasielewski (1897): 59.

284 Hummel (1827): 428.

285 See Strauss's article "Dirigentenerfahrungen mit klassischen Meisterwerken" in Strauss (1989): 57.

286 Czerny (1839): 4, 26.

he was 80 years old, the conductor and composer Carl Reinecke made piano roll recordings of several works by Mozart, including his own solo arrangements of the slow movements of the piano concertos K. 488 and K. 537 (as mentioned above, Reinecke had edited the piano works of Mozart for the first-ever critical complete edition). Reinecke is pilloried in *Über das Dirigieren* for his supposedly rigid approach to tempo. We cannot know exactly how he conducted, but his piano rolls prove that when he played, he engaged in all manner of *crescendi, decrescendi, arpeggiandi* and subtle tempo shifts quite unlike the stricter style of Mozart playing that became the norm in the 20th century.[287]

Given Reinecke's close friendship with members of the Brahms–Schumann circle and his position at the heart of German music-making—he conducted the Gewandhaus Orchestra for over three decades—we can assume that such liberties and fluctuations of dynamics and tempi were the norm in his time, not the exception. But since most critics of the day made specific reference to Wagner's own tempo fluctuations, we must also assume that Wagner's practices were even more extreme than those of his conducting contemporaries. Some critics—such as Henry Smart in London—might well have exaggerated the supposedly erratic nature of Wagner's tempo changes on account of some personal antipathy towards the man and his views, but Wagner's tempi must nevertheless have deviated considerably from what was considered the norm, as otherwise they would not have been remarked upon by so many different people at different times in different places.

If we wish to identify a concrete point of origin for Wagner's more rhapsodic practice, it might have been the 1840 biography of Beethoven by Anton Schindler, which offers numerous examples of the kind of tempo modifications that Beethoven supposedly wanted himself.[288] Schindler claims that: "Whatever I heard Beethoven play was, with few exceptions, free of any compulsion in matters of tempo; it was a 'tempo rubato' in the truest sense of the word."[289] The most extreme example given by Schindler is an excerpt from the slow movement of Beethoven's Second Symphony, whose rapid shifts in tempo, purportedly derived directly from Beethoven, are strangely prescient of later reports of how Wagner and his followers conducted Beethoven. In fact, though, Wagner himself never conducted either

---

287 See Da Costa (2019).
288 See Schindler (1840): 227–42; the *Eroica*'s first movement is discussed on 239.
     See also *Über das Dirigieren*, p. 57.
289 Schindler (1840): 228.

his First or Second symphonies, which he seems to have regarded as "naïve" in style—Classical in today's parlance—and thus, ironically, unsuited to precisely the kind of tempo modifications given in figure 5.18 by Schindler. Schindler also recommends slowing down for the second subject in the first movement of the *Eroica*, and the music example he gives here is the same we find in *Über das Dirigieren*, where Wagner clearly also expects a different tempo (p. 57 above). A few pages later, Wagner also recalls in horror how Dionys Weber had supposedly performed this symphony at a strict tempo throughout, in Prague in the early 1830s (p. 64). It is important to note that Schindler offers these detailed explanations of Beethoven's *rubato* as a riposte to Ferdinand Ries, whom he criticizes here for having claimed that Beethoven played his works "mostly strict in time," which Schindler says is simply wrong. Ries had died in early 1838 and so (conveniently) could not now reply, but the *Biographical Notes* by Ries and Franz Wegeler, published after Ries's death in 1838, were Schindler's direct competition on the market for Beethoveniana. In order to assert his primacy, Schindler had to give his own book a greater veneer of authenticity, and his insistence on Beethoven's excessive *rubati*, regardless of how authentic they might have been, were a useful means to this end. Schindler has long since been proven to be highly unreliable, but Wagner knew and admired the man and his book, and had even worked with Schindler's sister, a singer at the Magdeburg theater, in the mid-1830s.

Freedom, Control, and the "Two Cultures"

There are two other factors that might have induced Wagner to pursue his art of tempo modification with such vigor, though they are more biographical than musical—and they also provide an odd parallel with the argument over primacy in Beethoven interpretation between Schindler and Ries. Numerous sources testify to Mendelssohn having used *rubato* sparingly, preferring stricter tempi on the whole.[290] Given that Wagner was determined to set himself apart from his perceived rival to a degree that can best be termed pathological (besides Mendelssohn's importance to the infamous pamphlet *Jewishness in Music*, he all but haunts the pages of *Über das Dirigieren*), we should consider the possibility that Wagner used his tempi at least in part as a means of differentiation between them. If Mendelssohn was "strict," Wagner

---

290   See, for example, Brown (1999): 384–85.

Figure 5.18. Beethoven, piano reduction of the second movement of his Symphony no. 2 in D major, op. 36, mm. 55–75, as given in Anton Schindler's biography of 1840. None of the tempo markings are original, but have been added by Schindler.

would set music "free" (whether or not he was aware of echoing Schindler's stance towards Ries must remain a matter of speculation). Such "freedom," however, brings complications of its own, and this raises the second extra-musical factor that might have conditioned Wagner's tempo responses. The tempo modifications described by Czerny and Hummel refer primarily to piano music. If one is to perform orchestral music with even greater tempo fluctuations, this can only be done if there is one person in complete control, and if everyone submits to his will. As long as a work is played at a single tempo, then Schumann's conducting solution, mentioned at the outset above, is not impossible: you simply set the orchestra into motion, wait, and then make sure they finish together. But if an orchestra is to ebb and flow in tempo, it must be molded into a single unit, and cannot be left to its own devices.

The notion of the conductor as a figure of absolute power remains popular in our time—to prove it, one only needs to glance at the photos on any conductor's website, which almost inevitably include at least one action photo with raised right arm, more reminiscent of Heinrich Hoffmann's staged photos of Hitler the would-be orator in the 1920s than of anything musical.[291] But this is largely a fiction. Orchestral musicians simply ignore a conductor if he is uninteresting or mediocre, regardless of how demonstrative his gestures might seem (if the audience took the trouble to look more closely, they would find that hardly anyone behind the first desk of strings ever casts a glance at the man thrashing away on the podium if he is not up to par). When Elias Canetti wrote in his *Mass and Power* of the conductor as a "Führer," a would-be "master of the world,"[292] this was a figment of his own imagination, and proof that he himself had no practical experience of either conducting or playing in an orchestra. But if a conductor is competent and is constantly changing the tempo, then the orchestra will be on tenterhooks and will have little choice but to pay close attention to his baton, otherwise the performance will fall apart. Given Wagner's proven desire to control all aspects of his art, his preference for tempo modification—besides all the musical reasons he gives—might also have been a means of exercising a similar control in this particular field of activity.

---

291 Such conductor photos seem to have been popular on record covers from the early LP era onwards; any random Internet search will provide innumerable examples. The Hoffmann photos of Hitler can similarly be found online with ease.

292 Canetti (1980): 443–44.

This control extended into determining the vocabulary that Wagner used to describe his conducting. Just as Wagner appropriated the word "melos" to elevate and differentiate his own approach to melody, he also expanded his vocabulary to describe his tempo modifications. As far as the present writer has been able to determine, Wagner never used the phrase "*tempo rubato*" in his writings, though it had been in widespread use in Germany since the 18th century. Instead, he uses the straightforward term "Modifikation des Tempo's" or "Modifikation des Zeitmaaßes," both meaning modification of the tempo, for the Italian word "tempo" had in Germany long been interchangeable with its local equivalent, "Zeitmaß." Wagner also uses a second term, however—one that has no direct relationship to music, and no direct correlation in English: "Zartlebigkeit," which more or less means "possessed of fleeting life"; "volatile" comes perhaps closest, though this has connotations today that would not suit Wagner's context. It appears that Wagner has here created a noun from the adjective "zartlebig," which is also rare, though it is occasionally found in the scientific literature of his time, such as in a tract about microscopic organisms that was published in Bern in 1852 by one Maximilian Perty,[293] where it is used to denote the fragility and brief lifespan of those tiny creatures that die rapidly when observed in a drop of water. Perty was not unknown to Wagner; we find a later book of his in Wagner's Wahnfried library,[294] namely *Die mystischen Erscheinungen der menschlichen Natur*, which deals with matters of the occult, ghosts, the state of half-sleep, and other such phenomena.[295]

"Zartlebigkeit" first appears in Wagner's prose in the phrase: "hierzu gehört vor allen Dingen, dass das Zeitmaß von nicht minderer Zartlebigkeit sei, als das thematische Gewebe," for which my translation is: "above all, the tempo should be no less flexible than the thematic web" (see p. 59). This passage is in itself of special significance, for Wagner was writing not long after he had resumed composition of the *Ring* after a hiatus of over a decade, and was grappling anew with its own flexible "thematic web" of leitmotifs. It is something of a truism that when Wagner writes about other composers, he is usually also writing about himself. And in this passage, "Zartlebigkeit" for a moment serves not just to unite Beethoven and Wagner, but also to dissolve the boundaries between the actual work of art and the manner of its performance. As in the case of "melos," there is no

---

293 Perty (1852): 149–50.
294 See [Richard Wagner Museum Bayreuth] (n.d.): 286.
295 See Perty (1872).

musical reason for Wagner to use "Zartlebigkeit." But unlike "melos," it never caught on; short Greek words are better for that, as they can sound erudite in any language.

We have already discussed above how Ludwig Feuerbach had inspired Wagner to set about creating his own aesthetic vocabulary. It might also have been Feuerbach who prompted Wagner to expand his general reading into the sciences in order to bolster that vocabulary. Feuerbach had already compared his own approach in theology to that of the sciences. In the preface to his *Essence of Christianity* of 1841, for example, he had written that: "The method that the present writer pursues here is one that is thoroughly *objective*—the method of *analytical* chemistry."[296] But Wagner was not alone in introducing aspects of science into the aesthetic discourse. Eduard Hanslick did so in the very first edition of his book *Vom Musikalisch-Schönen* of 1854, though with the aim of actually denying science any validity in discussing music. He wrote how

> even the most abstract investigations gravitate noticeably towards the methods of the natural sciences. Even aesthetics, if they don't wish to lead a mere semblance of life, have to know both the gnarly root and the tender fiber that links every individual art to the foundations of nature.[297]

But Hanslick insists that music depends on nature merely for the materials we need for its physical instruments—wood, animal skins and the like—whereas "melody and harmony, the two main factors of the musical art, are not found in nature. They are the creation of the mind of man."[298]

Hanslick's insistence here on music's independence is in itself proof of how the arts and sciences had already become largely separate in the general discourse. Goethe's generation had seen no contradiction in straddling both, but by the mid-19th century, the split was already apparent in the western world between these "two cultures" (as C.P. Snow famously termed them over a century later).[299] Aesthetics will always remain a matter of debate, but as Hanslick intimates, science was already assuming its modern role as sole bearer of truth, and banishing falsehood in the process.

Wagner's engagement with the sciences intensified in his final years, as is obvious from his own writings and from Cosima's diary. They both

---

296 Feuerbach (1841): vi (italics in original).
297 Hanslick (1854): 83.
298 Ibid.: 84.
299 Snow (2010).

maintained friendly relations with assorted scientists from the 1870s onwards, and she specifically records meetings with luminaries such as Helmholtz, who attended Wagner's reading of the *Götterdämmerung* text in Berlin in January 1873. Wagner became increasingly skeptical about the dominance of science in society, harboring grave doubts about its claims to objective truth. But even he had to admit in his 1878 essay *Public and Popularity* that the natural sciences were now largely regarded as responsible for "progress" in society and for "abstract scientific knowledge." So while Wagner's use of scientific vocabulary to describe musical processes might at first glance seem to be harking back to the age of Goethe when those "two cultures" were ostensibly one, in fact he too is thereby affirming their separateness. His writings of these years leave little doubt about his determination to have his own interpretative practices recognized as possessing sole validity (hence all those passages in *Über das Dirigieren* denigrating almost everyone else). So perhaps by appropriating the language of science, Wagner hoped to partake in its "abstract" objectivity, and thereby assert an even greater control over the aesthetic discourse of performance.

Charles Darwin and the Imperceptible Art of Transition

"Zartlebigkeit" offers us just one example of how Wagner adopted scientific terminology to his own ends. But there are other, no less fascinating analogies to be found between the natural sciences and Wagner's understanding of his work as a creative artist.

> My subtlest, most profound art is what I would now like to call the art of transition [*Übergang*], because the whole tissue of my art [*Kunstgewebe*] comprises such transitions; what is abrupt and sudden is now abhorrent to me; it is often unavoidable and necessary, but even then it may not arise without the mood being so specifically prepared for this sudden transition that it comes as if of its own accord. My greatest masterpiece in the art of the subtlest, most gradual transition is surely the big scene in the second act of *Tristan und Isolde*.[300]

This passage, from a letter Wagner wrote to Mathilde Wesendonck from Paris on October 29, 1859, is one of the most often quoted of all his correspondence. The word "Übergang" (transition) had long been in currency in writing on music; we even find it used thus in Goethe, such as in his translation

---

300 SB 11: 329.

of Diderot's text *Rameau's Nephew*.[301] But we find it more often in Goethe's investigations of the natural world. In his *Versuch die Metamorphose der Pflanzen zu erklären* (An Endeavor to explain the Metamorphosis of Plants) of 1790, for example, Goethe used "Übergang" repeatedly to describe how one part of a plant merges into the next. He described the "secret relationships" that exist between the outer parts of a plant, and how nature can teach us "the laws of transformation, according to which one part brings forth another, illustrating the most varied patterns by modification of a single organ."[302] It was in part thanks to Goethe's influence that such an "organicist" approach (encompassing "unity in variety") also became important in the arts in the 19th century—not least though his notion of an "Urpflanze" (primordial plant) that might bear within it the traits of all other plants. Schenker, another keen organicist, surely had this term at the back of his mind when conceiving his *Urlinie* referred to above. Wagner was as beholden to an "organic" or "organicist" view as any of his artist colleagues of the day. We find a host of organic and biological metaphors already in his Zurich writings: witness his description of melody as itself "the expression of an inner organism,"[303] or his famous gendered explanation of text being the male sperm, fertilizing music-as-woman to create music drama in the "most heated moment of love's arousal," for which he uses the superlative "brünstigst," a word otherwise employed to describe male animals on heat.[304] (This probably makes Wagner the first-ever composer to describe composing itself as an orgasm.)

Wagner knew his Goethe, so was presumably familiar with his use of the word "Übergang" in both a scientific and an aesthetic sense (we know, for example, that Cosima and Wagner read *Rameau's Nephew* together).[305] But Wagner will also have come across the term elsewhere—one occurrence worth noting here is in the chapter entitled "Klingsohrs Märchen von Fabel und Eros" (Klingsohr's Fairy Tale of Fable and Eros) in the fragmentary novel *Heinrich von Ofterdingen* by Novalis, which was one of Wagner's sources for his opera *Tannhäuser*. Here, the author's description of the music of the spheres sounds almost like a precursor of Wagner's symphonic web of leitmotifs: "The music changed like the pictures on the table, unceasingly,

---

301 Diderot, trans. Goethe (1811): 171.
302 Goethe (1790): 2.
303 SSD 3: 314.
304 SSD 4: 103.
305 See CWT 2: 334 (April 20, 1879).

and however wonderful and abrupt the transitions often were, nevertheless a single, simple theme seemed to bind the whole together."[306]

Wagner used the word "Übergang" throughout his life, both in its musical and commonplace meanings, though sparingly at first; there are roughly half a dozen instances in his correspondence up to the mid-1850s, and a few in *Opera and Drama* and elsewhere. The word then appears with sudden frequency in his correspondence with Mathilde Wesendonck in 1859—twice in his letter to her of May 8, 1859, but a full seven times in the above quoted letter of October 29. He is admittedly insisting here on the newness of his art of transition as if he were a salesman, which can explain the word's mantra-like occurrence, though it is also tempting to discern some autobiographical intent. Wagner had not yet given up hope of convincing Mathilde to abandon Otto and join him instead, and he was presumably keen to put behind them their own "abrupt and sudden" break of the previous year, when Wagner had been compelled at short notice to leave Zurich, his home, and his wife after his passion for Mathilde had become public knowledge. But just because Wagner was himself prone to mixing life and art[307] does not mean we should be overly swift in constructing direct correlations between them, if it means we risk descending to the level of a tabloid Freud.

What is of relevance to us here is that this art of transition, this avoidance of abruptness, is just as central to Wagner's aesthetic of conducting as described in *Über das Dirigieren* as it is to his aesthetic of composing. We find it in his insistence on tempo modifications (whose "Zartlebigkeit" we have already discussed above), we find it in the annotations made at his behest to the orchestral parts in Zurich, and we find it his later alterations to Beethoven's scores. The marked-up parts copied by Adam Bauer for Mozart's *Jupiter* Symphony and for Wagner's own arrangement of Gluck's Overture to *Iphigenie in Aulis* consistently employ *crescendi* and *diminuendi* to negate the impact of the more sudden, terraced dynamics of the originals.[308] We find the same tendency to smooth out what Wagner perceived as abrupt in his amendments to Beethoven's Ninth, already discussed above—whether filling out the trumpet parts to avoid "gaps" in the original melody caused by using natural instruments, or adding *accelerandi* and *decelerandi*. Wagner's

---

306 Novalis (1802): 276.

307 See, for example, the references to Goethe's *Faust* or to Beethoven's letter to his "Immortal beloved" in his letters to Mathilde of 1858, before he was compelled to leave Zurich; these are discussed in Walton (2019).

308 See Walton (2007): 169–74.

intention each time is generally to provide a bridge from one idea to another. But this approach did not find approval with everyone. Heinrich Schenker for one was aghast. Just as he was opposed to Wagner's alterations to Beethoven's music to emphasize the "melos," Schenker was convinced that Beethoven's treatment of the woodwind and brass, with all their gaps and supposedly ungainly leaps, was an integral aspect of his compositional technique and a result of keen calculation. Adorno was of a similar opinion, writing in his marginal notes to *Über das Dirigieren* of "Wagner's transition mania. He is incapable of comprehending contrast as a means of connection … NB everything in Wagner is 'overdetermined,' his music drama is totality as tautology."[309]

Wagner's insistence on the art of transition in *Über das Dirigieren* again offers us a connection to the world of science, though this time to a contemporary scientist. We know that Wagner possessed German and French editions of books by Charles Darwin in his Bayreuth library.[310] Cosima's diary first mentions Wagner reading Darwin on June 29, 1872,[311] and he himself specifically mentions Darwin in the abovementioned essay *Public and Popularity* of 1878.[312] But it seems likely that Wagner had dipped into *Origin of Species* several years before (the earliest German translation of Darwin in his library was Heinrich Bronn's 1867 edition of *Origin of Species*).

In *Über das Dirigieren*, Wagner insists repeatedly that a tempo transition must be "unmerklich" (imperceptible). The word "unmerklich" occurs ten times in Wagner's writings in the near-thirty years before *Über das Dirigieren*, but seven times alone in this essay, each time referring to transitions of some form or other. This might well be an idea that Wagner either acquired from Darwin, or at the very least found confirmed there. In the second chapter of the abovementioned 1867 edition of Darwin's *Origin of Species*, differences among subspecies etc. are described thus: "Diese Verschiedenheiten greifen, in eine Reihe geordnet, unmerklich in einander, und die Reihe weckt die Vorstellung von einem wirklichen Übergang."[313] Darwin's original English contains no mention of any "imperceptible transition," no "unmerklich[er] … Übergang," instead running thus: "These differences blend into each

309 Adorno (2001): 45.
310 See [Richard Wagner Museum Bayreuth] (n.d.).
311 CWT 1: 541.
312 For example, SSD 10: 84.
313 Darwin, trans. Bronn (1867): 73.

other in an insensible series; and a series impresses the mind with the idea of an actual passage."[314]

There is a further correlation that is worthy of note. As mentioned above, Wagner used the term "Modifikation des Zeitmaaßes" or "Modifikation des Tempo's" when writing of his flexible tempi. "Modifikation" is a term we only find some five times in his extant letters and writings before *Über das Dirigieren*, but over twenty times in that essay. The word was hardly new (as we have seen above, it was used by Goethe in his study of plants), but it does seem as if something had suddenly convinced Wagner that the word now possessed special currency. So it is interesting to note that "modifizieren" is a term of crucial importance in Bronn's edition of Darwin, just as it is in the author's original English, for "descent with modification" is the latter's term for how a species evolves over several generations. Bronn's translation even sounds reminiscent of music if taken out of context—thus we find in it phrases such as "durch Variation modifiziert" (modified by variation),[315] and Bronn also uses the word "Abänderung" as a variant of "Modifikation"—a word that we find occasionally in Wagner's letters, but which is almost absent from his writings until his essay of 1873 on Beethoven's Ninth, where it appears four times to describe modifications to the melodic content.

Cosima's diaries record several further instances of Wagner reading Darwin's writings over the ensuing years (besides the *Origin of Species* in German and French, his Wahnfried library also holds German editions of *The Expression of the Emotions in Man and Animals* and the *Descent of Man*). Perhaps the most convincing connection between Wagner's art of transition and his interpretation of Darwin is to be found in his late aphorisms, published two years after his death in the *Bayreuther Blätter*, which bear the subsidiary title "Natura non facit saltus" (Nature does not make leaps). We find this phrase in assorted forms in the writings of several scholars of the 18th and 19th centuries, but it features prominently in Darwin's *Origin of Species*, which might be where Wagner first became properly aware of it. It is listed as one of the subheadings of Darwin's chapter 6, and in the chapter itself it is used to demonstrate how nature proceeds by means of "ganz allmähliche Übergänge"—thus the German translation in Wagner's library,

---

314 Darwin (1866): 60. I quote here from the fourth edition of *Origin of Species*, which was the edition translated by Bronn and Carus, though this passage is identical in Darwin's earlier editions.

315 Darwin, trans. Bronn (1867): 109.

meaning "very gradual transitions."[316] The English original, however, has merely "graduated steps."[317]

Linguistic similarities do not provide concrete proof of influence—Wagner's vocabulary naturally included words such as "allmählich" before he had read any Darwin, for example—though the abovementioned, sudden burst of Darwinian vocabulary in Wagner after the publication of Darwin's German editions is undeniable. And even if there were no direct connection, such passages suggest a remarkable convergence in the vocabulary of contemporaneous developments in both music and science. Just as Darwin wrote of an evolutionary, gradual, organic progression in the world, so does Wagner uphold an aesthetic of music as organic growth that would become central to Austro-German musical thinking over the ensuing decades, and that in the realm of conducting arguably found its final flowering in the work of Willem Mengelberg and Wilhelm Furtwängler.[318]

Wagner ex Cathedra

Wagner's late, critical engagement with the sciences went hand in hand with a similar approach to matters of religion, culminating in the so-called "regeneration writings" of his final years, whose strange, convoluted admixture of vegetarianism, racial purity, and Christianity formed a backdrop to the composition of *Parsifal*. This general interest also found a specific outlet in his increasing fascination with Martin Luther from the early 1870s onwards. On the one hand, Luther now formed part of a teleological interpretation of history that culminated naturally in Wagner and emphasized a supposedly Protestant triumph over Catholicism (summed up by Cosima on July 31, 1879, albeit without due regard for chronology, as "Luther, Goethe, Schiller, Dürer, Bach, *Parsifal*");[319] but on the other hand, Luther also served as a useful metaphor for Wagner's mistrust of the sciences. Thus in his essay *What Use is this Knowledge* (published in the *Bayreuther Blätter* in 1881 as a "supplement to *Religion and Art*"), Wagner implicitly placed his own antipathy to science on a par with Luther's opposition to the extremes of Roman Catholicism. Just as letters of indulgence had once falsely promised relief

316 Darwin, trans. Bronn (1867): 240.
317 Darwin (1866): 232.
318 See, e.g., Allen (2018).
319 CWT 2: 390.

from sin, claimed Wagner, so now did the new belief systems of physics and chemistry erroneously offer "salvation from evil."[320]

Wagner's obsession with religion and science as failed or failing harbingers of man's salvation was inextricably bound up with his belief in the revelatory, salvational power of (his) art. Thus in *Religion and Art* of 1880 he expressly suggests that the latter's use of mythical symbols might enable it to "salvage" the essence of the former.[321] But just as his antipathy towards science seems not to have prevented him from seeking and finding correlations between his own aesthetic and the teachings of Darwin and others, Wagner also seems to have sought to emulate the example of the Church in his endeavors to ensure the permanent, future success of his oeuvre. Both Wagner and Cosima followed the course of the First Vatican Council of 1869–70 with a fascinated horror, as we can see from the sheer number of times that Cosima's diary refers to the "infallibility" of the Pope, both before and after the actual confirmation of it in the decree *Pastor aeternus* of July 18, 1870 (she mentions it no less than eight times between May and August 1870). But this fascination with "infallibility" seems to involve more than a knee-jerk rejection of Catholic dogma. We have already noted how Wagner was keen to portray his own aesthetic views as possessing sole validity, and it is almost as if he now envied the Pope his means of ensuring the general acceptance of his *ex cathedra* statements. As a Catholic monarch, Ludwig II was compelled to engage with the developments emerging from the Vatican Council (opposition to Papal Infallibility was strong in Munich, resulting in the establishment of a breakaway faction calling themselves "Old Catholics," who refused to accept the new doctrine). After complaining in a letter to Wagner on May 2, 1870 of "devilish political and infallibly papal matters,"[322] Ludwig wrote to him a month later on June 5 to assure him—with an obvious reference to Peter, the Rock of the Church—that "I have a rock-solid belief in your infallibility (and in no other)."[323] Just three months later, on September 8, 1870, Cosima's diary mentions infallibility and her husband's *Beethoven* essay in more or less the same breath: I "do not believe that this emptiness can be filled by a belief in [Papal] infallibility. (R. reads me the close of his *Beethoven*)."[324] Three months after that, on December 4, she quotes Wagner's criticism of the

---

320 SSD 10: 256.

321 SSD 10: 211.

322 Wagner and Ludwig II (1936): 2, 304–5, here 305.

323 Ibid.: 2, 309–10, here 310.

324 CWT 1: 282.

natural scientists who in his opinion are now also claiming "infallibility," and continues "the print of *Beethoven* has arrived."[325] What in each case seems a *non sequitur* is not; it is as if a mention of "infallibility" prompts her to think of Wagner's interpretation of Beethoven in some odd, Pavlovian reaction that is presumably in turn a response to Wagner's own opinion of himself.

Unlike the Protestant Church of Luther, which gives primacy to scripture, the Roman Catholic Church has always acknowledged three sources of divine revelation: scripture, tradition, and the Magisterium (i.e., the teachings of the Church). We know that Wagner in his later years saw his own artistic project increasingly in religious terms (hence those late essays on art and religion), and the methods he adopted to ensure his legacy display a remarkable convergence with those of the Catholic Church. Wagner had long been aware that his musical texts alone (his scripture, in our chosen terminology) might not thrive on their own. They needed not just a physical home of their own (the Festspielhaus as a kind of basilica for the faithful) but also a set of teachings (a Magisterium in Catholic parlance) to show future generations how to interpret them, and a living tradition to perpetuate them. Wagner's major theoretical writings of the late 1840s and 1850s were by turns reflective and speculative—explaining why he was who he was, and what he felt sure would be the future of his art—but when he returned to regular activity as an essayist in the late 1860s, he began engaging in detail with concrete, practical issues of performance (most notably in the writings translated in the present volume). All the while, he was also planning a complete edition of his writings, realizing it in collaboration with the Leipzig publisher Fritzsch from 1871 onwards (the first nine volumes were published by 1873, with the tenth appearing shortly after Wagner's death in 1883). Wagner was also busy dictating his autobiography to Cosima (it was his third autobiography, as we already noted above, but by far the longest), and he had it printed privately in over a dozen copies—just enough to ensure its survival, though few enough to ensure that it did not enter the public domain too soon. Throughout these years, Cosima was also keeping her own diary in order to record for posterity the Master's everyday sayings and doings. Wagner was also able to employ assistants to codify and publish his performance instructions—first and foremost Heinrich Porges, whose accounts of Beethoven's Ninth at Bayreuth in 1872, referred to above, and of the rehearsals for the *Ring* in 1876 remain key texts. Wagner also found a further willing helper in Hans von Wolzogen, whom he appointed to manage and edit

---

325   CWT 1: 320.

his own journal, the *Bayreuther Blätter*, from 1878 onwards. Wagner was clearly keen to leave nothing to chance to ensure that his own "teachings" were preserved. If Jesus Christ had been similarly perspicacious—dictating the Gospel to Mary Magdalen, perhaps, or getting Matthew, Mark, Luke, and John to publish his parables within weeks of telling them—the history of the Church could have been far less complicated.

When it came to creating a living tradition for his oeuvre, Wagner went about matters no less assiduously. He was at first unsuccessful—as outlined above, he had tried and failed to organize his own music school in Munich in the mid-1860s (that *Report to His Majesty*), which is presumably one of the reasons for the vitriol he shows towards the Leipzig Conservatory and its graduates in *Über das Dirigieren*. Ideally, Wagner would have liked his own son to carry on his work (dynasty-forming was very much on his mind in 1869 and 1870).[326] But since he was nearing 60 when Siegfried was born, he could not anticipate still being around when the boy would reach an age mature enough to grasp what his father wanted to teach him. So Richard had to have a back-up plan. In fact, he had several of them.

Wagner's School of Capellmeisters

In his review of Wagner's performance of the *Eroica* on May 12, 1872, Hanslick wrote that

> If Wagner's principles "of conducting" were generally adopted, the doctrine of tempo change would open up the floodgates to an unbearable capriciousness; we would soon no longer be hearing symphonies by Beethoven, but freely based on Beethoven.[327]

Wagner would have argued that there was nothing "capricious" about his approach, but otherwise his aim was precisely what Hanslick feared: the general adoption of his principles. Wagner's writings on performance at this time were indeed focused more on how to perform Beethoven than on how to perform his own works. To some extent, Wagner really does seem to have seen his oeuvre as the "fulfillment" of Beethoven (with Beethoven a kind of John the Baptist anticipating Wagner-as-Christ), but I believe that

---

326 See my chapter "Richard Wagner's Dynastic Dreams" in Walton (2014): 11–30.

327 Hanslick (1872).

there was a deeper reason for this obsessive engagement with the symphonies. Wagner was convinced that the success of his operas depended on their being performed the right way (i.e. *his* way). But his *Ring* had not even been premiered yet, his other works were simply not given frequently enough in enough opera houses to ensure the emergence of a standard, Wagnerian manner of interpretation, nor was he of an age at which he might have contemplated touring the opera houses of Europe as a guest conductor to establish a unified approach to his works. His plans for a music academy of Wagnerian performance had also come to nothing. How, then, might he nevertheless ensure that everyone knew the right way to play his music?

Beethoven provided him with an answer. He was the most widely performed orchestral composer of the western canon by the 1860s—neither Mozart nor Haydn came anywhere close. If Wagner could somehow establish a widespread performance tradition for *Beethoven* whereby the man's symphonies were regularly performed as if they were music by *Wagner*, then when those same conductors came to perform Wagner's own operas, they would already have internalized his ideas about "melos" and tempo modification, and would apply these naturally to the Wagnerian oeuvre too. So when Wagner writes in *Über das Dirigieren* of how "since Beethoven a quite fundamental shift has occurred in the treatment of musical material and its performance" (see p. 58), what I suggest he really means is "since Wagner," though he backdated that "shift" in order to bring the performance of Beethoven's symphonies into line with how he wanted to hear his own works. Hanslick feared that such an approach could result in "symphonies ... based on Beethoven," but what Wagner implicitly wanted were Beethoven symphonies based on Wagner.

Hanslick was not alone in bemoaning how Wagner saw everything through the prism of his own oeuvre. Forty years later, Heinrich Schenker wrote in his monograph on the Ninth as follows:

It's as if fate played a bitter trick on him [Wagner], because however and whatever he thought about Beethoven, all his thoughts culminated unconsciously and involuntarily in the artistic goal that he himself had in mind. He went out to seek Beethoven, but kept finding only himself.[328]

---

328 Schenker (1912): 45.

In my reading, however, there was no trick, bitter or otherwise, nor anything "involuntary," because Wagner only ever went out to seek himself; he just happened to keep finding Beethoven along the way.

Wagner early on stepped back from conducting the world premieres of his own works, delegating the task to von Bülow and others, as detailed above. This might seem odd for a man so convinced of his own conducting prowess and so keen to control all aspects of his art; but it was one of the most astute decisions he ever made—after all, if he were to establish a tradition of performance, it meant actually getting others to perform for him. He had enjoyed the services of perhaps the finest German conductor of the age in Hans von Bülow, but when he began enjoying Hans's wife, too, his relationship with his former protégé was doomed. He was soon hunting for suitable replacements.

Wagner had always exerted a magnetic attraction on gifted young musicians—after all, it was he who had convinced von Bülow to dedicate himself to music in the first place, and he went on to mentor other young men such as Wendelin Weissheimer, Peter Cornelius and Carl Tausig, all of whom helped him out as copyists in Vienna in the early 1860s. Had Wagner played his cards right in his early days in Munich, he could have used King Ludwig's support to gather around him all the men he needed, but his machinations soon compelled him to leave and set up home in Tribschen instead, by which time his former assistants had fallen away. Tausig was now running a music school in Berlin, Cornelius and Weissheimer had both married and had to earn their living, and Weissheimer in any case sided with von Bülow after his separation from Cosima. Hans-Joachim Hinrichsen has suggested that Wagner's publications of the late 1860s (including *Über das Dirigieren* and the republication in extended, book form of *Jewishness in Music*) were a vehement reaction to feelings of utter isolation. He was stuck in Swiss exile in a lakeside house, and the only two conductors he felt he could have trusted to establish a performing tradition faithful to his ideals—Hans von Bülow in Munich and Heinrich Esser in Vienna—abandoned their respective posts in July and November 1869 respectively[329] (in the case of von Bülow, of course, it had been Wagner's own act of personal betrayal that caused the break between them).

Not for the first time, Wagner now began reinventing his life. Tribschen might have been in the middle of nowhere in cultural terms, but Wagner found that being settled in one place, having a family, a representative

---

329 See Hinrichsen (2016): 95.

residence, a stable home life, and a royal patron actually made it easier to establish the kind of semi-permanent team of acolytes that he needed for his work. So he now began systematically acquiring a new band of talented, young helpers. Friedrich Nietzsche and Hans Richter were two of the first. Richter became a kind of man-about-the-house and musical dogsbody to the Master, Nietzsche helped to proofread *Mein Leben*, and when the Wagners moved to Bayreuth in 1872, this circle of young men grew (albeit now *sans* Nietzsche) and acquired a title: the "Nibelungenkanzlei" (the Nibelungen Chancellery) was what Wagner called them in his correspondence with Ludwig II. Not unlike their predecessors in Vienna over a decade before, they helped to copy scores and parts, played music to delight the Master and his family in their leisure hours, and later helped to coach the singers for the Bayreuth Festival and even work backstage where necessary. In return, they had easy access to the man increasingly regarded as the foremost musician of the age, and could rely on a recommendation from him whenever they moved on. Wagner proudly emphasized the international nature of the group to his patron—they comprised, he wrote, a Saxon (Hermann Zumpe), a Hungarian (Anton Seidl), a Russian (Joseph Rubinstein) and a Macedonian (Demetrios Lalas). Others came and went in the Chancellery, and Wagner seems to have made full use of his personal charm to draw talented young musicians into his copying team if they came to sing or play for him while passing through Bayreuth. Thus when Adolf Wallnöfer arrived to audition for the part of Donner in 1874, two years after singing in the chorus for the Ninth in Bayreuth, Wagner rejected him gently, but convinced him to join his band of copyists instead.[330]

Getting talented, enthusiastic musicians to copy his scores free of charge, in-house, was astute on Wagner's part for several reasons. First, it meant he did not have to send his precious scores to some outside copyist and risk them getting lost along the way; secondly, he had direct supervision of the copying process; and thirdly, a band of committed young enthusiasts, eager to please the Master, would probably take greater care and make fewer mistakes than an outside professional whose rate of pay depended on how swiftly he could deliver. There seems to have been a further reason, however: Wagner wanted his young charges to go out into the world and conduct his works. There is no better way to get to know a complex score than to copy it out, part by part, internalizing the details of its structure and orchestration in the process. Wallnöfer wrote in his memoirs of how he and his fellow copyists

---

330 CWT 1: 825 (June 3, 1874); also Wallnöfer's diary (manuscript), June 3, 1874.

would avidly discuss the intricacies of Wagner's orchestration amongst themselves, and how they would play through sections of the *Ring* on evenings, with Wagner or Richter singing the vocal parts—which also meant they got first-hand instruction in how Wagner wanted his works interpreted, especially with regard to tempi. And Wallnöfer also records how Wagner repeatedly urged him to embark on a conducting career. "All these young people [i.e., the Chancellery members] would soon get excellent jobs [he said]. He believed that I understood him and his works."[331]

Wagner complained to Cosima in 1878 that his friends used to "give up on him when he thought they could achieve more than they were capable of, like [Georg] Herwegh, [Wilhelm] Baumgartner, Cornelius, Weissheimer, [Karl] Ritter etc."[332] But in his late years at least, he chose his disciples very well. Hermann Zumpe later became a court capellmeister, first in Stuttgart and then in Munich in 1900, where he was responsible for numerous Wagner productions at the new Prinzregententheater. Hans Richter became the main conductor at the Court Opera in Vienna before moving to England where he dominated the country's music life for several years, running the Hallé Orchestra in Manchester, co-founding the London Symphony Orchestra, and conducting Wagner's operas regularly at Covent Garden. As already mentioned above, Adolf Wallnöfer became one of the great heldentenors of the age, singing all the main Wagner roles in Angelo Neumann's touring Wagner ensemble, then across the world from Russia to the USA. Anton Seidl was appointed chief conductor of Neumann's troupe before moving to New York in 1885 to become principal conductor at the Met (where he conducted 295 Wagner performances)[333] and later of the New York Philharmonic; more than anyone, Seidl was responsible for popularizing Wagner in the USA. Felix Mottl's initial tasks in Bayreuth included copying in the Chancellery, coaching the singers, and wheeling the Rhinemaidens around on stage. He later became one of Cosima's favorite conductors for the festival. He also conducted Wagner in London and New York, and in his later years ran the Court Opera in Munich and the Royal Music Academy there. Arthur Nikisch played the violin under Wagner in his Viennese concert of May 12, 1872, for his Bayreuth performance of Beethoven's Ninth ten days later, and then again in the Bayreuth pit for the *Ring* under Richter. He became chief conductor of the Leipzig Gewandhaus and Berlin Philharmonic orchestras, and

---

331 Wallnöfer (n.d.): 21.
332 CWT 2: 177 (September 16, 1878).
333 Vazsonyi (2013): 527.

his recording of Beethoven's Fifth Symphony of 1913 is famous for its tempo modifications in line with Wagner's suggestions in *Über das Dirigieren*.

The spread of Wagner's conducting ideas was so successful that just twelve years after the composer's death, Ashton Ellis could write in his introduction to his fourth volume of Wagner translations that "most of us are old enough to recognize the change in the whole spirit of 'conducting' that arrived with the public appearance of men who had come under [Wagner's] influence, and one at all events—the late Hans von Bülow—under his personal *tuition*."[334] As far as we can judge from contemporary accounts, von Bülow took several aspects of Wagner's conducting style to excess, most notably his tempo modifications (for which Weingartner criticized him heavily). But as the leading conductor of his day, von Bülow had a significant impact on his contemporaries and on the younger generation. His two main protégés, Mahler and Strauss—appointed chief conductor at the Vienna Court Opera and the Berlin Court Opera in 1897 and 1898 respectively—were as fervent as any of the abovementioned in their devotion to Wagner's ways (or what they imagined these to be). Strauss wrote in later life that he had copied out all of von Bülow's annotations in his own Beethoven scores; this is important to note, because only a Seventh Symphony has survived with Bülow's own annotations. (Von Bülow did give an annotated copy of Beethoven's Ninth Symphony to Leopold Damrosch, who described it somewhat superficially in an article for the *Musical Quarterly* in 1927, but the score itself is no longer extant.[335]) As we have already noted, Strauss and Mahler followed the Wagnerian and von Bülowian example of tempo modifications and of "retouching" Beethoven's orchestration to "improve" it, both of them referring explicitly to Wagner's example as they did so. They clearly did not adopt everything that their mentor had practiced, however; Strauss later wrote that von Bülow's tempo changes had sometimes tended to "dissect" the music (he names the first movement of the *Eroica* in particular), and that he preferred more unified tempi overall.[336]

By the close of the 19th century, Wagner's disciples were essentially running all the top music centers of the Germanic and Anglo-Saxon worlds. Vienna, Munich, Berlin, Leipzig, London, and New York were all dominated by men who openly adhered to Wagner's aesthetic as expounded in the texts published in the present volume. What's more, in discussion with Heinrich

---

334   Wagner trans. Ellis (1895): xvi (his italics).

335   See Damrosch (1927).

336   Strauss ed. Schuh (1989): 61.

Ehrlich in 1897, Giuseppe Verdi spoke of how Wagner's ideas on tempo modification were already common practice outside Germany: "it's also rampant in Italy too; it's almost funny to see how many a young capellmeister of ours changes the tempo every ten measures in every insignificant aria and in every orchestral piece, trying to bring wholly new nuances to it," said Verdi. Ehrlich apparently interviewed him in French, but wrote up his report in German; whether it was Verdi or Ehrlich who used the word "nuance"—one of Wagner's favorites—remains unclear.[337] Wagner's practices even spread to Russia; the conductor Nikolai Golovanov (1891–1953) left us few recordings of the German repertoire, but his *Egmont* Overture by Beethoven and his Wagner excerpts (mostly overtures and preludes to *Meistersinger*, *Tannhäuser*, *Tristan* etc.), all made with the Moscow Radio Symphony Orchestra after the Second World War, are extraordinary in their tempo modifications. They are arguably closest to Mengelberg's, but even more extreme—though Mengelberg is overall much more precise.

Wagner in Translation

French was the only foreign language that Wagner ever mastered, more or less (judging from his own letters in the language). As noted above, there are also scatterings of English, Italian, Latin, and Greek in his writings and letters, though these instances generally confirm his inadequacy in them. Wagner notoriously had a love-hate relationship with France and the French, trying and failing over the space of some four decades to achieve success in Paris, the one city that clearly really mattered to him. The first-ever translations of his prose into any language were also into French, organized by Wagner himself when he published a number of articles in the Parisian *Revue et gazette musicale* from 1840 to 1842, in an effort to earn some money during his fraught, first sojourn in the city. His translator at the time was Henri-Joseph-Maria Duesberg, who worked for the *Revue*. The next French translations of Wagner's writings coincided roughly with his two subsequent attempts to establish himself in Paris. His plans to conquer the capital in 1850 involved getting his prose works put into French, as he confirmed in a letter to his Dresden friend Theodor Uhlig of December 27, 1849, just weeks before he set out for Paris.[338] In fact, the next translation of his prose

337 Ehrlich (1897): 327.
338 SB 3: 194–202, here 196.

to appear in French was only of his (still anonymous) *Jewishness in Music*, which *La Belgique musicale* and *La France musicale* both published in late 1850. The ensuing years saw an increased interest in his theoretical writings in the French-speaking world, though when François-Joseph Fétis published translations of excerpts from them into French in 1852, this was in the context of a highly critical series of articles for the *Revue et gazette musicale* that did Wagner little good.[339]

When Wagner next set out to win over the French, this time by staging his *Tannhäuser* in Paris in 1861, he managed to achieve what he'd wanted over a decade earlier by publishing a major summary of his ideas in French: his essay *Music of the Future*, which appeared along with four of his opera texts in a translation by Paul Challemel-Lacour. *Tannhäuser* flopped, but Wagner and his ideas at least found one important supporter in the shape of Charles Baudelaire, who became the first of many major converts to his art. Wagner's increasing international fame over the course of the next decade is reflected in a growing number of French translations of his writings. His main essays on conducting were first published in French not long after they originally appeared in German. In the fall of 1874, Maurice Kufferath published translations of Wagner's 1846 program for Beethoven's Ninth and of his 1873 *On Performing Beethoven's Ninth Symphony*, and preceded them with a summary of Wagner's *Report on the Performance of Beethoven's Ninth Symphony in Dresden in 1846*.[340] That same fall, Guy de Charnacé published four of Wagner's prose works in abridged versions as the second volume of his *Musique et Musiciens*. These were: *On German Music, On the Overture, Opera and Drama* and *Über das Dirigieren*. Charnacé (1825–1909) had studied in Dresden in the mid-1840s and had there become acquainted with German literature and opera, including the works of Wagner. He later had a varied career as a writer, agronomist, inspector of railways, and much else.[341]

Charnacé seems not to have liked Wagner much. This is not a little ironic; not only did they share a dreadful anti-Semitism (see Charnacé's novel *Le Baron vampire* of 1885), but they were actually brothers-in-law, for Charnacé had married Cosima's half-sister, Claire d'Agoult, in 1849. He and Wagner met at least once—in a letter to Otto Wesendonck from Paris of October 5,

---

339 See Fétis (1852) and Josephson (1972–1973).

340 See Wagner, trans. [Kufferath] (1874).

341 See "Charnacé (Ernest-Charles-Guy de Girard, marquis de)" in Henry Carnoy, ed.: *Dictionnaire biographique international des écrivains*, vols. 1–4. Hildesheim etc., Georg Olms Verlag: 1987, 198–200.

1859, Wagner mentioned having "been delighted to meet [Claire d'Agoult's] very educated young husband."[342] But like a good many of his countrymen, Charnacé was probably peeved by Wagner's satirical play *Eine Kapitulation* of 1870, which took the defeat of France in its war against Prussia as an occasion to exercise revenge for Wagner's personal defeats in Paris. Having never conquered Paris himself, he was determined to enjoy Bismarck's success in that endeavor (Wagner's satire accordingly has more nastiness than wit about it; the cast includes a chorus of large rats alongside Victor Hugo, Jacques Offenbach, and other historical figures). It has been argued cogently by Manuela Schwartz that the upset caused by this satire was one of the main reasons for the relative infrequency of Wagner productions in Paris until the 1890s.[343]

By the time he published his abridged translations of Wagner's writings in 1874, Charnacé clearly had a frosty view of the man and his ideas, though this very fact makes him worth reading, as his approach is far removed from the hero-worship of later French Wagnerites. Charnacé's preface explains that he is publishing these essays in shortened form for reasons of copyright: had he wished to publish them complete, he claims, he would have had to ask permission from Wagner, which he is sure would not have been forthcoming. His translation of *Über das Dirigieren* suffered less under the translator's knife than other essays in the book, though Charnacé does omit all the music examples. He also adds his own footnotes on occasion. When Wagner complains that conductors don't understand rhythm because they do not understand singing, Charnacé adds a sarcastic note in the bottom margin that "Mr. Wagner alone understands everything."[344] The closing decades of the 19th century saw a number of further translations of Wagner's essays into French, though the first attempt to publish them entire began only in 1907 with the *Oeuvres en prose de Richard Wagner* of Jacques Gabriel Prod'homme, a project not completed until 1925.

By the late 19th century, Wagner's works were staples of the operatic repertoire throughout Europe, though this fact was not matched by any similar endeavor to make his prose works accessible in the other main languages of continental Europe. None of the writings relevant to our topic here—the essays on conducting—were published in Italian or Spanish, for example, until well into the 20th century (there is still no complete translation of

---

342 SB 11: 278.
343 See Schwartz (1999): 51.
344 Charnacé (1874): 286.

Wagner's writings in either of these languages). The main essay in the present volume, *Über das Dirigieren*, was first published in Spanish in 1925 in a translation by Julio Gómez,[345] but it did not appear in Italian until 1940, when, like the proverbial English bus, two versions appeared at once. The first was by Adriano Lualdi and was published as part of a large-scale study of conducting entitled *L'arte di dirigere l'orchestra. Antologia e guida.*[346] In the first section, the "guide," comprising some 140 pages, Lualdi discusses a wide spectrum of issues pertaining to interpretation and conducting, with music examples ranging from Cherubini to Richard Strauss and contemporary Italian works, including Lualdi's own; the latter half of the book—the "anthology," some 250 pages in length—comprises brief, hitherto unpublished essays on conducting by Vittorio Gui and Tullio Serafin, and Italian translations of assorted other essays on conducting and/or the art or interpretation, closing with Lualdi's translation of *Über das Dirigieren*. His book was published by Hoepli in Milan, the same company that had been responsible for bringing many of Mussolini's writings into the world. It came onto the market just as Ferruccio Amoroso was correcting the proofs of his own translation of *Über das Dirigieren* for Bompiani, also in Milan; Amoroso added an endnote criticizing Lualdi for "many errors and oversights."[347] His own book also included translations of five further essays from Wagner's late years (these were: *On the Destiny of Opera, On Actors and Singers, The Stage Festival Theater in Bayreuth, Public and Popularity*, and *On the Application of Music to Drama*).

It was arguably in the English-speaking world that Wagnerism put down the quickest, deepest roots outside Germany (aided, perhaps, by Wagner lacking any antipathy to things English comparable to his dislike for the French). The first-ever English translations of any of Wagner's texts were published by the London weekly journal *The Musical World* in 1855, to coincide with Wagner's engagement to conduct the "Old Philharmonic" Orchestra that year. As discussed in detail above, these concerts were extensively reviewed in the journal, which gave much space in spring 1855 to discussions of his theories (or at least what people believed them to be). *The Musical World* also published the libretto of his *Lohengrin* in translation, in separate installments, from April onwards. It offered biographical information, and allowed space for a lively debate among his adherents (such as Ferdinand Praeger—see p.

---

345 Gómez (1925).
346 Lualdi (1940).
347 Amoroso (1940): 374.

152 above), his detractors (often anonymous), and those who were simply intrigued by the hype and wanted to find out more for themselves.[348] The editor of *The Musical World*, James William Davison, harbored many reservations towards Wagner, but remained impartial enough to commission an English translation of *Opera and Drama*, which was published over a year in installments beginning on May 19, 1855 (thus long before the work was published entire in any language outside German). The translator is not named explicitly, but was apparently John Vipon Bridgeman (1819–89), a contributor to *The Musical World* for many years and an author and translator in his own right, whose later oeuvre included several farces (such as *Where's Your Wife?*, *A Good Run for It*, and *Matrimonial—A Gentleman*), two libretti for Michael William Balfe (*The Puritan's Daughter* and *The Armourer of Nantes*) and an English adaptation of the libretto for Offenbach's *La Périchole*.[349] He struggled with Wagner, however. In a footnote to his second installment on May 26, 1855 explaining the use of the word "Erscheinung," Bridgeman wrote:

> If the opposition offered to Herr Wagner's musical theories is as great as the difficulties presented by his literary style, it will be some time before the "Music of the Future" is firmly established in England. Herr Wagner is very fond of making use of words admitting of a vast diversity of meaning, and of the most transcendental description, so that a poor commonplace and common-sense translator stands but little chance with him.[350]

Nearly four decades later, William Ashton Ellis (1852–1919) suggested that this translation of *Opera and Drama* in *The Musical World* was in fact part of an insidious plot to make Wagner and his music seem ludicrous,[351] though after having translated the same book himself a year later, Ellis admitted that he felt a "greater lenience—*not* towards the editor of that journal—but towards the earlier translator of this book … For a work of

---

348 See, for example, the letters by Praeger and "An Amateur" in *The Musical World* 33/12 (March 24, 1855), 189.
349 These and other works can be found in the online catalogue of most large libraries in the English-speaking world, e.g. the British Library's http://explore.bl.uk/.
350 Footnote to Wagner: "Opera and Drama. Part One. Opera and the constitution of music," *The Musical World* 33/21 (May 26, 1855), 322–24, here 322.
351 Ellis (1892): 15–18.

this kind is enough to knock the vanity out of any man."[352] The original translator, far from being "commonplace" as he self-deprecatingly claims, was probably doing as best as anyone could in the circumstances. The prose style of *The Musical World* was generally entertaining and argumentative, but often erudite and witty, and a world away from the serious style of, say, the *Neue Zeitschrift für Musik*, which had become Wagner's favored organ for his smaller-scale essays. Wagner's repetitious prose and his convoluted arguments (regardless of the language in which they were expressed) must have been so far removed from the experience of the readers of *The Musical World* that many probably gave up after reading the first paragraph of *Opera and Drama*. Perhaps they even assumed that such dense prose was just a general Teutonic trait.

The same London journal published Wagner's *Jewishness in Music* over nine issues from May to July 1869, again translated by Bridgeman. And again it made an effort to achieve a balance of opinions by publishing a translation of Hanslick's reply to it, along with articles by Henry Chorley, who excoriated Wagner and his racist obsessions in a prose as measured and succinct as Wagner's was emotive and prolix.[353]

Bridgeman was also the first to translate anything from *Über das Dirigieren* into English, though these were merely the excerpts quoted by Ferdinand Hiller in his long, scathing review of that essay from the *Kölnische Zeitung* of April 1870, and published in translation by *The Musical World* in two installments, on May 14 and June 11, 1870 (it was reprinted in *Dwight's Journal* in Boston on June 4 and July 2). Bridgeman once more admitted to his struggles with Wagner's prose, and in the second installment of Hiller's review, he resorted to retaining the original German for one of Wagner's superlatives—"einzig berufenster," referring to Hans von Bülow as Liszt's anointed successor—and added the following footnote:

> "Solely most-having-a-call," a pretty specimen of Wagnerian style. Despite a fearful martyrdom while translating *Opera and Drama*, and other works of the Lucerne Anchorite, I am not even yet *quite* perfect in the language invented by him, to supply the place of German … It may be wisdom clothed in mystic garb, but, to the uninitiated, it resembles exceedingly unmitigated nonsense. Disbelievers adopt the theory that the Musician of the Future pads his sentences with grand words, to make believe that beneath them lurks a finely developed thought, just as some

---

352 Wagner trans. Ellis 1900: xviii.
353 See Hanslick (1869a) and Chorley (1869).

beauties call in the aid of cotton-wool to supply the place of certain charms which would otherwise be prominent only by their absence.[354]

On June 18, 1870, just one week after this final installment of Hiller's review was published in London, *Dwight's Journal of Music* in Boston began serializing its own English translation of Wagner's essay itself. These installments continued until late August, when the endeavor came to a premature halt. No translator is named, which presumably means that he was the founder-editor of the journal himself, the remarkable John Sullivan Dwight (1813–93): a Harvard graduate, Unitarian minister and transcendentalist who often translated from the German for his journal and elsewhere[355] (though he is perhaps best known today for his free English translation of the popular French carol "O holy night"). On July 2, 1870 (as mentioned in the Introduction to this book), *The Musical World* printed a brief notice expressing astonishment that Dwight should be investing time and energy into translating "that miserable piece of egotistical coxcombry and absolute nonsense ... What, in the name of Music, does any sensible American care about such stuff?"[356] On July 30, 1870, after a total of two excerpts from his translation had appeared, Dwight offered an extensive reply in which he largely concurred with his fellow editor across the water:

> Our friend ... wonders that we waste our time in the translation of ... "the pamphlet called *Ueber das Dirigeren*" ... Pray do not be alarmed; we never dreamed of undertaking to translate the whole work, or even the larger part of it; that would indeed be a thankless and a dreary task.[357]

Dwight went on to make clear his "distrust of [Wagner's] principles [and] our distrust for his practice."[358] Two more installments of his translation appeared, but then nothing more. This is a pity, for while it is often heavy going, it is not without its idiomatic moments. Excerpts of his excerpts were then reprinted in the London journal *The Orchestra* that same summer.[359]

354 Hiller, trans. Bridgeman (1870): 393.
355 See Thomas (1950).
356 Anon.: "Occasional notes," *The Musical World* 48/27 (July 2, 1870), 446–8, here 447.
357 [Dwight] (1870), 286.
358 Ibid.
359 In *The Orchestra* 14/353, 231 (July 1, 1870); 14/357, 300 (July 29, 1870); and 14/365, 427 (September 23, 1870).

In 1870–71, *The Musical World* continued its series of Bridgeman's Wagner translations with *A Communication to my Friends*, again published over several months—yet another "English perversion," thus Ashton Ellis,[360] though even a cursory perusal of this version and Ellis's own, completed over two decades later, confirms that his predecessor was qualitatively not as far removed from his own efforts as Ellis would like to have imagined. Perhaps Ellis's negative reaction was in part because of the journal's continuing disparagement of Wagner elsewhere in its pages, such as in asides referring to "the great Musician of the Future, alias the Lion of the Present."[361] As Richard Kitson has noted, Davison, the editor of *The Musical World*, "located many derogatory articles and news pieces about the German composer and republished them."[362] Some of these are witty, others plain silly—such as the "news" item on June 11, 1870 reporting that "a dog, having caught sight of a page of [*Die Meistersinger*], immediately bit twenty people, and was knocked on the head."[363] But for all his antipathy to things Wagnerian, Davison kept his public well informed about Wagner's activities, and was from today's perspective remarkably even-handed towards the new-fangled notions emerging from the German-speaking world at this time.

The first man to translate Wagner into English who possessed both a fine literary sensibility and real empathy towards his ideals was the pianist, conductor, and writer Edward Dannreuther (1844–1905). He was born to a German father in Strasbourg (then still a French city), but his family moved to Cincinnati in the USA when he was small, which meant that Edward grew up fluent in both German and English.[364] He moved back to Europe on his own when only in his teens, enrolling at the Leipzig Conservatory in 1860 (the same institution that Wagner attacks in *Über das Dirigieren*). While there, he became friendly with Edvard Grieg, Arthur Sullivan, and others, and attended the performance of Wagner's *Meistersinger* Overture that was later mentioned by Wagner himself in *Über das Dirigieren* (see p. 101). Dannreuther moved to London in 1863 at the invitation of Henry

---

360 Ellis (1893): 19.

361 See Anon.: "Music at Berlin," *The Musical World* 49/19 (May 13, 1871), 293.

362 Kitson (2006): xv.

363 [The editor?]: "Occasional notes," *The Musical World* 48/24, 399.

364 The biographical information on Dannreuther here is taken largely from the anonymous article on him—presumably penned by the editor of the journal, though edited by Dannreuther himself—published in the *Musical Times* on October 1, 1898: Anon (1898).

Chorley, thereafter settling permanently and enjoying a significant career as a pianist and teacher. He was a professor of piano at the Royal College of Music for many years, where his students included men such as Hubert Parry. Dannreuther was an early adherent of Wagner's in England, a prime mover in the London Wagner Society, and he conducted the first performance in England of the *Meistersinger* Overture in 1873. He attended the Bayreuth Festival in 1876, and when Wagner visited London in 1877, he and Cosima stayed with Dannreuther and his wife in Bayswater. But Dannreuther was no mere partisan, for his friends included staunch Mendelssohnians such as Chorley, he gave the first British performances of Tchaikovsky's Piano Concerto no. 1 and Grieg's Piano Concerto, and his published writings also include praise of Brahms and other composers whom Wagner preferred to excoriate.[365]

Dannreuther's first publication on Wagner, a book entitled *Richard Wagner: His Tendencies and Theories*, appeared in 1873, and included a remark that "the pamphlet on conducting should be translated entire,"[366] which might well have been a reference to Dwight's translation of excerpts back in the summer of 1870. He then proceeded to give an excellent, nine-page summary of its content that focused on all its salient points, such as Wagner's insistence on tempo modification in Beethoven's orchestral works. Dannreuther also noted certain similarities between Wagner's ideas of tempo and Anton Schindler's first-hand accounts of hearing Beethoven play his own sonatas.[367] Dannreuther's bilingual background meant he was ideally situated to understanding the intricacies of Wagner's prose. His first major translation of Wagner into English was also published in 1873, namely *The Music of the Future.*

Two years after Dannreuther wrote of the need to translate *Über das Dirigieren*, the London journal *The Musical Standard* embarked on just such an undertaking. It published a first installment, "Translated for the *Musical Standard* by Walter E. Lawson," on August 27, 1875, but after two more installments, the serialization stopped—just after the episode in which Wagner describes having brought joy to the composer Philip Potter (see p. 43 above).[368] Lawson clearly struggled with Wagner's syntax, resulting in odd inversions of subject and object and occasionally over-complex formulations,

365 See, for example, Dannreuther (1893): x and 99.
366 Dannreuther (1873): 80.
367 Ibid.: 83.
368 See Wagner, trans. Lawson (1875).

but he still manages a considerable degree of clarity in conveying the content of the essay. His other extant translations from the German include *Aesthetics of Musical Art* by Ferdinand Hand (1786–1851).[369]

Dannreuther returned to his task of translating Wagner in 1880, when he published his English version of the *Beethoven* essay of 1870. And in 1887 he became the first to fulfill his own early exhortation that *Über das Dirigieren* should be translated entire; a second edition followed in 1897. We are here obviously concerned with this essay, not with Dannreuther's previous two Wagner translations. His prose is smooth and idiomatic, though he often paraphrases heavily. He omits Wagner's many repetitions, but also much more besides. Nevertheless, his translation was reviewed positively by George Bernard Shaw in the *Pall Mall Gazette* of May 28, 1887 (Shaw presumably did not compare its content all too closely with Wagner's original German).

The next English translation of *Über das Dirigieren* to be published was by William Ashton Ellis. He included it in the fourth volume of his translations of Wagner's works, published in London by Kegan Paul, Trench, Trübner & Co. in 1895. Ellis also published translations of the other essays included in the present volume. *Mementoes of Spontini* appeared in volume three in 1894, *The Rendering of Beethoven's Ninth Symphony* in volume five in 1896; and his *Report on the Performance of Beethoven's Ninth Symphony in Dresden in the year 1846* in volume seven in 1898. Ellis is something of a mystery. His training was in medicine, and no one really knows where he acquired his knowledge of either music or German. It seems he became obsessed by Wagner in the mid-1870s, though he never actually met the man, and apparently failed to capitalize on Wagner's visit to London in 1877. Ellis was the founder, editor, and principal author of the English-language quarterly Wagner journal *The Meister*, which ran from 1888 to 1895. He published his eight volumes of Wagner's translated writings from 1892 to 1899, and in 1900 embarked on a translation of C.F. Glasenapp's vast biography of Wagner. The original author's name disappeared from the fourth volume onwards because the work had by now become more Ellis than Glasenapp (one wonders if Vladimir Nabokov knew this before writing his 1962 novel *Pale Fire*, in which an acolyte's annotations overwhelm the work of the poet he adores). Ellis's other interests included theosophy and various aspects of

---

369 Hand, trans. Lawson: *Aesthetics of Musical Art; or, the Beautiful in Music.* London: Reeves, 1880.

the occult and the esoteric.[370] At the risk of being unfair, he comes across as the kind of fellow who, if alive today, would be an avid attendee of *Star Trek* conventions, wearing Spock ears and reciting *Tristan* in Klingon. His translations of Wagner's works have been often pilloried for their idiosyncratic style, though he approached his task with an open mind and few illusions as to the enormity of his ambitions. His paper on "Richard Wagner's Prose," given to the Royal Musical Association on December 13, 1892, remains relevant today and is highly readable. What's more, given the convoluted syntax of the originals, it is impossible not to admire Ellis's industry and achievement. His remains the only hitherto attempt at a complete English edition of Wagner's principal prose works. The eight volumes he published were reprinted by the University of Nebraska Press in the 1990s, and are still often used.

The most recent translations of *Über das Dirigieren* and of the 1873 essay on Beethoven's Ninth are by Robert L. Jacobs, and were published together with his translation of *Music of the Future* as *Three Wagner Essays* in 1979.[371] A close perusal of Jacobs's text shows that he has often heavily paraphrased the original, if not as extensively as Dannreuther. Jacobs admits to taking two "liberties": one of omission, the other of inclusion. He excised the anti-Semitic diatribes from *Über das Dirigieren*, but added numerous music examples to better illustrate Wagner's text. Wagner's music examples are indeed extremely cursory. Since he first published his essays on conducting and on Beethoven's Ninth in separate installments in music journals, he might have felt constrained in the amount of space he could use for his examples, though he also seems to have felt no compunction in cutting them off at the end of a measure, regardless of whether or not the musical phrase continues to the next downbeat. Perhaps he was confident, as Jacobs suggests, that "the reader would be ... so familiar with the music referred to that he would need no more than an occasional brief quote."[372] But the music examples given in the original text sometimes confuse things, such as in his essay on the Ninth, where his assessment of what is, and his suggestions for what should be, are given in fragmentary, almost haphazard fashion, occasionally without regard for musical chronology. Since Wagner knew the symphony by heart,

---

370 The most extensive study of Ellis's life and work remains that of David Cormack, who in 2014 updated and expanded two articles he had published on Ellis in the journal *Wagner* in 1993 and 1994, and placed the result online. See Cormack (2014).

371 Wagner, trans. Jacobs (1979).

372 Ibid.: x.

his mind was apparently free to wander back and forth across the details of the score as if music were to him a spatial art, free of the constraints of time, like a Gurnemanz leading his reader-as-Parsifal to the Castle of the Grail.[373]

The Triumph of Time

The success of Wagner's conducting aesthetic in the late 19th century was in part a result of his ability to promote himself in print, and to prompt others to debate him in the press of the day. The existence of a discourse on any topic depends largely on written texts, and it is a simple fact that we know so much about Wagner's approach to conducting because he himself told us about it, and did so with such vigor that others felt compelled to join in the argument. With the exception of Berlioz (who in any case—as explained above—concentrated more on basic technical matters of conducting, and less on interpretation), none of Wagner's contemporaries or competitors took the trouble to commit their conducting ideas to paper. Neither Weber, Mendelssohn, Spohr, Spontini nor Habeneck made any similar effort to codify their art of performance. When Ferdinand Gassner published the first-ever book on conducting in 1844, his preface closed with a tribute to the leading conductors of his day: Spohr, Mendelssohn, and Reissiger.[374] Half a century later, the discourse had become so skewed towards the Wagnerian that no one would ever be able to leave him unmentioned again. And this was despite the fact that his interpretive ideas were soon being upheld by many (like Strauss) who had never actually seen him conduct. Perhaps the story of conducting in the later 19th and early 20th centuries is not too different from the reception history of Beethoven's Ninth, only writ large: although that work had been "rediscovered" and fêted under Habeneck in Paris and Nicolai in Vienna, their stories were all but forgotten after they were supplanted by Wagner's tale of his own rediscovered, fêted Ninth in Dresden. We cannot exclude the possibility that Wagner's apparent domination of the conducting scene in circa 1900 is a similar sleight of hand, with all other voices simply drowned out by the deafening roar of the big beast of Bayreuth. Alternative histories are popular at present, and while even their most successful instances in fiction and TV drama can rarely avoid a whiff of

---

373 As noted in the Introduction above, I follow Jacobs in expanding several of the music examples in this book.

374 Gassner (1844): vi.

the absurd, it is fascinating to postulate an alternative 19th century in which Mendelssohn lived long enough to publish a guide to conducting for the students of his conservatory in Leipzig, and in which his aesthetic of stricter tempi became dominant across Europe. But he didn't. It was Wagner's story and his tempo modifications that emerged triumphant.

Regardless of the means he employed, the success of Wagner's endeavor in promoting his art of interpretation is little short of breath-taking. The present writer can think of no other instance in the history of western music when the aesthetic ideas of one man have seemed to reign so supreme on the international music scene within just a few years of his death. Perhaps the only comparable instances are the spread of Schoenbergian dodecaphony and its serial offshoots in the 1950s and early 1960s, or the success of the Historical Performance Practice movement in the late 20th and early 21st centuries. But the former soon dwindled in the face of Minimalism, Post-Modernism and audience antipathy, while the latter in any case never originated as the vision of a single creative artist. The closest comparisons to Wagner's posthumous supremacy are perhaps to be found not in the arts, but (once again) in religion—witness the spread of Christianity via the Apostles after the death of Christ, or of Islam in the decades after the death of the Prophet. And through the students and disciples of those first- and second-generation Wagnerians—most notably Wilhelm Furtwängler, who was Nikisch's successor in Leipzig and Berlin, and Willem Mengelberg, Mahler's champion in Amsterdam—Wagner's *rubato* style continued to be heard in the concert halls and opera houses of Europe until the mid-20th century. As Hans-Joachim Hinrichsen has rightly observed,[375] we must retain a healthy measure of skepticism about just how much Wagner or von Bülow we can discern through listening to the recordings of their students or successors, as we can never hope to find our way through the many quasi-archaeological layers of interpretation back to some putative, pure, Ur-Wagner. Nor can those recordings in themselves provide any undiluted experience of how these conductors performed the repertoire in the concert hall or the opera house. As Leon Botstein pertinently writes, recordings in themselves constitute only "incomplete fragments of a musical culture."[376]

If we want proof of the diversity that can co-exist within a specific performing tradition, we need only consider three conductors who were all mentored in some way by Gustav Mahler, and whose artistic legacy they

[375] See Hinrichsen (2011), especially 31.
[376] Botstein (1999): 5.

RICHARD WAGNER AND THE ART OF CONDUCTING &♦ 273

all revered to the end of their lives: Willem Mengelberg, Bruno Walter, and Otto Klemperer. They were born within fourteen years of each other (in 1871, 1876 and 1885 respectively), but came to represent very different aesthetics, ranging from the ultra-Romanticism of Mengelberg to the *Neue Sachlichkeit* of Klemperer, as we can hear if we compare their recorded interpretations of the Classical and Romantic repertoire. But all the same, if one reads Wagner's texts on conducting and then listens to the ebb and flow of Beethoven's Fifth Symphony under Nikisch in 1913, Mengelberg's recordings of Beethoven's symphonies, or even Furtwängler's *Tristan* of 1952, it is impossible not to feel that there is some deep, underlying interpretive tradition connecting them all.[377]

To sum up: despite their turgid prose, their repulsive anti-Semitism, their intellectual insecurities, and their haphazard organization, Wagner's essays on conducting succeeded in exerting a huge influence on the art of performance, far beyond the circle of those who ever saw and heard their author conduct in person. From his notions of critical fidelity to the musical text while preserving interpretive flexibility to his descriptions of fluid tempi, his insistence on the primacy of a melodic core in the symphonic repertoire, and his creation of an aesthetic vocabulary for interpretation: conductors have been engaging with Wagner's ideas ever since. One might agree with them or reject them, but it is impossible to ignore them.

---

377 For those interested in close comparisons of Beethoven's Fifth in recordings from Nikisch onwards (including Furtwängler, Mengelberg and other representatives of the "Wagnerian" *rubato* tradition), see Laubhold (2014).

Bibliography

Sound Recordings

The archival recordings to which I refer in this book have in many cases been released and re-released several times. Most of them are easily accessible online today, via YouTube, Spotify or elsewhere, which is why we here refrain from offering more precise discographical information.

The Willem Mengelberg Society maintains a website on which one can stream his extant recordings (see www.willemmengelberg.nl/?q=discografie), while the various Wilhelm Furtwängler Societies (of Germany, France, Japan, and elsewhere) variously offer online discographies besides actually releasing recordings themselves (see, for example, https://furtwangler.fr/en/list-of-recordings/ by the French Society, and https://furtwaengler.org/cdEN.html by the German Society). The bibliography below also includes numerous books with extensive conductor discographies: see, for example, Hunt (2015), Obert and Schmidt (2009), Zwart (2019) etc.

Annotated Scores

Many of the annotated scores consulted and referenced here are available online today. Numerous conductors' archives are listed in Bloch (2006) below. I here name the principal holding institutions for the annotated scores referred to in this edition:

Bülow, Hans von: Staatsbibliothek zu Berlin
Furtwängler, Wilhelm: Zentralbibliothek Zürich; Staatsbibliothek zu Berlin
Kletzki, Paul: Zentralbibliothek Zürich
Mahler, Gustav: New York Philharmonic Orchestra; Österreichische Nationalbibliothek
Mengelberg, Willem: Niederlands Muziek Institut, Den Haag
Strauss, Richard: Richard Strauss Archiv, Garmisch
Toscanini, Arturo: New York Public Library

Wagner, Richard: Zentralbibliothek Zürich; Richard Wagner Museum mit Nationalarchiv der Richard-Wagner-Stiftung, Bayreuth

Walter, Bruno: Universitätsbibliothek der Universität für Musik und darstellende Kunst, Vienna

Books and Articles

Adorno, Theodor Wiesengrund, ed. Henri Lonitz (2001): *Zu einer Theorie der musikalischen Reproduktion. Aufzeichnungen, ein Entwurf und zwei Schemata. Nachgelassene Schriften. Abteilung I: Fragment gebliebene Schriften*, vol. 2. Frankfurt am Main: Suhrkamp.

Aldrich, Richard (1941): *Concert life in New York, 1902–1923*. New York: G.P. Putnam's Sons.

Allen, Roger (2018): *Wilhelm Furtwängler: Art and the Politics of the Unpolitical*. Woodbridge: The Boydell Press.

Amoroso, Ferruccio (1940): *L'ideale di Bayreuth (1864–1883). Prose di Riccardo Wagner a cura di Ferruccio Amoroso*. Milan: Valentino Bompiani. Includes translations of *Über das Dirigieren, Über die Bestimmung der Oper, Über Schauspieler und Sänger, Das Bühnenfestspielhaus zu Bayreuth, Publikum und Popularität* and *Über die Anwendung der Musik auf das Drama*.

Anon. (1843): "Über eine Aufführung des Don Juan auf dem Dresdner Hoftheater am 26. April," *Zeitung für die elegante Welt* 19 (May 10), 463–64.

Anon. (1853): "Aus Düsseldorf," *Niederrheinische Musik-Zeitung für Kunstfreunde und Künstler*, 1/20 (November 12), 157–59.

Anon. (1872): "Die Festtage in Bayreuth," *Neue Zeitschrift für Musik* 39/23 (May 31), 231–32; 39/24 (June 7), 243–45. The second installment ends with the remark "conclusion to follow," but this last section seems only to appear in 39/32 (August 2), 317–18, as an untitled appendix to Porges' report on the Ninth Symphony in Bayreuth.

Anon. (1898): "Edward Dannreuther," *The Musical Times and Singing Class Circular* 39/668 (October 1), 645–54.

Anon. [Friedrich Chrysander?] (1870): "H. Esser und R. Wagner," in *Allgemeine musikalische Zeitung* 5/22 (June 1), 175.

Aristotle, trans. Arthur Platt (1912): *De generatione animalium*, in J.A. Smith and W. D. Ross, eds., *The Works of Aristotle*, vol. 5. Oxford: The Clarendon Press.

Beethoven, Ludwig van, ed. Ernst Herttrich (2019): *Symphonie Nr. 8 F-Dur Opus 93*. Munich: Henle.

Berlioz, Hector (1843): *Grand traité d'instrumentation et d'orchestration modernes*. Paris: Schonenberger.

————— (1855): *Grand traité d'instrumentation et d'orchestration modern … suivie de l'Art du chef d'Orchestre*. Paris: Schonenberger.

————— (1856a): *Le Chef d'orchestre, théorie de son art*. Paris: Schonenberger.

—————, trans. Mary Cowden Clarke (1856b): *A treatise upon modern instrumentation and orchestration*. London: Novello.

—————, trans. Johann Christoph Grünbaum (1856c): *Die moderne Instrumentation und Orchestration … 2te Ausgabe vermehrt durch … Der Orchester-Dirigent …* Berlin: Schlesinger.

————— (1862): *À travers chants*. Paris: Michel Lévy.

—————, trans. Richard Pohl (1864): *Gesammelte Schriften*, vol. 1: *À travers chants*. Leipzig: Gustav Heinze.

————— (1870): *Mémoires*. Paris: Michel Lévy.

—————, ed. Pierre Citron (1989): *Correspondance Générale*, vol. 5, 1855–1859. Paris: Flammarion.

—————, ed. Katherine Kolb (2015): *Berlioz on Music: Selected Criticism 1824–1837*. Oxford: Oxford University Press.

Blitz, Édouard (1887): *Quelques considérations sur l'art du chef d'orchestre*. Leipzig and Brussels: Breitkopf & Härtel.

Bloch, Henry (2006): *Directory of Conductors' Archives in American Institutions*. Lanham, Maryland etc.: The Scarecrow Press.

Bloom, Peter (2000): "Berlioz and Wagner: Épisodes de la vie des artistes," in Peter Bloom, ed.: *The Cambridge Companion to Berlioz* (*Cambridge Companions to Music*). Cambridge: Cambridge University Press, 235–50.

Botstein, Leon (1999): "Musings on the History of Performance in the Twentieth Century," *The Musical Quarterly* 83/1 (Spring 1999), 1–5.

Boult, Adrian (1920): *A Handbook on the Technique of Conducting*. Oxford: Hall.

Bowen, José Antonio (1993): "Mendelssohn, Berlioz, and Wagner as Conductors: The Origins of the Ideal of 'Fidelity to the Composer,'" *Performance Practice Review* 6/1, 77–88.

————— (2001): "The Missing Link: Franz Liszt the Conductor," *Basler Jahrbuch für historische Musikpraxis* 24, 125–50.

—————, ed. (2003): *The Cambridge Companion to Conducting*. Cambridge: Cambridge University Press.

Braam, Gunther (2015): *Richard Wagner in der zeitgenössischen Fotografie*. Regensburg: ConBrio.

Brown, Clive (1999): *Classical and Romantic Performing Practice 1750–1900*. Oxford etc.: Oxford University Press.

Brown, Jonathan (2012): *Great Wagner Conductors. A Listener's Companion*. Canberra: Parrot Press.

Brügger, Joachim, Wolfgang Gratzer and Thomas Hochradner, eds. (2008): *Mozarts letzte drei Sinfonien. Stationen ihrer Interpretationsgeschichte*. Freiburg im Breisgau etc.: Rombach Verlag KG.

Cahn-Speyer, Rudolf (1919): *Handbuch des Dirigierens*. Leipzig: Breitkopf & Härtel.

Canetti, Elias (1980): *Masse und Macht*. Frankfurt am Main: Fischer Taschenbuch Verlag.

Charnacé, Guy de (1874): *Musique et musiciens*. Vol. 2. *Fragments critiques de M. Richard Wagner. Traduits et annotés*. Paris: P. Lethielleux. Contains abridged translations of *Über deutsches Musikwesen, Über die Ouvertüre, Oper und Drama* and *Über das Dirigieren*, with a critical commentary.

Chevalley, Heinrich, ed. (1922): *Arthur Nikisch. Leben und Wirken*. Berlin: Bote & Bock.

Chorley, Henry Fothergill (1869): "Judasim in Music," review, *The Musical World* 47/18 (May 1), 312.

Christensen, Jesper B. (2001): "'Del modo di guidare colla battuta e senza.' Francesco Maria Veracini über das Dirigieren," *Basler Jahrbuch für historische Musikpraxis* 24, 49–69.

Cook, Nicholas (1993): *Beethoven: Symphony no. 9*. Cambridge: Cambridge University Press.

———— (1995): "Heinrich Schenker, Polemicist: A Reading of the Ninth Symphony Monograph," *Music Analysis* 14/1 (March 1995), 89–105.

Cormack, David (2014): "Faithful, all too Faithful. William Ashton Ellis and the Englishing of Richard Wagner," *The Wagner Journal*, http://www.thewagnerjournal.co.uk/cormackonellis.html (accessed December 2018).

Courvoisier, Carl (1873a and 1873b): "Über das Dirigiren. Bemerkungen vom Standpuncte des Orchesterspielers," *Musikalisches Wochenblatt* 4/21 (May 23), 305–8 and 4/23 (June 6), 337–41.

Czerny, Carl (1839): *Vollständige theoretisch-practische Pianoforte-Schule … in 4 Theilen*. Vienna: Diabelli.

Damrosch, Walter (1927): "Hans von Bülow and the Ninth Symphony," *The Musical Quarterly* 13/2 (April 1927), 280–93.

Dannreuther, Edward (1873): *Richard Wagner: his Tendencies and Theories*. London: Augener & Co.

———— (1893 and 1895). *Musical Ornamentation*, 2 vols. London and New York: Novello, Ewer & Co.

Darwin, Charles (1860): *On the Origin of Species by Means of Natural Selection, or the Preservation of Favored Races in the Struggle for Life*. 2nd edition. London: John Murray.

Darwin, Charles, trans. Heinrich Georg Bronn, revised Julius Victor Carus (1867): *Über die Entstehung der Arten durch natürliche Zuchtwahl oder die Erhaltung der begünstigsten Rassen im Kampfe um's Dasein. Nach der vierten englischen Auflage mit einer geschichtlichen Vorrede und andern Zusätzen des Verfassers für diese deutsche Ausgabe aus dem Englischen übersetzt und mit Anmerkungen versehen*. Stuttgart: E. Schweizerbart'sche Verlagshandlung.

Deathridge, John and Carl Dahlhaus (1984): *The New Grove Wagner*. London: Macmillan.

Deldevez, Édouard-Marie-Ernest (1878): *L'Art du chef d'orchestre*. Paris: Firmin-Didot & Cie.

Devrient, Eduard (1869): *Meine Erinnerungen an Felix Mendelssohn-Bartholdy und seine Briefe an mich*. Leipzig: J.J. Weber.

Di Profio, Alessandro and Arnold Jacobshagen, eds. (2017): *Maestro! Dirigieren im 19. Jahrhundert*. Würzburg: Königshausen & Neumann.

Döge, Klaus (2016): "Wagner (Komponisten und Regisseure), Richard, WERKE, Schriften," in Laurenz Lütteken, ed.: *MGG Online*. Kassel, Stuttgart, New York: Bärenreiter, Metzler, RILM. www.mgg-online.com/mgg/stable/49968 (accessed April 2019).

Döge, Klaus, Christa Jost and Peter Jost, eds. (2002): *"Schlagen Sie die Kraft der Reflexion nicht zu gering an." Beiträge zu Richard Wagners Denken, Werk und Wirken*. Mainz etc.: Schott.

Dorn, Heinrich (1870a and 1870b): "'Über das Dirigiren' von Richard Wagner. Ein Mahnruf," *Neue Berliner Musikzeitung* 24/7 (February 16), 49–50, and 24/8 (February 23): 57–58.

Drescher, Thomas (2001): "Dirigieren als Kunst. Zu den Anfängen der neuzeitlichen Orchesterleitung bei I.F.K. Arnold (1806)," *Basler Jahrbuch für historische Musikpraxis* 24, 7190.

Drieberg, Friedrich von (1835): *Wörterbuch der griechischen Musik in ausführlichen Artikeln*. Berlin: Schlesinger.

Drüner, Ulrich (2016): *Richard Wagner: die Inszenierung eines Lebens*. Munich: Blessing.

[Dwight, John Sullivan] (1870): "Richard Wagner," in *Dwight's Journal of Music*. 30/10 (July 30, 1870), 286–87. *See also* Wagner, trans. [Dwight].

Eatock, Colin Timothy (2009): *Mendelssohn and Victorian England*. Farnham: Ashgate.

Ehrlich, Heinrich (1897): "Beim 84jährigen Verdi," *Deutsche Revue über das Gesamte Nationale Leben der Gegenwart* 22/2 (April to June 1897), 325–28.

Eichhorn, Andreas (1993): *Beethovens Neunte Symphonie. Die Geschichte ihrer Aufführung und Rezeption (Kasseler Schriften zur Musik* 3). Kassel etc.: Bärenreiter.

Ellis, William Ashton (1892): "Richard Wagner's Prose," *Proceedings of the Musical Association* 19, 13–33.

——— (1900–1908): *Life of Richard Wagner. Being an authorised English version by Wm. Ashton Ellis of C.F. Glasenapp's "Das Leben Richard Wagner's."* 6 vols. London: Kegan Paul, Trench, Trübner & Co., Ltd.

Fairtile, Linda B. (2003): "Toscanini and the Myth of Textual Fidelity," *Journal of the Conductors Guild* 24/1–2, 49–60.

Fay, Amy (1883): *Music Study in Germany*. 5th edition. Chicago: Jansen, McClurg & Company.

Federhofer, Heinrich, ed. (1990): *Heinrich Schenker als Essayist und Kritiker. Gesammelte Aufsätze, Rezensionen und kleinere Berichte aus den Jahren 1891–1901*, Hildesheim etc.: Georg Olms Verlag.

Fétis, François-Joseph (1852): "Richard Wagner," *Revue et Gazette Musicale de Paris* 19/23 (June 6) to 19/32 (August 8).

Feuerbach, Ludwig (1841): *Das Wesen des Christentums*. Leipzig: Otto Wigand.

Fischer, Jens Malte (2015): *Richard Wagners Das Judentum in der Musik. Eine kritische Dokumentation als Beitrag zur Geschichte des Antisemitismus*. Würzburg: Königshausen & Neumann.

Föttinger, Gudrun (2011): "'Ich bin zu wechselnd in meinem Ausdrucke.' Neuere Anmerkungen zur Wagner-Ikonografie," *wagnerspectrum* 7/1, 143–70.

Fricke, Richard (1906): *Bayreuth vor dreissig Jahren: Erinnerungen an Wahnfried und aus dem Festspielhause*. Dresden: Richard Bertling.

Friedrich, Sven (1999): "*Das Buch eines edlen Geistes ist der kostbarste Freund*. Wagner und seine Bibliotheken," in Döge, Jost and Jost (2002): 11–20.

Furtwängler, Wilhelm (1956): *Vermächtnis. Nachgelassene Schriften*. Wiesbaden: Brockhaus.

Galkin, Elliott W. (1988): *A History of Orchestral Conducting in Theory and Practice*. New York: Pendragon Press.

Gartmann, Thomas, and Daniel Allenbach, eds. (2019): *Rund um Beethoven. Interpretationsforschung Heute* (*Musikforschung der Hochschule der Künste Bern* 14). Schliengen: Argus.

Gassner, Ferdinand Simon (1844): *Dirigent und Ripienist für angehende Musikdirigenten, Musiker und Musikfreunde*. Karlsruhe: Groos.

Glasenapp, Carl (1923): *Das Leben Richard Wagners*. 6 vols. 5th edition. Leipzig: Breitkopf & Härtel.

Goehr, Alexander (2004): "Introduction," in Julian Littlewood, *The Variations of Johannes Brahms*. London: Plumbago Books, ix–x.

Goethe, Johann Wolfgang von (1790): *Versuch die Metamorphose der Pflanzen zu erklären*. Gotha: Carl Wilhelm Ettinger.

Goldsmith, Melissa U.D., Paige A. Willson and Anthony J. Fonseca, eds. (2016): *The Encyclopedia of Musicians and Bands on Film*. Lanham, etc.: Rowman & Littlefield.

Gollmick, Carl (1848): *Carl Guhr. Ein Nekrolog*. Frankfurt am Main: Fr. Benj. Auffarth.

Gounod, Charles (1874): "La neuvième symphonie de Beethoven," *Le Ménestrel* 40/24, 189–90.

Gray, Andrew (1988): "On Translating Wagner," *The Opera Quarterly* 6/1, 22–28.

Grove, George (1896): *Beethoven and his Nine Symphonies*. London: Novello and Company.

Gui, Vittorio (1940): "Come si studia una partitura," in Lualdi (1940): 191–207.

Hanslick, Eduard (1854): *Vom Musikalisch-Schönen*. Leipzig: Rudolph Weigel.

———— (1865): *Vom Musikalisch-Schönen*. 3rd, improved edition. Leipzig: Rudolph Weigel.

————, trans. Anon (1869a): "Richard Wagner's *Judaism in Music*," *The Musical World* 47/16 (April 17, 1869), 263–64.

———— (1869b): *Geschichte des Concertwesens in Wien*. Vienna: Braumüller.

———— (1870): "Hofoperntheater," in *Neue Freie Presse. Morgenblatt*. June 2.

———— (1872): "Das Wagner-Concert im grossen Musikvereinssaal," in *Neue Freue Presse. Morgenblatt*. May 14.

Hardenberg, Georg Philipp Friedrich von: *see* Novalis.

Harten, Ch. (1983): "Proch, Heinrich," in *Österreichisches Biographisches Lexikon 1815–1950*. Vienna: Verlag der Österreichischen Akademie der Wissenschaften, 1983, vol. 8, 290–91.

Hartmann, Ludwig (1870): "Musikbrief aus Dresden," in *Musikalisches Wochenblatt* 1/20 (May 13), 312–13.

Heinel, Norbert (2006): *Richard Wagner als Dirigent*. Vienna: Praesens Verlag.

Heyworth, Peter (1983 and 1996): *Otto Klemperer: His Life and Times*, 2 vols. Cambridge: Cambridge University Press.

Hiller, Ferdinand (1868): *Aus dem Tonleben unserer Zeit. Gelegentliches*. Vol. 2. Leipzig: Hermann Mendelssohn.

———— (1876): "Über das Auswendig-Dirigieren," in *Musikalisches und Persönliches*. Leipzig: Breitkopf & Härtel, 132–42.

————, trans. John Vipon Bridgeman (1870): "Musical letters. New series, no. III," *The Musical World* 48/20 and 48/24 (May 14 and June 11, 1870), 329–30 and 393–94.

Hinrichsen, Hans-Joachim (1999): *Musikalische Interpretation. Hans von Bülow*. Stuttgart: Franz Steiner Verlag.

———— (2011): "Kann Interpretation eine Geschichte haben? Überlegungen zu einer Historik der Interpretationsforschung," in Loesch and Weinzerl (2011), 27–37.

———— (2016): "Die Praxis des Dirigierens und die Politik der Interpretation. Wagners polemisches Mendelssohn-Bild als Strategie der produktiven Zerstörung," *wagnerspectrum* 12/2, 79–97.

Holden, Raymond (2005): *The Virtuoso Conductors. The Central European Tradition from Wagner to Karajan*. New Haven and London: Yale University Press.

————, ed. (2007): *Glorious John. A collection of Sir John Barbirolli's Lectures, Articles, Speeches and Interviews*. Ottoxeter: The Barbirolli Society.

———— (2011a): "The Iconic Symphony: Performing Beethoven's Ninth Wagner's way," *The Musical Times* 152/1917 (Winter 2011), 3–14.

———— (2011b): *Richard Strauss. A Musical Life*. New Haven and London: Yale University Press.

Hollaender, Alexis (1875): "Über die Vorschläge zu Änderungen in Beethoven's Compositionen," *Neue Berliner Musikzeitung* 29/1 (January 7), 1–3 and 29/2 (January 14), 9–11.

Holoman, D. Kern (2001): "Berlioz als Dirigent," *Basler Jahrbuch für historische Musikpraxis* 24, 105–24.

Huebner, Steven (2013): "Édouard Dujardin, Wagner, and the Origins of Stream of Consciousness Writing," *19th-Century Music* 37/1 (Summer 2013), 56–88.

Hueffer, Franz (1874): *Richard Wagner and the Music of the Future. History and Aesthetics.* London: Chapman and Hall.

Hummel, Johann Nepomuk (1827): *Ausführliche theoretisch-practische Anweisung zum Piano-Forte-Spiel.* 2nd edition. Vienna: Tobias Haslinger.

Hunt, John (2015): *The Furtwängler Sound.* 7th edition. London: Travis & Emery.

Jacobshagen, Arnold (2003): "Vom Feuilleton zum Palimpsest: Die 'Instrumentationslehre' von Hector Berlioz und ihre deutschen Übersetzungen," *Die Musikforschung*, 56/3 (July–September 2003), 250–60.

Jahn, Otto (1866): *Gesammelte Aufsätze über Musik.* Leipzig: Breitkopf & Härtel.

Janz, Curt Paul (1997): "David Friedrich Strauss—Richard Wagner—Friedrich Nietzsche—Basel," *Basler Zeitschrift für Geschichte und Altertumskunde* 97 (1997), 171–81.

Jaschinski, Andreas (2016): "Musikwissenschaft," II.1., in Laurenz Lütteken, ed., *MGG Online.* Kassel, Stuttgart, New York: Bärenreiter, www.mgg-online.com/ mgg/stable/14613 (accessed September 2018).

Josephson, Nors S. (1972–1973): "François-Joseph Fétis and Richard Wagner," in *Revue belge de Musicologie / Belgisch Tijdschrift voor Muziekwetenschap* 26 and 27, 84–89.

Jost, Christa and Peter Jost (1997): *Richard Wagner und sein Verleger Ernst Wilhelm Fritzsch.* Tutzing: Hans Schneider.

Jost, Peter (2002): "Zu den französischen Übersetzungen von Wagners Schriften zu Lebzeiten," in Döge, Jost and Jost, eds. (2002), 32–47.

Kietz, Gustav Adolph, as written up by Marie Kietz (1905): *Richard Wagner in den Jahren 1842–1849 und 1873–1875. Erinnerungen.* Dresden: Carl Reissner.

Kirchmeyer, Helmut (1967): *Situationsgeschichte der Musikkritik und des musikalischen Pressewesens in Deutschland, dargestellt vom Ausgang des 18. bis zum Beginn des 20. Jahrhunderts. Das zeitgenössische Wagner-Bild*, vol. 2: *Dokumente 1842–1845.* Regensburg: Gustav Bosse.

——— (1968): *Situationsgeschichte*, vol. 3: *Dokumente 1846–1850.* Regensburg: Gustav Bosse.

——— (1972): *Situationsgeschichte*, vol. 1: *Wagner in Dresden.* Regensburg: Gustav Bosse.

Kitson, Richard (1991): *Dwight's Journal of Music (1852–1881).* Ann Arbor: Répertoire international de la presse musicale.

——— (2006): *The Musical World*, www.ripm.org/pdf/Introductions/MWO1866-1891introEnglish.pdf

Klemperer, Otto (1993): *"Anwalt guter Musik." Texte aus dem Arbeitsalltag eines Musikers*. Berlin: Henschel Verlag.

Klemperer, Victor (1996): *LTI. Notizbuch eines Philologen*. Leipzig: Reclam.

Kloss, Erich, ed. (1909): *Richard Wagner an Freunde und Zeitgenossen*. Berlin: Schuster und Loeffler.

Köhler, Joachim (2012): *Der lachende Wagner*. Munich: Wilhelm Heyne Verlag.

Kolb, Katherine (2009): "Flying Leaves: Between Berlioz and Wagner," *19th-Century Music* 33/1 (Summer): 25–61.

Kondrashin, Kirill (1989): *Die Kunst des Dirigierens*. Trans. (into German) from the Russian by Elisabeth Heresch. Munich and Zurich: Piper.

Koury, Daniel J. (2010): *Orchestra Performance Practices in the Nineteenth Century. Size, Proportions, and Seating*. Rochester: University of Rochester Press.

Kreowski, Ernst and Eduard Fuchs (1907): *Richard Wagner in der Karikatur*. Berlin: Behr's Verlag.

Kufferath, Maurice (1890): *L'art de diriger l'orchestre. Richard Wagner et Hans Richter (extrait du "Guide musical")*. Paris: Librairie Fischbacher.

——— (1909): *L'art de diriger*. 3rd edition. Paris: Librairie Fischbacher.

Kunt, Carl (1843): "Philharmonisches Concert. Die neunte Symphonie von Beethoven," *Wiener Zeitschrift für Kunst, Literatur, Theater und Mode*, 60 (March 25, 1843), 475–78.

La Mara: *see* Lipsius, Ida Marie

Laubhold, Lars E. (2014): *Von Nikisch bis Norrington. Beethovens 5. Sinfonie auf Tonträger. Ein Beitrag zur Geschichte der musikalischen Interpretation im Zeitalter ihrer technischen Reproduzierbarkeit*. Munich: edition text + kritik.

Lessmann, Otto (1872): "Pfingsten 1872 in Bayreuth," *Neue Berliner Musikzeitung* 26/23 (June 5), 178–80.

[Lipsius, Ida Marie, ed.] (1898): *Briefwechsel zwischen Franz Liszt und Hans von Bülow*. Leipzig: Breitkopf & Härtel.

Liszt, Franz (1853): "Ein Brief von Franz Liszt." *Neue Zeitschrift für Musik* 39/25 (December 16), 267–68.

Loesch, Heinz von and Stefan Weinzerl, eds. (2011): *Gemessene Interpretation. Computergestützte Aufführungsanalyse im Kreuzverhör der Disziplinen*. Mainz etc.: Schott.

Lualdi, Adriano (1940): *L'arte di dirigere l'orchestra: antologia e guida:* Milan: Hoepli.

Macdonald, Hugh (2002): *Berlioz's Orchestration Treatise. A Translation and Commentary*. Cambridge etc.: Cambridge University Press.

Malloch, William (1960): "I remember Mahler." KPFK radio station, Los Angeles.

Mann, Thomas (1975): *Doktor Faustus*. Frankfurt am Main: Fischer Taschenbuch Verlag.

Martin, James Michael (1976): "A Comparison of Interpretations of Viennese Symphonies by Selected Conductors based upon Recordings." Doctoral thesis, University of Cincinnati.

Martner, Knud (2010): *Mahler's Concerts*. New York: Kaplan Foundation and The Overlook Press.

Melichar, Alois (1981): *Der vollkommene Dirigent. Entwicklung und Verfall einer Kunst*. Munich and Vienna: Langen-Müller.

Metzger, Heinz-Klaus (1985): "Restitutio Musicae. Zur Intervention Kolischs," in Metzger and Riehn (1985), 54–69.

Metzger, Heinz-Klaus and Rainer Riehn (1985): *Beethoven. Das Problem der Interpretation* (*Musik-Konzepte* 8). Munich: edition text + kritik.

Mikorey, Franz (1917): *Grundzüge einer Dirigierlehre. Betrachtungen über Technik und Poesie des modernen Orchester-Dirigierens*. Leipzig: C. F. Kahnt.

Millington, Barry (2012): *The Sorcerer of Bayreuth. Richard Wagner, his Work and his World*. New York: Oxford University Press.

Moor, Christoph (2019): "'Und spurlos verschollen ist hiervon die Tradition.' Die Aufführungs- und Rezeptionsgeschichte von Mozarts Jupiter-Sinfonie im Prisma der Wagnerschen Dirigier- und Interpretationsästhetik bis zum Einsetzen der historisch informierten Aufführungspraxis." Doctoral thesis, University of Bern/Bern University of the Arts HKB. https://biblio.unibe.ch/download/eldiss/19moor_ch.pdf (accessed October 2019).

Mungen, Anno (1995): "Richard Wagners 'grauenvolle Sympathie' für Spontini. Deutungsversuch einer erfindungsreichen Studie Wagners," *Die Musikforschung* 48/3 (July–September), 270–82.

Navarre, Jean-Philippe, ed. (2005): *E.-M.-E. Deldevez. L'art du chef d'orchestre (1878); De l'exécution d'ensemble (1888)*. Sprimont: Mardaga.

Nietzsche, Friedrich (1886): *Die Geburt der Tragödie aus dem Geiste der Musik*. New edition. Leipzig: Fritzsch.

——— (1992): *Unzeitgemässe Betrachtungen*. Munich: Goldmann.

———, ed. Paolo D'Iorio (2009–): *Digitale Kritische Gesamtausgabe. Werke und Briefe*, based on the critical text by G. Colli and M. Montinari, Berlin and New York: de Gruyter, 1967–. www.nietzschesource.org/#eKGWB (accessed September 2019).

Nikisch, Arthur (1920): "Erinnerungen aus meiner Wiener Jugendzeit," *Melos* 1/3 (March 1, Arthur Nikisch issue): 71–72.

Nohl, Ludwig (1870): "Beethoven's hundertjähriger Geburtstag. Ein Neujahrswort zur vorbereitenden Orientirung," *Neue Zeitschrift für Musik* 66/1 (January 1, 1870), 1–4.

Nottebohm, Gustav (1865): *Ein Skizzenbuch von Beethoven. Beschrieben und in Auszügen dargestellt*. Leipzig: Breitkopf & Härtel.

Novalis (1802): *Heinrich von Ofterdingen. Ein nachgelassener Roman*. Berlin: Buchhandlung der Realschule.

Obert, Simon and Matthias Schmidt (2009): *Im Mass der Moderne. Felix Weingart-ner—Dirigent, Komponist, Autor, Reisender*. Basel: Schwabe Verlag.

Pembaur, Josef (1892): *Über das Dirigieren. Die Aufgaben des Dirigenten beleuchtet vom Standpunkte der verschiedenen Disciplinen der Kompositionslehre*. Leipzig: Leuckart.

———— (1907): *Über das Dirigieren. Die Aufgaben des Dirigenten beleuchtet vom Standpunkte der verschiedenen Disziplinen der Kompositionslehre*. 2nd edition. Leipzig: Leuckart.

Peres da Costa, Neal (2019): "Carl Reinecke's Performance of his Arrangement of the Second Movement from Mozart's Piano Concerto k. 488. Some Thoughts on Style and the Hidden Messages in Musical Notation," in Gartmann and Allen-bach (2019): 114–49.

Perty, Maximilian (1852): *Zur Kenntniss kleinster Lebensformen: nach Bau, Funktio-nen, Systematik, mit Spezialverzeichniss der in der Schweiz beobachteten*. Bern: Jent & Reinert.

———— (1872): *Die mystischen Erscheinungen der menschlichen Natur*. 2nd, expanded edition. Leipzig & Heidelberg: Winter'sche Verlagshandlung.

[Pohl, Richard] (1854): "Die Manie des Dirigirens," in *Neue Zeitschrift für Musik* 40/1 (January 1, 1854), 5–6; 40/2 (January 6, 1854), 16–18; 40/3 (January 13, 1854), 24–25; 40/4 (January 20, 1854), 37–40.

Pohl, Richard (1872): "Das Wagner-Concert in Mannheim," *Neue Zeitschrift für Musik* 68/2 (January 5, 1872), 13–16; 68/3 (January 12, 1872), 25–29.

Praeger, Ferdinand (1892): *Wagner as I Knew him*. New York: Longmans, Green & Co.

Recktenwald, Fritz (1929): *Über das Dirigieren. Praktische Ratschläge für Kapellmeis-ter, Chormeister und solche, die es werden wollen*. Vienna: Verlag Adolf Robitschek.

[Richard Wagner Museum Bayreuth]: Katalog der Wahnfried-Bibliothek. Bayreuth: n.d., https://www.wagnermuseum.de/wp-content/uploads/sites/17/2019/01/bestandsliste_wahnfried.pdf / (accessed September 2020).

Riehn, Rainer (1985): "Beethovens Verhältnis zum Metronom," in Metzger and Riehn (1985), 70–84.

Rimsky-Korsakov, Nikolay, trans. Ely Halpérine-Kaminsky (1909): *Ma vie musicale*. Paris: Pierre Lafitte & Cie.

Rovaart, M.C. van de (1928?): *De orkestdirigent*. Hilversum: Harmonia-uitgave.

Saminsky, Lazare (1958): *Essentials of conducting*. London: Dennis Dobson.

Seaman, Christopher (2013): *Inside Conducting*. Rochester: University of Rochester Press.

Schenker, Heinrich (1901): "Beethoven-'Retouche,'" article from the *Wiener Abend-post* (January 9), reprinted in Federhofer (1990), 259–68.

Schenker, Heinrich (1912): *Beethovens neunter Sinfonie. Eine Darstellung des musi-kalischen Inhaltes unter fortlaufender Berücksichtigung auch des Vortrages und der Literatur*. Vienna & Leipzig: Universal-Edition.

Scherchen, Hermann (1929): *Lehrbuch des Dirigierens*. Mainz: Schott.

Schilling, Gottfried Wilhelm Fink etc. (1841): *Encyclopädie der gesammten musikalischen Wissenschaften oder Universal-Lexicon der Tonkunst*. New edition, vol. 4. Stuttgart: Köhler.

Schindler, Anton (1840): *Biographie von Ludwig van Beethoven*. Münster: Aschendorff.

Schmitz-Berning, Cornelia (2007): *Vokabular des Nationalsozialismus*. Berlin: Walter de Gruyter.

Schopenhauer, Arthur, ed. Julius Frauenstädt (1874): *Sämmtliche Werke*, vol. 6: *Parerga und Paralipomena* vol. 2. Leipzig: Brockhaus.

———, ed. Julius Frauenstädt (1877), *Sämmtliche Werke*, vol. 5: *Parerga und Paralipomena* vol. 1. Leipzig: Brockhaus.

Schroeder, Carl (1921): *Handbuch des Dirigierens und Taktierens (Der Kapellmeister und sein Wirkungskreis)*. Berlin: Max Hesses Verlag.

Schubert, Franz Ludwig (1864): *Der praktische Musikdirektor oder Wegweiser für Musik-Dirigenten. Auf Erfahrung gestützte Bemerkungen*. Leipzig: C. Merseburger.

Schubert, Giselher (2014): "Wagners Hiller-Polemik," in Peter Ackermann, Arnold Jacobshagen, Robert Scoccimarro and Wolfram Steinbeck: *Ferdinand Hiller. Komponist, Interpret, Musikvermittler (Beiträge zur Rheinischen Musikgeschichte 177)*. Kassel: Merseburger, 501–11.

Schuller, Gunther (1997): *The Compleat Conductor*. New York and Oxford: Oxford University Press.

[Schumann, Robert] (1836): "Vom Dirigiren und insbesondere von der Manie des Dirigirens," *Neue Zeitschrift für Musik* 4/31 (April 15), 129–30.

Schünemann, Georg (1913): *Geschichte des Dirigierens*. Leipzig: Breitkopf & Härtel.

Schwartz, Manuela (1999): *Wagner-Rezeption und französische Oper des Fin de siècle. Untersuchungen zu Vincent d'Indys Fervaal (Berliner Musik Studien 18)*. Sinzig: Studio.

Schwarze, Friedrich Oskar von, ed. (1876): *Das Strafgesetzbuch für das Deutsche Reich vom 15. Mai 1871*. Leipzig: Fues's Verlag.

Seidl, Anton (1895a): "On Conducting," in Anton Seidl, Fanny Morris Smith, Henry Krehbiel and W.S. Howard, eds.: *The Music of the Modern World*. 2 vols. New York: D. Appleton and Company, vol. 1, 100–106.

——— (1895b): "About Conducting. II," Anton Seidl, Fanny Morris Smith, Henry Krehbiel and W.S. Howard, eds.: *The Music of the Modern World*. 2 vols. New York: D. Appleton and Company, vol. 1, 201–14.

——— (1900): "Über das Dirigiren," *Bayreuther Blätter* 23/10 (October–December), 291–320. The German original of the article Seidl published in America in 1895.

Sessa, Anne Dzamba (1979): *Richard Wagner and the English*. Cranbury and London: Associated University Presses.

Siepmann, Jeremy (2003): "The history of Direction and Conducting," in Bowen, ed. (2003), 112–25.

Solie, Ruth A. (1980): "The Living Work: Organicism and Musical Analysis," *19th-Century Music* 4/2 (Autumn), 147–56.

[Spitzer, Daniel] (1877): "Briefe Richard Wagner's an eine Putzmacherin," *Neue Freie Presse. Morgenblatt* (June 16–17).

Stefan, Paul (1911): *Oskar Fried: das Werden eines Künstlers*. Berlin: Erich Reiss Verlag.

——— (1935): *Arturo Toscanini*. Vienna etc.: Herbert Reichner Verlag.

Stollberg, Arne, Jana Weissenfeld and Florian Henri Besthorn, eds. (2015): *DirigentenBilder: Musikalische Gesten—verkörperte Musik*. Basel: Schwabe.

Strauss, David Friedrich (1865): *Der Christus des Glaubens und der Jesus der Geschichte: eine Kritik des Schleiermacher'schen Lebens Jesu*. Berlin: Duncker.

Strauss, Richard (1931): "Vorwort," in Hans Diestel: *Ein Orchestermusiker über das Dirigieren. Die Grundlagen der Dirigiertechnik aus dem Blickpunkt des Ausführenden*. Berlin: Edition Adler, 5–7.

Strauss, Richard, ed. Willi Schuh (1989): *Betrachtungen und Erinnerungen*. Munich and Mainz: Piper & Schott.

Strecker, Ludwig (1951): *Richard Wagner als Verlagsgefährte: eine Darstellung mit Briefen und Dokumenten*. Mainz: Schott.

Strobel, Otto (1952): *Richard Wagner. Leben und Schaffen. Eine Zeittafel*. Bayreuth: Verlag der Festspielleitung.

Swarowsky, Hans, ed. Manfred Huss (1979): *Wahrung der Gestalt. Schriften über Werk und Wiedergabe, Stil und Interpretation in der Musik*. Vienna: Universal Edition.

Tappert, Wilhelm (1872): "Die Festtage in Bayreuth," *Musikalisches Wochenblatt*, 3/23 (May 31), 358–59; 3/24 (June 7), 375–76; 3/25 (June 14), 391–94; 3/26 (June 21), 407–10.

——— (1877): "Wagner und Hanslick," *Musikalisches Wochenblatt* 8/28 (July 6), 388–89.

——— (1883): *Richard Wagner, sein Leben und seine Werke*. Elberfeld: S. Lucas.

Thienemann, Alfred (n.d.): *Die Kunst des Dirigierens*. No place, no publisher.

Thomas, J. Wesley (1950): "John Sullivan Dwight: A Translator of German Romanticism," *American Literature* 21/4 (January), 427–41.

Trémine, René (1997): *Wilhelm Furtwängler. Concert Listing 1906–1954*. [Paris]: TAHRA Productions.

Trimble, Michael, Dale C. Hesdorffer, Robert Letellier and Gordon T. Plant (2019): "In Wagner's Eyes: Casting Light on a Disputed Portrait," *The Wagner Journal* 13/3: 20–31.

Trippett, David (2013): *Wagner's Melodies. Aesthetics and Materialism in German Musical Identity*. Cambridge etc.: Cambridge University Press.

Uhlig, Theodor (1852: I–IV): "Über den dichterischen Gehalt Beethoven'scher Tonwerke," *Neue Zeitschrift für Musik*, I: 37/13 (September 24), 131–33; II: 37/14 (October 1), 143–46; III: 37/16 (October 15); 163–66; IV: 37/19 (November 5), 196–99.

Vazsonyi, Nicholas (2010): *Richard Wagner. Self-Promotion and the Making of a Brand*. Cambridge etc.: Cambridge University Press.

———, ed. (2013): *The Cambridge Wagner Encyclopedia*. Cambridge: Cambridge University Press.

Vosteen, Annette, ed. (2001): *Neue Zeitschrift für Musik 1834–1838*. 4 vols. Baltimore: NISC.

Wagner, Cosima, ed. Martin Gregor-Dellin and Dietrich Mack (1976 and 1977): *Die Tagebücher*. 2 vols. vol. 1, 1869–1877; vol. 2, 1878–1883. Munich & Zurich: Piper. Cited as CWT.

Wagner, Richard ([1911]): *Sämtliche Schriften und Dichtungen*. 6th edition (*Volksausgabe*). 16 vols. Leipzig: Breitkopf & Härtel, [1911]. Cited as SSD.

——— (1967–): *Richard Wagner: Sämtliche Briefe*. 25– vols. Vols. 1–9 edited by Hans-Joachim Bauer, Klaus Burmeister, Johannes Forner, Gertrud Strobel, and Werner Wolf. Leipzig: Deutscher Verlag für Musik, 1967–2000. Vols. 10–25 edited by Martin Dürrer, Margret Jestremski, Isabel Kraft, Andreas Mielke, and Angela Steinsiek. Wiesbaden: Breitkopf & Härtel, 2000–. Cited as SB.

———, ed. Martin Gregor-Dellin (1977): *Mein Leben*. Munich: List Verlag. Cited as ML.

———, ed. Sven Friedrich (2004): *Werke, Schriften und Briefe* (*Digitale Bibliothek* 107). Berlin: Directmedia.

———, ed. Egon Voss (2015): *Über das Dirigiren (1869)*. Tutzing: Hans Schneider.

———, trans. [John Sullivan Dwight] (1870): excerpts from *Über das Dirigieren*, published in 4 installments in *Dwight's Journal of Music* as: "Wagner on Conducting I," 30/7 (June 18), 257–58; "Wagner on Conducting II," 30/8 (July 2), 265–66; "Further specimens of Wagner on Conducting III," 30/11 (August 13), 289–90; "Specimens of Wagner on Conducting IV," 30/12 (August 27), 297.

———, trans. Guy de Charnacé (1874): *see* Charnacé (1874).

———, trans. [Maurice Kufferath] (1874): "Richard Wagner et la 'neuvième' IV," *Le guide musical: revue hebdomadaire des nouvelles musicales de la Belgique et de l'étranger* 20/39 (September 24); 20/41 (October 8); 20/42 (October 15); 20/43 (October 22); no page numbers. Nos. I to III of this series of articles entitled "Richard Wagner et la 'neuvième'" were devoted to Kufferath's comments on Wagner's report on conducting the Ninth in Dresden in 1846: I, 20/33 (August 13) and 20/34 (August 20); then to a translation of Wagner's program written for that performance: II, 20/35 (August 27) and 20/36 (September 3); and III, 20/37 (September 10).

————, trans. Walter E. Lawson (1875): "Richard Wagner on Conducting," *The Musical Standard* 9/578 (August 28), 126–27; 9/579 (September 4), 142–43; 9/580 (September 11), 158.

————, trans. Edward Dannreuther (1887): *On Conducting.* London: William Reeves.

————, trans. Émile Guilliaume (1888 and 1889): "Sur l'art de diriger l'orchestre," in *Annuaire du Conservatoire royal de musique de Bruxelles,* vol. 12 (1888), 134–84 and vol. 13 (1889), 133–201.

————, trans. William Ashton Ellis (1892–99): *Richard Wagner's Prose Works,* tr. and ed. William Ashton Ellis, 8 vols. London: Kegan Paul, Trench, Trübner & Co., Ltd (facsimile repr. 1993–95, Lincoln and London: University of Nebraska Press). 2nd edition, 8 vols., 1895–1912. London: Kegan Paul, Trench, Trübner & Co., Ltd.

————, trans. William Ashton Ellis (1895): "About Conducting," in *Richard Wagner's Prose Works,* 1st edition, vol. 4: *Art and Politics,* 289–64.

————, trans. William Ashton Ellis (1900): *Opera and Drama,* in *Richard Wagner's Prose Works,* 2nd edition, vol. 2: *Opera and Drama.*

————, trans. Anon. (1911): *My Life.* London: Constable & Company Ltd.

————, trans. Jacques Gabriel Prod'homme (1907–25): *Oeuvres en prose de Richard Wagner.* Paris: Delagrave.

————, trans. Julio Gómez (1925): *El arte de dirigir la orquesta.* Madrid, L. Rubio. An online transcription is available at: https://solfeando.files.wordpress.com/2018/07/ueber-das-dirigieren_cast.pdf (accessed February 2020).

————, trans. Ferruccio Amoroso (1940): *see* Amoroso, Ferruccio (1940).

————, trans. Adriano Lualdi (1940): *see* Lualdi, Adriano (1940).

————, trans. Robert L. Jacobs (1979): *Three Wagner Essays.* London: Eulenburg Books.

————, trans. Andrew Gray, ed. Mary Whittall (1983): *My Life.* Cambridge: Cambridge University Press.

————, trans. Roger Allen (2014): *Richard Wagner's* Beethoven *(1870).* Woodbridge: The Boydell Press.

Wagner, Richard, Cosima Wagner and Charles Nuitter (2002): *Correspondance. Réunie et annotée par Peter Jost, Romain Feist et Philipp Reynal.* Sprimon: Mardaga.

Wagner, Richard, and Ludwig II, ed. Otto Strobel (1936): *König Ludwig und Richard Wagner. Briefwechsel.* 4 vols. Karlsruhe: Braun.

Wagner, Siegfried (1923): *Erinnerungen.* Stuttgart: J. Engelhorns Nachf.

Wallnöfer, Adolf, ed. Klaus Wallnöfer (n.d.): *Autobiografie.* [Munich]: self-published.

Walter, Bruno (1947): *Thema und Variationen. Erinnerungen und Gedanken.* Frankfurt am Main: S. Fischer Verlag.

———— (1957): *Von der Musik und vom Musizieren,* Frankfurt am Main: Fischer.

Waltershausen, Hermann Wolfgang von (1954): *Die Kunst des Dirigierens.* 2nd expanded edition. Berlin: Walter de Gruyter & Co.

Walton, Chris (2002): "Wagner's Peculiar Oboist: Philipp Joseph Fries," *Fontes artis musicae* 49/4, 271–84.

——— (2007): *Richard Wagner's Zurich. The Muse of Place.* Rochester: Camden House.

——— (2010): "Mendelssohn on the Mersey: the Lives and Work of Jakob Zeugheer," *The Musical Times* 151/1912, 25–40.

——— (2012): "Upstairs, Downstairs: Acoustics and Tempi in Wagner's 'Träume' and *Siegfried Idyll*," *The Musical Times* 153/1918, 7–18.

——— (2014): *Lies and Epiphanies. Composers and their Inspiration from Wagner to Berg.* Rochester: University of Rochester Press.

——— (2019a): "Von innen und von aussen: Beethovens neunte Sinfonie und die 'Wagnersche' Dirigiertradition," in Gartmann and Allenbach (2019), 218–37.

——— (2019b): "Manhandling Mahler," in *Opera* 70/12, 1524–29.

——— (2020): "Gender and Sexuality in Wagner's *Ring des Nibelungen*," in Mark Berry and Nicholas Vazsonyi, eds.: *The Cambridge Companion to Wagner's "Der Ring des Nibelungen."* Cambridge: Cambridge University Press.

Wasielewski, Wilhelm (1897): *Aus siebzig Jahren.* Stuttgart & Leipzig: Deutsche Verlags-Anstalt.

Weber, Solveig (1993): *Das Bild Richard Wagners. Ikonographische Bestandsaufnahme eines Künstlerkults.* 2 vols. Mainz etc.: Schott.

Wegeler, Franz Gerhard and Ferdinand Ries (1838): *Biographische Notizen über Ludwig van Beethoven.* Coblenz: Bädeker.

Weingartner, Felix (1896): *Über das Dirigieren.* Leipzig: Breitkopf & Härtel.

——— (1906): *Ratschläge für Aufführungen der Symphonien Beethovens.* Leipzig: Breitkopf & Härtel.

——— (1923): *Ratschläge für Aufführungen klassischer Symphonien*, vol. 3. *Mozart.* Leipzig: Breitkopf & Härtel.

Weissheimer, Wendelin (1898): *Erlebnisse mit Richard Wagner, Franz Liszt und vielen anderen Zeitgenossen nebst deren Briefen.* Stuttgart and Leipzig: Deutsche Verlags-Anstalt.

Westernhagen, Curt von (1966): *Richard Wagners Dresdener Bibliothek 1842–1849. Neue Dokumente zur Geschichte seines Schaffens.* Wiesbaden: F.A. Brockhaus.

Widmer, C. (1868): *Wilhelm Baumgartner: Ein Lebensbild.* Zurich: David Bürkli.

Ziegler, Theobald (1908): *David Friedrich Strauss.* Strasbourg: K.J. Trübner.

Zimmermann, Werner G. (1986 and 1988): *Richard Wagner in Zürich: Materialien zu Aufenthalt und Wirken*, 2 vols. Zurich: Hug.

Zopff, Hermann (1881): *Der angehende Dirigent.* Leipzig: Carl Merseburger.

Zwart, Frits, trans. Cynthia Wilson (2019): *Conductor Willem Mengelberg, 1871–1951.* 2 vols. Amsterdam: Amsterdam University Press.

Index